The Last Days of the Afghan Republic

THE LAST DAYS OF THE AFGHAN REPUBLIC

A Doomed Evacuation Twenty Years in the Making

ARSALAN NOORI

AND

NOAH COBURN

ROWMAN & LITTLEFIELD
Lanham • Boulder • New York • London

Published by Rowman & Littlefield
An imprint of The Rowman & Littlefield Publishing Group, Inc.
4501 Forbes Boulevard, Suite 200, Lanham, Maryland 20706
www.rowman.com

86-90 Paul Street, London EC2A 4NE

British Library Cataloguing in Publication Information Available

Library of Congress Cataloging-in-Publication Data
Names: Noori, Arsalan, 1987– author. | Coburn, Noah, author.
Title: The last days of the Afghan republic : a doomed evacuation twenty years in the making /
   Arsalan Noori and Noah Coburn.
Description: Lanham : Rowman & Littlefield, 2023. | Includes bibliographical references and
   index.
Identifiers: LCCN 2023005077 (print) | LCCN 2023005078 (ebook) | ISBN 9781538178089
   (cloth) | ISBN 9781538178096 (epub)
Subjects: LCSH: Afghan War, 2001–2021—Evacuation of civilians. | Afghanistan—Biography.
   | Afghanistan—Civilization—Western influences. | Afghan War, 2001–2021—Influence.
   | Refugees—Afghanistan—Biography. | Afghans—Foreign countries—Biography. |
   Afghanistan—Social conditions—21st century.
Classification: LCC DS371.415 .N66 2023 (print) | LCC DS371.415 (ebook) | DDC
   958.104/7—dc23/eng/20230214
LC record available at https://lccn.loc.gov/2023005077
LC ebook record available at https://lccn.loc.gov/2023005078

To the youth of Afghanistan,
who deserve better than this.

Contents

CHARACTERS

Names and identifying details of some of those in the book, who are not widely known political figures, particularly those who remain in Afghanistan, have been changed to protect them. In other cases, characters have explicitly asked that we identify them by their names.

Those looking to escape and those left behind:

Arsalan Noori—A social science researcher, who was raised just north of Kabul, and coauthor of the book. **Farah**—Arsalan's wife and **Yousuf**—his brother.

Dr. Amena—A medical doctor, who grew up a refugee in Iran and ended up working for the Ministry of Public Health. **Murtaza Hakimi**—Amena's husband and **Ismaeil**—a legal scholar, who narrowly escapes an attack on the Ministry of Justice, and Murtaza's father and Amena's father-in-law.

Najeeb—A translator for the US military first based in Kandahar and then Kabul. **Haseeb**—his brother, also a translator, who is held in Abu Dhabi.

Zeinab—A student at the American University of Afghanistan and a triathlete. **Ali**—her husband.

Munir—The youngest of three brothers from a poor area in Wardak who eventually works for UNICEF (United Nations Children's Fund) helping Afghan children.

Sahar and **Jalil**—A young couple and friends of Arsalan, who get caught in the airport.

Kabir—A fixer with close ties to the Taliban

Zabi—A businessman

National and International Figures:

Hamid Karzai—First president of the Islamic Republic of Afghanistan (2002–2014)

Ashraf Ghani—Academic, former World Banker, and second president of the Islamic Republic of Afghanistan (2014–2021)

Hamdullah Mohib—Afghan ambassador to the United States, later national security advisor and key Ghani advisor in the final days of the republic, along with **Fazel Fazly**—the head of the administrative office of the president

Zalmay Khalilzad—US ambassador to Iraq, Afghanistan, and the United Nations, before becoming special representative for Afghanistan reconciliation and leading the US side of negotiations for drafting the Doha Agreement with the Taliban

David Petraeus—US CentCom (Central Command) commander under President Obama and director of the CIA under President Trump, promoted a counterinsurgency, "hearts and minds" approach to the war in Afghanistan

Abdul Ghani Baradar—Longtime deputy to Mullah Omar and eventual key negotiator on the Taliban side of the Doha Agreement

Other Internationals:

Noah Coburn—Arsalan's longtime research partner and friend, and the other coauthor

Jackie—Zeinab's training partner and friend, who founded the NGO (nongovernmental organization) She Can Tri.

TIMELINE

The Lead-Up

1979–1989—Soviet Occupation of Afghanistan

1989–1996—Afghan Civil War between various jihadi parties

September 1996—The Taliban take Kabul for the first time.

September 11, 2001—The September 11 attacks, which were planned in Afghanistan but not carried out by Afghans, strike New York, Washington, and Pennsylvania.

The US War

October 7, 2001—The US bombing campaign of Afghanistan begins.

November 13, 2001—The Taliban flee Kabul.

December 2001—Taliban head Mullah Omar escapes from Kandahar to Pakistan, and a US operation in the Tora Bora mountains fails to capture the al Qaeda leader, Osama bin Laden.

March 2003—The United States invades Iraq, diverting resources from Afghanistan.

January 2004—Afghanistan holds a constitutional convention.

October 9, 2004—Afghanistan holds first presidential elections.

December 2007—The Taliban take Musa Qala as part of a wider Taliban resurgence that produces increased instability across the south and east of Afghanistan.

January 2008—Special Immigrant Visa (SIV) program is extended from Iraq to include Afghans in danger due to their work with the US government.

February 11, 2009—Attack on the Ministry of Justice in downtown Kabul, which Ismaeil escapes

December 1, 2009—President Obama announces a surge in US troops, eventually to 100,000, which leads operations in the south and east of the country to ramp up.

January 2012—The Taliban open an office in Qatar.

May 27, 2014—President Obama announces a timeline for withdrawing US troops.

September 29, 2014—Ashraf Ghani is inaugurated as second president of the Islamic Republic of Afghanistan.

August 24, 2016—Attack on the American University of Afghanistan, which Zeinab escapes, kills thirteen.

August 21, 2017—President Trump announces his own surge of US troops into Afghanistan.

February 29, 2020—Doha Agreement is signed between the United States and the Taliban, but it does not include Afghan government representatives.

September 7, 2020—President Trump claims to have invited Taliban leaders to Camp David.

September 12, 2020—Talks between the Taliban and Afghan government begin but make little progress.

April 14, 2021—President Biden announces all US troops will depart Afghanistan by September 11, 2021.

August 2, 2021—Secretary of State Anthony Blinken announces a new "Priority 2" status for Afghans who supported the United States but do not qualify for the Special Immigrant Visa, part of a wider Operation Allies Refuge program.

The Withdrawal and Collapse

August 15, 2021—The Taliban arrive in Kabul; Ashraf Ghani flees the country.

August 26, 2021—An IS-K (Islamic State–Khorasan Province) suicide bomber kills 183 at Abbey Gate at the Kabul airport.

August 29, 2021—A US drone attack in Kabul in retribution for the IS-K bombing kills ten, including seven children, none of whom had any connections with IS-K.

August 30, 2021—The last US plane departs from Kabul airport.

Acronyms

ANA   Afghan National Army
ANP   Afghan National Police
AUAF   American University of Afghanistan
CCAP   Citizens' Charter Afghanistan Program, a World Bank assistance program set up in 2016 building on the NSP model
HKIA   Hamid Karzai International Airport, Kabul
IOM   International Organization for Migration
IRAP   International Refugee Assistance Project, a legal rights group
ISAF   International Security Assistance Forces, an international coalition of NATO and allied troops in Afghanistan
IS-K   Islamic State–Khorasan Province (the Afghan branch of the Islamic State)
KPF   Khost Protection Force
MRRD   Ministry of Rural Rehabilitation and Development
NOLB   No One Left Behind, a charity
NSP   National Solidarity Project, a rural assistance program run by the World Bank and Afghan government starting in 2003
P-2   Priority Two, an alternative US visa pathway
SIV   Special Immigrant Visa
UNAMA   United Nations Assistance Mission in Afghanistan
UNHCR   United Nations High Commissioner for Refugees
UNICEF   United Nations Children's Fund
USAID   United States Agency for International Development

THE LAST FLIGHT OUT OF HKIA

ARSALAN—AUGUST 18, 2021:

The first time my family fled the Taliban, in 1997, I was eleven years old. Taliban troops had started raiding homes in our area, taking any men of fighting age away in their trucks, and we made the hasty decision to flee.

We walked fifteen miles south from my father's village to Kabul, taking only what we could carry on our backs. The rockets from the Taliban and the Northern Alliance resisting them caused the ground to shake around us.

We walked in a large group made up of people from the villages near ours and other refugees fleeing from the north. We carried bags and bundles of clothes. Some even brought animals. We passed close to Bagram Air Base, where the United States would eventually return to run their war. We crossed vineyards and orchards studded with Soviet land mines. We walked slowly because of the mines, but also because my mother was eight months pregnant with my younger sister.

As the eldest son of my family, I remember trying to appear as brave as I could, but then, there was an explosion just ahead of us. A farmer was walking his cows and one of them stepped on a land mine and was torn into pieces. The smell of it was a mixture of burnt meat and singed hair. Sometimes now when I walk by a kebab shop and they've left the meat on too long, it pulls me back to that day.

We arrived at my grandfather's small mud house in Kabul. There were smokey woodburning heaters that we huddled around to keep warm. The rooms were constantly cloudy with smoke. My sister was born there a few days later. With little space, my parents tried to figure out where to go next.

The second time I tried to flee the Taliban, in 2021, it was very different.

On August 15th, as the government collapsed, I stood with some colleagues in the garden outside of our office, where I was head of research, watching smoke rise from the US embassy. At first, we had no idea what it could mean, probably a bombing, we thought. The United States had announced it would finish its withdrawal of troops by August 31, and some thought that the government might fall then, but none of us expected it all to happen so quickly.

Around 9:30 a.m. or so, we started to get some odd reports from colleagues who were out of the office. One of our staff called and said they had seen Taliban fighters just driving around Kabul. The women in the office panicked, and my boss suddenly became quite concerned. I got calls from my brother, who was at his office. My father was with my sister. They were out to collect their passports at the passport office. Suddenly everyone was rushing around the streets and the major roads were entirely blocked. My father and sister couldn't actually make it home, but my uncle's house was not far from where they got stuck, so they went there instead to wait and see if the roads cleared.

I remained at the office, helping to organize transportation for everyone else. Our priority was getting our international staff out. As the top Afghan, I felt it was my duty to them—these foreigners who had worked with us for so long, but focusing on the details of organizing cars and getting information about what routes were open also helped me stay calm. Some embassies seemed to be allowing people to take refuge there, but others, like the United States, had already announced that all Americans should stay where they were. We made sure my Australian boss went back to his house since if the Taliban found a foreigner in our office somehow, that would have been even more problematic for all of us. After that we started making sure that all of our female staff were on their way home.

In the meantime, the guards were also panicking, asking, what should they do with their guns? After spending years worrying about Taliban attacks and making sure our guards were constantly checking the streets, it suddenly felt safer not to have guns. What should we say if anyone comes here and asks what we do? Should we leave? There were also more and more helicopters and planes flying in the sky, and it almost seemed as if we could hear everyone leaving.

Once we got home, I sat there, unsure of what to do next. I called my colleagues, checked in with the guards, and messaged Noah and other internationals I knew.

"Have you received any news from the embassy? Do you have a visa?"

"Should I go to the airport?"

"The Taliban have just come to the office asking whether we work with the foreigners."

"How did this happen?"

The text messages came faster than I could answer them. My boss was hoping to take refuge in one of the embassies, but no one in my family had any foreign passports or connections good enough to get one of the Western embassies to take us in. So, my wife, my brother, my parents, and I decided to remain where we were. We texted friends on WhatsApp and checked in on family and friends by Facebook.

Some were terrified: One friend posted that he had watched his neighbor's house be looted. Others were angry: "Those hypocritical Taliban, they came to our office and stole our cars 'in the name of the Islamic Emirate of Afghanistan.'" Others shared pictures from the road outside the airport where there were high-end armored cars that had been simply abandoned in the middle of the road. Other photos showed abandoned police vehicles and Humvees.

There were darker posts talking about government officials being targeted and killed, but there were few details. I scrolled through Twitter, looking for some hopeful news. I couldn't find any. Taliban militias continued to converge from all over the country, and since few were wearing uniforms, we were worried that fighting might even break out between these various groups.

At my house, we rotated who got to use the charger and kept checking to make sure the Taliban had not yet cut the internet. I talked on the phone with friends who were trying to make it out of the country—a few had actually made it inside the airport but were not sure they would be allowed on planes.

Many of my friends and colleagues sent me messages asking if I could help them.

"Can I have a letter saying that I worked with your organization for USAID?"

"Do you have a contact in the US embassy? How about the British or the Germans?"

"I heard the Canadians said they were going to evacuate 20,000 people, but you need to submit an online application right away."

"There's a long line at the internet cafe by my house where these guys are handing over their documents and asking the internet cafe staff to apply for evacuations for them."

"Are there any flights at all available?"

I clicked refresh on the US embassy website, rereading the same dense instructions on how to apply for a visa. I had worked on a series of US-funded projects, and since the US government had changed the regulations earlier that summer, it seemed like I was eligible for the Special Immigrant Visa (SIV), set up to help Afghans like me who had supported the US government. Since I had not worked directly for the government, but instead had worked as a subcontractor for several companies, it was not clear which employer I should use to confirm my employment. The HR offices of the employers I tried to reach did not respond. The US government had also recently announced a Priority 2 visa for Afghans, but with a completely different application process. The website said the wait time for those applications was twelve to fourteen months. Joe Biden said in a press conference that the United States would "protect the Afghan allies" who had worked with them, and despite the fact I had worked exclusively on internationally sponsored projects for the past twelve years, there was no help on those webpages for me it seemed.

As the first week of the chaotic evacuation passed by, rumors grew. I couldn't sleep. I skipped meals. My beard started to grow out. I'm almost always clean-shaven, so this made me look like I was losing my mind, my wife said. She said that she was more worried about my mental health than she was about the Taliban.

It felt like my house had become like a call center, with relatives and friends asking for help. I wanted to submit my own application, but I worried that it needed to be perfect. What if I forgot to include everything? How could I be sure they understood my case? I froze up, and distracted myself by helping others.

As I helped friends and relatives fill in visa applications and various Google forms that embassies were allegedly sending around, it was so hard to tell what was true and if any of this could really help us escape. Some said there was a family of airline workers who lived near the airport who could sneak you inside the airport for $4,000. Another friend heard that the French would help you if you could get to the border in Tajikistan. We debated among ourselves what the Taliban would do next. Young men from the country patrolled our neighborhood with assault rifles. They looked frightening, but also somehow lost in the big city. We began to count down the days until, as Biden promised, the final American troops would leave.

My mother looked out the window as a plane passed overhead: "That is the sound of people leaving, the sound of people dying, the sound of people falling from the skies."

She pulled the curtain shut.

Introduction: The Final Days

Munir hesitated for one last moment on the ramp of the airplane. Other families pushed past him, climbing up into the back of the C-130.

He had called home just minutes before asking his family whether he should stay or go. His brother-in-law, a journalist, was convinced that he should take the opportunity. "You have to take this chance, it could only come once," he said. "Who knows what will happen with P-2 or any of these ways. They have not even responded to you, despite so many emails, so many channels." His mother and sister were both against it. His wife was torn.

"I cannot say," she said. "You have to make the decision."

He strode onto the airplane.

He sat down on the floor—there were no seats. Families crowded around him, shoulder to shoulder.

On the flight were also twenty-eight unaccompanied minors who had ended up at the airport without parents or guardians. A few of these kids had been separated from their parents who had already made it out on earlier flights, but some were street children who had snuck onto the grounds of the airport during the rush. The US military didn't seem to know what to do with them. The children didn't want to leave the airport, and it seemed wrong to throw them out, so now they were being evacuated to Qatar. But then what?

Munir worked for UNICEF, the United Nations' program that supports children worldwide. He had been tasked with registering each of the minors, getting them on the plane, and returning to his office in Kabul. Now, instead, he was leaving on the same plane as they were.

Many of the adults around him were clutching small bags or backpacks, but not Munir. In his pocket was his cell phone and wallet, but everything else was still sitting in the makeshift UNICEF workspace he had left just a few minutes before. He was wearing an outfit of traditional Afghan robes, which he had worn to the airport that morning in the hope that he would not appear to be the UN contractor that he was.

UNICEF had already let staff know that they were prioritizing the evacuation of non-Afghans over the Afghans who worked with them, so Munir had been searching for other options. Over the past eight days, he had tried desperately to get the company that he worked for in the earlier years of the war to provide him with employment verification, but they wouldn't even respond to his emails. He sent message after message to the HR email address and the personal email addresses of his former bosses and colleagues, but heard nothing. The Afghan staff at the UN repeatedly asked the internationals in charge what the plan was to protect them, but they received no answer. For the most part, they were busy making sure they had their own flights out of the country.

As he was giving the paperwork for the children to the US Marine who was handing out tickets to those who had the right paperwork to board the plane, the Marine looked at Munir and said, "Do you want one?" He saw the surprise on Munir's face and said, as if to justify it, "It would probably be good for you to accompany them to Qatar."

Before that moment, he had not considered that he might be able to simply board one of the flights and leave. Security was so tight and leaving seemed like a distant dream. He also had four small children and a respectable job. His English was good, but he knew other Afghans who had left and were now working landscaping jobs or driving for Uber. People had jumped onto random flights in the first days of the evacuation, but now things were more orderly, and Munir had not been granted permission by anyone to depart. Then again, there was no clear order to how certain people were being prioritized as plane after plane filled and left.

Munir looked at the piece of paper in his hand and called his family.

He thought, "If the UN is not going to evacuate me, perhaps I just need to evacuate myself."

The plane engines kicked on. The plane lurched forward, bodies pushing into one another since there were no seat belts or seats. A few minutes later the vibrations of the engines intensified, and Munir could feel an emptiness deep in his belly as the plane lifted up and he left his family, his phone charger, and everything else behind.

His regret was immediate.

**

It is difficult to overstate the chaos of August 2021 for many of those living in Afghanistan, particularly those who lived in Kabul and had worked closely with the international community there. In a matter of days, an insurgency that had quietly picked up steam threw out a government that the international community had spent twenty years and tens of billions of dollars supporting. A government that had stated it stood for women's rights, education, and a litany of other ideals was replaced by one that did not allow girls to attend secondary school. A university that was built by the American government at a cost of hundreds of millions of dollars was now being used to house members of the militias supporting the Haqqani network, a criminal, tribal band that had supported the return of the Taliban and carried out many of their most brutal attacks over the past two decades. In the place of President Ashraf Ghani, a former professor at Johns Hopkins, was Mullah Haibatullah Akhunzada, who had been educated in Islamic seminaries and had come to power after leading the Taliban's religious council.

Afghans, Americans, and much of the rest of the world watched for two weeks in August as crowds rushed the airport, young bodies fell from planes, a suicide bomber killed civilians and soldiers at one gate, and a baby was handed to a Marine over a barbed-wire wall. The agony of lives so clearly destroyed, as people tried to flee their homeland with little to nothing, felt like images that we see only in the wake of natural disasters.

And yet, this was not a natural disaster. It was also completely avoidable.

Not everyone was shocked by the events. Military experts had been warning that the American withdrawal could exacerbate the violence in the country. The Afghan National Army had expanded and several of their Special Forces units were highly trained and efficient, but their ranks were also filled with ghost soldiers, invented names so that corrupt officials could steal their salaries. Toward the end of June 2021, *Long War Journal*, which was considered one of the most reliable trackers of the insurgency, estimated that only 80 of 407 districts were under government control, while the Taliban controlled 160 districts, leaving half of the Afghan population living in the remaining disputed areas.

Many of the Afghans in these rural areas were not particularly surprised by the speed by which the Taliban took the country either. The Taliban were brutal, but in many areas their shadow governments had been seen as more effective and less corrupt than the official Afghan counterparts for the past decade. Yet, for many Afghans living in more urban areas, areas that had expanded under twenty years of international intervention, where working with foreigners, buying products made abroad, and listening to the daily flights of American helicopters had become a way of life, the collapse was more shocking.

What was so surprising about that August, particularly for the Afghans living in Kabul, was just how quickly the Ghani government crumbled and how unprepared for those final events the American government seemed to be. Even as the Taliban were taking provincial capitals, it was thought that surely some sort of truce would be signed or there would be some transition of power. The day before the Taliban entered Kabul, we were on the phone with each other speculating who might be in an interim government composed of both Afghan Republic officials and members of the Taliban. Ghani had said in an interview he was prepared to die protecting his country. No one expected the president to just get on a helicopter and leave.

Similarly, most Afghans who had worked for the United States over the past twenty years expected the US government to have a plan in place for a scenario like this. Surely there would be some last-minute negotiations to help protect those who had worked for the US government. The US government (and others) had hundreds of millions of dollars in ongoing development projects in the country, they weren't just going to leave those for the Taliban, were they? There must have been a plan in place for the collapse of the armed forces. There must have been a list of those who would be evacuated, right?

No, there was no list.

In fact, the evacuation played out just as much of the past twenty years in Afghanistan had for the US government: There was plenty of good intentions and money (and guns), but the strategy was not fully thought out. There was no endgame in place, government agencies were awful at cooperating, bureaucracies were slow to make decisions, and the politics and culture of Afghanistan were fundamentally misunderstood time and time again. And all this ended up costing Afghan and American lives.

It also destroyed the chances that a compromise could be reached between those who supported the democratic government of the Islamic Republic of Afghanistan (as it was formally known) and Taliban hard-liners. The evacuation of so many of Afghanistan's educated young people and the political elite of the past twenty years meant that when the dust settled, there were none with the power to stand up to the Taliban. Those who did try were often quickly detained and tortured and then disappeared.

Many in the US government cared deeply about the success of the US mission in Afghanistan. They worked hard to protect those Afghans they had worked alongside, and since 2008, some of these Afghans had been eligible to receive Special Immigrant Visas if they could show their lives were threatened. But this program was, in many ways, emblematic of everything that was wrong with the US time in Afghanistan: It was poorly designed, never fixed, and provided only minimal help, often to the educated and wealthy, not to those who needed it most. At the time of the evacuation, if the program had been well-run, it could have contributed to an orderly prioritization of those most at threat. Instead, the evacuation was marked by fake visas, bribes paid for access to the airport, and painful scenes of Afghans pleading for their lives.

The case of the Special Immigrant Visa (SIV) program itself tells much of the broader story of the US presence in Afghanistan. For years, the US government realized that simply working alongside Americans was enough to get an Afghan killed, but the US government was incapable of pushing back hard enough on the Taliban to make the country safe for those who worked with the United States. Official reports were written and news articles were published about translators who had been murdered by the Taliban, but the US government wasn't interested in evacuating more than a small percentage of those who were at risk, so nothing meaningful was done to fix the SIV process until it was too late.

The US presence in Afghanistan as well as its hasty withdrawal impacted groups unevenly. Many of those living in rural areas who had suffered from drone strikes but received little development aid were happy to see the Americans leave. Those living in the cities, accustomed to things like women going to schools and working in government jobs, were going to see their lives completely reshaped by a new, but very unchanged, Taliban regime.

In the rushed final days of August, during the painful American evacuation from Afghanistan, very few Afghans made it out. Desperate families lined up outside the Kabul airport, hoping to somehow slip through. Instead, a suicide bomber killed more than 170 Afghans and 13 US service members. The new Taliban occupation continued to assert its control, beating journalists and protestors. Those who made it out relied on personal connections, guile, and luck.

The collapse of the Ghani government and the return of the Taliban affected everyone in Afghanistan in some way, but Arsalan, Munir, and others from their generation—from their mid-twenties to their mid-forties—were rather uniquely impacted. Older Afghans had memories of navigating the previous version of the Taliban and the even more violent era of the Civil War. Younger Afghans had fewer memories of the optimism of the early 2000s. Their memories are more of widespread corruption, civilian casualties, and a combination of economic stagnation and constant fear of violence that pervaded the 2010s.

Both Arsalan and Munir, however, remember the oppression of the first Taliban era and when the Americans arrived in 2001. They took advantage of the schools the Americans opened, the newspapers they sponsored, and the democracy they promised. The internationals who came with the American soldiers told them that if they studied hard, worked for democracy, human rights, and freedom that eventually their lives would improve and they would prosper. For those in this book, their lives played out exactly as those internationals had promised.

Until they didn't. And it all fell apart over a few weeks in August.

The stories of Arsalan, Munir, Zeinab, Amena, Najeeb, and others tell a dark history of how the US intervention went so wrong, leaving hundreds of thousands of Afghans, in the United States, Afghanistan, and scattered around the globe, trying to make sense of how to put back together their careers, their families, and their lives.

Part I

A Failed Intervention?

ARSALAN—SEPTEMBER 5, 2021:

As we have adjusted to life with the Taliban, my wife and I have ventured out on occasion, but when we travel now, it is like we are in a new country. I recognize many of the places, but it is as if they have all been somehow changed.

The other day, I realized that we were driving by a park where I used to purchase firewood when I was a young boy during the first Taliban period. I hadn't thought about that time in years. Since we were barely bringing in enough money to feed our family, we couldn't order wood in bulk like ordinary people do. Instead, I was sent every day or two to buy a buji, or a sack of wood, and bring it home to my mother. Some days the sticks were thin, but on the better days we were able to buy large chunks and break them up. They would burn for longer. As I thought back to those days, I started to wonder if I would have to do that again, and I began to cry.

My wife sometimes jokes that I am cheap, because I negotiate the price on everything, even though we are now fairly well off by Afghan standards—we have a nice home, a car, and, until the Taliban returned, few concerns about food or heat. That need to negotiate, however, stayed with me. Now, I think that it all goes back to those days, when literally every stick of firewood counted.

Even though my family had some farmland in one of the districts just north of Kabul, the Civil War period in the 1990s was difficult for everyone. This was when the Soviet troops withdrew and the various Afghan militias began to fight for control of the country. It was the chaos of those militias fighting each other that gave rise to the Taliban the first time. Even though the Islam that the Taliban preached was radical and far from anything we believed, people were just so tired of war and destruction that few people had the energy to oppose them.

Life in Kabul in the 1990s under the Taliban was not much better than during the Civil War. In two years, my family moved houses six or seven times. One of the houses was basically a mud hut, and my sisters and I spent weeks cleaning the yard and planting a garden so that it would be more bearable. Then the landlord visited, saw how nice the garden was, and raised the rent, so we had to move again.

Another of the houses didn't have a real door, but only scrap metal that we hung in the doorway. I remember feeling shame as I went to school since the neighbors' houses all looked better than ours, even though, in reality, everyone back then was suffering.

My father is a veterinarian, but during those years he did embroidery since this was the only work he could find that would pay enough to feed our family. We didn't have electricity, however, so he had to bike an hour and a half across the city each morning to a workshop in a neighborhood that had more reliable power. Then he would pedal home each night.

During that time, I was a good student overall, but I was particularly intense in my focus on learning English. Looking back on it, I'm not sure why I put so much emphasis on it. We were cut off from the rest of the world then. No internet, no TV. There were no jobs for people who spoke English, and not many people thought about going abroad. Yet, for some reason, I understood that English was a way to prove myself somehow. I took my lessons very seriously and never missed a class, even when the roads were covered with snow and the fighting between the Taliban and the Northern Alliance intensified.

I would finish up my regular school classes and immediately ride my bike over to a tutor's house for another two hours of schoolwork. One day a rocket crashed into my neighborhood. It was bigger than most of the usual ones and left a smoking crater ten feet deep. I barely paid attention as I pedaled through the dusty haze, worried I would be late for my English lesson. The bomb, it turned out, had landed just a hundred yards away from the building where I received my lesson. When I got there, the gatekeeper shouted at me, "Are you crazy? What are you doing here? Lessons are canceled!" So instead, I went off and went to see where the rocket had landed, and I stood with a crowd near *the big crater. I don't know what my parents were thinking, letting me go out at a time like that.*

After visiting the site of the rocket strike, I rode down the road to my aunt's house. She lived about half a mile away and when I arrived, I saw that the doors had been blown off their hinges and all of her windows broken. Still, I was mostly upset that I had missed my lesson.

After a few more years of study, the work started to pay off, and I began earning a bit of money by providing lessons for younger students. I enjoyed this, plus it was nice to have something to contribute to my family's expenses.

I remember the day the first Taliban government left Kabul in 2001 in part because it was so sudden. During those years the Taliban required that all men and older boys wear large turbans made from four feet of cloth. They were heavy and I hated mine. We had to have them on at school as well as traveling back and forth, but often we would fool around and we liked to try to knock them off of each other. We would chase each other and try to grab them too. We would often take them off once we were in our neighborhood where we thought we wouldn't be noticed by any of the Taliban soldiers, but because of these games, we were often losing them.

Every time I lost mine, my mother would get upset since it would mean she would have to buy me a new one and they weren't cheap. The day before the Taliban fled from Kabul in late 2001, I had lost mine again. I was worried because I didn't want to tell my mother and was already stressed about what my punishment might be. The next morning, we woke up and all the news was that virtually overnight, almost all of the Taliban soldiers and government officials had vanished, most heading out of town southward. My first reaction was elation, not that they were gone, but that I would not need to buy a new turban and that my mother would not punish me.

That feeling of relief was something I connected with this new sense of freedom.

In those early days things changed slowly. We did not have regular electricity. Schools were still taught in tents, and a growing number of returning refugees flooded the city, setting up informal towns on the mountain slopes above the city center. But there was a new optimism that was particularly strong in 2004 when we voted in our first presidential election. Hamid Karzai had been the interim president of the Afghan Transitional Administration, but after the election he was the first president of the Islamic Republic of Afghanistan. It felt like a new era.

In 2005, I got an entry-level admin job for a Turkish construction company, since I had studied Turkish in high school. At first, I was excited, since I got to travel to Farah, one of the remote provinces on the border with Iran. It was my first time on a plane. The thing that surprised me, however, was that even though I was just an eighteen-year-old kid, since my title was "administrative officer," I was treated with respect by many of my other colleagues. When we landed on the dirt runway, we were met by a convoy of five armored vehicles, and one of the guards opened the door for me, so I could climb into the big vehicle. I remember that moment because the door was armored and heavy, and I had never seen a door like that before.

The Turkish company was working as a subcontractor for Louis Berger on the ring road that linked the remote desert province to the rest of the country. The construction projects had three camps that were right next to one another and each had its own dining hall, but these were all strictly segregated between Afghans, Americans, and other internationals, such as Turks. Since I was in management, I got to eat at the Turkish dining hall where most of the mid-level managers were. The Americans working for Louis Berger ate in a much nicer dining hall and were always talking about the steaks that they had just gotten flown in. In contrast, the food for the Afghan workers was barely edible, and some of the workers complained it was making them sick.

In the months before I arrived, an ambush had killed one of the Turkish engineers. In retaliation, the head of security, who was South African, took some of the security guards and they went out and leveled some buildings where the attack was said to have been planned. We never figured out whether the people who owned those buildings were connected to the attack, but mostly it seemed like the security team was trying to send a message to the local Afghan communities: Don't mess with the internationals.

Riding in the armored convoy, the security contractors drove aggressively, cutting other drivers off since they were worried about attacks from other vehicles, particularly those on motorbikes. We would blow by other cars and those walking alongside the road, kicking up dust on them. It was the first time I felt really disconnected from my fellow Afghans.

But only a few months after I was hired, the company started downsizing and, as one of the youngest there, I was pretty sure I was going to be fired. That's when a friend called me. He knew I gave English classes and wanted to know if I had ever taught foreigners. "Sure, sure. I've done that," I said somewhat cautiously.

In reality, I had helped some of the Turkish teachers at my high school with their English on a few occasions. They weren't really lessons, but my friend was in a rush and he didn't ask any follow-up questions about my experience.

"Listen," he said, "there's this American guy who needs a tutor right away. Can you help him out?"

I assumed the money would probably be better than what I was earning. Why not give it a try?

I met Noah at an international guesthouse near the city center, and at first, his Dari was not good, but the garden was pleasant and we would drink coffee and work on vocabulary. We met every day in those first months, and as he improved, he talked more about his research on culture and markets in Afghanistan. Later, I went with him as he started his research in a small village of potters, north of Kabul, not far from where I had grown up. He was interested in the history of the town and its bazaar. This was a new experience for me, particularly since Noah was interested in strange things.

"They say the woman buried at this shrine was British, but converted to Islam a hundred years ago. Let's ask them more about that."

"But it's not true," I said. "There's no way a British woman was here then. They say she was magically transported here by a local Sufi saint. It's impossible."

"Perhaps it's not true, but look at how they are connecting their history to British history, and showing how the British, in the end, come to believe what they believe. It's an interesting story, particularly when you consider that many of the young men here want to migrate to places like the UK."

So, we would go and interview some of the old men at the shrine.

The other new experience was the internationals Noah introduced me to. After he began spending more time conducting research, I started to give language lessons to other people he introduced me to. They were aid workers, artists, and architects. Some knew a lot about Afghanistan, others knew very little.

At first, I was expecting them to be similar to Noah, always studying and asking questions. I was in for something of a shock when I met Klaus, a German potter working for a development organization. Klaus always brought a snack to our lessons and seemed completely unbothered by the fact that he was not progressing much.

In our first class, we went over some of the sequences of basic greetings:

"Salaam Aleikum, Shoma chetor hastin? Khub hastin? Famil-eton jur ast?"

"Peace be upon you. How are you? Are you well? Is your family healthy?"

Almost every Dari speaker would go through these questions when greeting each other, and the ritual was important. For foreigners, learning this exchange was a good first step to showing the Afghans you work with that you were making an effort. With Klaus we went through the greetings on the first lesson and then repeated them again on the second lesson. And the third. And the fourth. He just couldn't seem to remember them, and if he couldn't even greet Afghans, how was I going to teach him to have an actual conversation? He seemed content to enjoy his snack and sit in the garden. But there were others who were even stranger.

One was an American who was blue. Actually blue. Noah told me he took colloidal silver, and really, that made him blue. I didn't know whether one could ask about something like this—is it rude to ask, "Why are you blue?" but he brought it up himself and tried to tell me that I should take it to prevent infections too.

Noah would sometimes say, "Not everyone in the West is like this, Arsalan."

But it did seem like the internationals I tutored, who were mostly working for NGOs, doing development work, were a strange bunch.

This was the beginning of my time working with internationals in Afghanistan, and by the time the Taliban returned I'd probably worked with at least a thousand. Now, however, they are all gone. My Australian boss, the aid workers, the diplomats, Klaus, and the blue man. After working closely with them for twenty years, it is a feeling of loss, abandonment, and confusion.

As we continue driving by the park, my wife asks me what is wrong, and I don't know exactly what to say. Partly I am afraid we will go back to those days of scraping together just enough to survive, but more, maybe, is that my life now seems to be divided into two parts: before and after.

CHAPTER I

A Land of Opportunity?

AMENA WAS ONE OF A MILLION AND A HALF AFGHAN REFUGEES LIVING in Iran before the United States started its invasion of Afghanistan in October 2001. Growing up as an outsider, she was accustomed to needing to assert herself and she does not hide her emotions. "I was angry growing up in Iran," she recalled. "Afghans were always last to get bread at the bakery, and we had to push to make sure we got our share. Nothing felt fair in Iran."

She was born in Iran and, like many Afghans in those years, never visited Afghanistan, only hearing stories of Bamiyan, the high mountain valley province where her family came from. Her parents were Hazaras, members of the long-persecuted Shia minority in Afghanistan, and they had fled the country under the Soviet regime in the early 1980s. Things for Hazaras had only gotten worse since then, with the Taliban brutally oppressing this minority that they did not consider real Muslims.

During this period Hazaras were almost constantly targeted and not allowed to openly practice their faith. It was worse perhaps for Hazara women, since Hazaras tend to be the group in Afghanistan that is also most tolerant of women having active social and professional lives outside of their homes. In Afghanistan, under the Taliban Ministry for the Propagation of Virtue and the Prevention of Vice, girls' schools were closed and women could be beaten for leaving the house without a male relative.

At the same time, however, Amena recalled, things in Iran were not good either. Afghans were treated as barely tolerated, uninvited guests.

They were paid less than Iranian citizens were to do the same jobs, and the only work they could find was often construction if you were a man, and maybe cleaning houses as a woman.[1] The questionable legal status of Afghans there made them constant targets. The police harassed Afghans frequently and threatened them with arrest if they did not have the correct documents. She and her seven brothers and sisters had problems with school officials while trying to do simple things like register for classes.

One day, a friend of Amena's was late for school. A typical Iranian student just would have been chided for such an offense, but Amena's friend was forced to stand in the courtyard for the entire day, students and teachers walking past her between classes, not allowed to sit. It was bordering on torture and a disgrace for the friend's entire family, but this is how official Iranians tended to treat Afghans, like they weren't real people.

Like many refugees, Amena's family waited a bit after the fall of the Taliban before returning, concerned that the US invasion might trigger another civil war. But things seemed stable, and they left Tehran in October of 2004. For Amena, a whole new world of possibilities began to open up.

***

While policy makers will debate in op-eds for years to come whether the American war in Afghanistan was "worth it," for millions of women and men in Afghanistan, the decades of American occupation between 2001 and 2021 provided opportunities they simply could not have imagined before. These transformations were not always predictable. They were marred by corruption, mismanagement, and violence, but particularly for those in urban areas, life in Afghanistan was completely transformed by the international presence.[2]

The Taliban first collapsed in November 2001, when the United States and, later, other NATO allies invaded the country ostensibly to punish the Taliban for harboring Osama bin Laden and other members of al Qaeda. Of course, the Taliban and al Qaeda were entirely separate organizations, with very different goals and orientations. The Taliban were a conservative Pashtun group with strong religious values, but whose aim was primarily to rule Afghanistan. Al Qaeda's goal was to reinstate the Islamic Caliphate and overthrow secular governments everywhere by building an international terrorist network. In these early days, however, the two groups often were conflated to justify the invasion.[3]

This led to a mishmash of goals and approaches. Yes, the military was there to punish the Taliban for harboring Osama bin Laden, but US president George W. Bush, and his wife, Laura, in particular, repeatedly referred to protecting Afghan women. Development experts warned that the new government was incapable of feeding its population, plus there were three million refugees who would be returning to the country soon. Human rights experts saw this as an opportunity to protect the most vulnerable, such as the Hazara, and advance women's rights. At the same time, a slew of private military and development contractors saw the invasion, and the emphasis on a "light footprint," as an opportunity to get the US government to pay them to do the things that American presidents did not want to risk US soldiers doing.[4]

In the years that followed, haphazard progress was made on some of these projects with remarkable speed: Roads were built, elections were held, a constitution was drafted, girls went to school, and, of course, money was made.

And so, while this is primarily a story about what went wrong in Afghanistan, it's worth considering what went right—at least at first, as Amena's story suggests.

***

Amena and her family were not alone in returning to Afghanistan. At the height of the Soviet occupation there were more than 6 million Afghan refugees living primarily in Pakistan and Iran. While some of those had repatriated during the first Taliban period in the 1990s, there were still 3.6 million Afghans living outside of the country, 2 million of whom were in Pakistan (with only 4,300 in the United States), when the Taliban government crumbled in 2001.[5] The UN and other international groups worried that the massive return of these migrants would create a humanitarian disaster and lead to violence. While there were instances of land disputes between returnees and the communities they were settling in, the gradual return of most of these refugees was one of the great success stories of the early years of the international intervention. Still, for some of the Afghans, arriving in Afghanistan for the first time was a shock.

As Amena described it, "When I first came to Afghanistan, I realized I was a seventeen-year-old girl who was visiting her own country for the first time. I was happy and worried at the same time."

The family, like many refugees, did not return to the rural province they had lived in previously but moved to Kabul and joined one of the rapidly expanding, primarily Hazara neighborhoods on the western side of the city. It was a real shift from Iran. In Iran, Amena had worn a headscarf, but not the heavy burqa cloth that covers the entire body, favored in more conservative, particularly Pashtun, areas of Afghanistan. One of the things that jumped out at her almost immediately was the openly hostile way men treated women on the streets, leering and occasionally yelling at them, even when a woman was walking with her father. "After that when I bought a burqa, I felt more comfortable because no one was looking at me," she said.

As a returning refugee and a woman, her family's expectations of her were that she would primarily remain at home and support her family as she could—at least until she was married. Her father had done tailoring work in Iran, and while Amena was allowed to get some basic schooling, it was assumed that she would eventually find work doing tailoring as well. When Amena began school, she thought she would be behind the other students, but it turned out her school experience in Iran had put her ahead, and she ended up in a classroom with girls who were three years older than she was.

Amena was not impressed by these girls. "All they talked about were upcoming weddings and engagement parties, how to get engaged faster, and how they might leave the country with their future husbands," Amena said.

Amena's cousins always talked about makeup and henna, but Amena preferred to study, and much of her family thought this was odd. One of her relatives used to tease her, asking her whenever he saw her, "How are your books? How is your computer?"

Her father had picked up more tailoring work now that they were back in Afghanistan, and every day when she came home from school, he expected her to work with him, often until 11:00 at night. Only then could she start her homework. Still, when grades were posted on the wall at school, Amena swelled with pride when she saw that she was the top student in her class. Despite that the pace of the work was exhausting, when she heard of a private center offering English classes near her home in the early mornings, she quickly signed up, telling the rest of her family nothing about it. She found that she was good at languages and picked up new vocabulary easily. When her father discovered she was secretly taking courses, he beat her for it. Still, Amena remained undeterred.

The next morning, she convinced him to let her continue her studies since she had already paid for the rest of the term. At the time, she had no idea all this would lead her to jobs with internationals. Later, looking back, she realized that this decision and her ability to quickly pick up languages put her on a track to join the cohort of Afghans working most closely with the Americans.

***

In the years following the US invasion, the rhetoric of "saving Afghan women" helped raise tens of millions of dollars in private and government funds, while also doing much to provide political cover and justification for the war efforts.[6] Many of these initiatives did little to change the actual legal protections women needed or dramatically impact the lives of women in many rural parts of the country and portrayed Afghan women as helpless victims.[7] However, some of these programs did provide opportunities for more urban women like Amena and allowed them to imagine their own versions of what it might mean to be a strong Afghan feminist.[8] This was particularly true in Kabul, since many organizations found that working outside the city was inconvenient and, at times, dangerous and that rural communities were far less interested in the Western version of women's empowerment that many of these NGOs were promoting.

The number of programs with international funding grew rapidly, and around this time Amena became involved in a youth parliament program set up by USAID, where student leaders from across the city worked in a model parliament and were given workshops in activism and organizing. It was an eye-opening experience for Amena, in part because it was the first time she could act out a role that was different from the women in her family whom she was familiar with. "We were conducting the meetings and designing and hanging up campaign posters just the same way real parliament members were doing," Amena said. "I presented my political platform and wrote down all the things related to my past and future goals. I hung them on the school walls."

When the vote was held, Amena received more ballots than any other candidate from her school, male or female. She and the top vote getters from other schools were taken to the real national parliament building, where they were allowed to sit in the actual chairs that the recently elected parliamentarians sat in and meet with ministers.

Her head began to swim as she, and thousands of other young Afghan women, started to think differently about their futures.

***

International funds during these early years were also going to help fund Afghanistan's university system, and as she reached the end of high school, Amena started exploring her options. To get into college in Afghanistan, you must take the Kankor exam—Afghanistan's version of the SATs, and every summer, tens of thousands of students would cram classrooms, fields, and other makeshift testing sites to take the exam. While rumors of corruption and the purchasing of positions have always been common, the test was generally the only way that entrance into Afghanistan's free public universities happens. The process itself was supposed to be democratizing: The poor shepherd in the most rural village should have the same opportunity as the rich, urban student, and, in many cases, poor students who studied hard were rewarded.

At the same time, however, the fact that admissions comes down largely to one test, in addition to the fact that results are announced publicly, puts an incredible amount of pressure on students. A top score could get you into the medicine track. A lower score might enable you to study something like history. And for plenty of test takers, an even lower score would mean no college at all. Many students in more urban areas enroll in Kankor prep courses, which often start at 5:00 a.m., so that students can still make it on time for their regular classes at 8:00. Since Amena's family was so ambivalent about her desire to continue her education, she could not afford the prep courses, but she did study nightly on her own after she had finished helping her father with his tailoring.

When the day arrived, she was incredibly nervous, but as she sat down with the test, she pushed her worries about her future and her family's expectations to the side and tried to clear her mind of everything but the questions in front of her. She moved quickly through the pages.

Weeks later, when the test results were returned, Amena had earned one of the very top scores in the country. She was ecstatic since this qualified her to study medicine, something only available to the very best students. Her joy, however, was short-lived.

"I cannot forget that moment when I told my father about my results," Amena said. "He looked at me and asked, 'What is the point of all this? Why waste another seven years of your life in school?' He wanted me to continue working with him, doing tailoring, and to get married.

"I was nervous that he might completely prevent me from beginning my medical studies, so during my first two years, I agreed to continue helping him every night after I returned from the university. But, even while I kept working for him, he grew distant and even colder towards me during those days, not even greeting me when I would say 'Salam' to him. He treated me like I didn't exist.

"By the end of my second year, I couldn't take it anymore, but, luckily, because I had worked on my English so hard, I was able to start doing some translation work, which paid well. There was a local TV station that did translation of international documentaries, and I could do this at home in my free time and eventually pay for my final years of study."

Studying at the university was not easy. There were 120 students in her class, most of them men. Amena was impressed by the other women in her class, who were talented and intelligent, but she still felt marginalized. The other women would make snide comments about her Iranian accent and imply that she was not actually Afghan. She was also the only Hazara woman in her class, and they would comment on that.

It was assumed by professors and other students alike that most women in the medical school would go into maternal health, but perhaps because she was used to defying expectations, Amena decided she wanted to specialize in surgery. This was a far more difficult exam to pass, but Amena liked pushing herself and the idea of challenging the assumptions that others had about her. She also felt that performing surgery was the real work of being a doctor. Still, her relationship with her family continued to deteriorate. By this point, most women her age were married, and she was reminded constantly of this by her family, who would bring home suitors for her. Each one she turned down and, these refusals, she said, "destroyed my relationship with my father."

As Amena gained more experience, she picked up some additional work with a Massachusetts-based international organization called Management Science for Health (MSH). They worked primarily on sending medicines to rural provinces, and Amena enjoyed working with the internationals at the organization who seemed genuinely concerned about the fate of public health across the country. It also got her thinking on a deeper level about how best to support women in rural areas who did not have easy access to the urban hospitals that she was working in. While there were more freedoms for women then than under the Taliban, many families still did not allow their women to travel alone, even for health care, so MSH and the Ministry of Public Health worked to design programs that sent medicine to them in their homes.

While working with MSH, Amena passed her specialization exam in surgery and was qualified to join one of the big hospitals as a surgeon. In those government hospitals, however, the pay was meager, there was a shortage of equipment, and Amena worried about being treated poorly by male doctors and nurses who didn't think a woman should be a general surgeon. She also realized working for MSH that she could impact far more women by running one of these programs than she could ever treat as a doctor. So, when MSH offered her a full-time position managing some of their medicine distribution programs, she felt this type of work was far more rewarding, not to mention it would pay her enough to be independent.

Her position at MSH was to work primarily with the Ministry of Public Health even though she was not a direct employee of the ministry. There were many international agencies, like MSH, that would embed these privately paid experts into the ministries. While there were certain upsides, such as the fact that these contracted experts could assist the ministries in areas where they had great need, at the same time, it created a very uneven system. The actual government employees were often resentful of these outside contractors who might be earning ten times what they were, and the external consultants lasted only as long as the project they were working on, and, as a result, many consultants hopped between positions, always looking for a longer-term project that would pay more. The entire system was aimed at short-term fixes, but after almost ten years of this type of outsourcing, the government became accustomed to running in this haphazard and disjointed way.

At the Ministry of Public Health, Amena was employed in part to support resources for doctors or nurses in remote areas. All of the medical textbooks in Afghanistan assumed the doctors using them had access to the technical equipment available in city hospitals. Doctors in rural areas, of course, did not. So Amena worked on writing and updating a textbook aimed at those doctors who did not have these resources. She went "hospital to hospital and ward to ward," speaking to doctors to get a sense of what was needed in the book. It focused on many of the diseases and other illnesses that are prevalent in remote areas, but it also focused on how to treat them with limited resources.

Amena's work was a part of a broader effort that truly revolutionized health care for those who could access it—by bringing resources to rural areas, instead of making those in remote areas travel to the cities, and initially, there were some real advances.

In 2000, 9.5 out of every 100 infants died before reaching their first birthday, and life expectancy was only age fifty-six. By 2019, life expectancy had climbed to age sixty-four and fewer than half as many infants were dying before reaching the age of one. Much of this had to do with the work that Amena was a part of. The ministry, supported by numerous international organizations, had built up facilities and programs across the country. By 2018, the World Health Organization (WHO) reported that there were 3,135 health facilities across the country that the ministry was supporting, with 87 percent of the total population able to access these sites.[9] These facilities were supported by doctors, but also health workers who had more basic training and could reach more remote areas where doctors were often unavailable.

At the same time, however, this progress was uneven. The health care system favored the wealthy and those in urban centers. While there were government hospitals in cities, you often had to purchase medical supplies and bring them with you. Despite the international funds pouring into the health sector, a Ministry of Public Health survey found that 76 percent of all costs were paid by the patients. In 2019, 32 percent of those reporting receiving treatment said they had to borrow money to do so and 6 percent reported selling an asset like a car or livestock to pay for medical expenses. In many rural areas, hospitals were simply too far and too expensive to be accessed by much of the population.

When it came to education, there were similar advances and challenges. The Communist governments had promoted education and women's literacy, and when the Taliban first took Kabul in 1995 there were 100,000 girls in Kabul's public schools and 7,800 female teachers.[10] A year later these girls were all banned from studying in public schools, essentially bringing these numbers to zero for the next five years. Over the two decades after the US invasion, the number of schools and students studying there shot up. By 2019 the Ministry of Education was overseeing 11,628 public and 1,245 private schools,[11] and according to USAID, an estimated 9 million children were in schools, 3.5 million girls.[12] By 2020 there were 100,000 women enrolled in universities, up from 15,000 in 2012 and 6,000 in 2005.[13] Many of these schools were set up using international funds, and USAID and other international donors set up numerous higher education programs that particularly targeted women.

Who knows what might have happened if the momentum of those early years had been sustained. Amena and many of her female colleagues had begun to make great strides for Afghanistan. There were women entering politics, journalism, and other fields that had been exclusively male domains, but by the end of the 2010s, however, the war had crept back north. Amena and her colleagues in Kabul felt the effect primarily through sporadic suicide attacks in Kabul, but it was the south and the east of the country where the Taliban started to gain the most ground, building on resentment of an increasingly corrupt Afghan government and a US military that seemed to favor the local warlords over bringing real changes to the rural areas themselves.

By the end of the Bush presidency in 2008, the Taliban had started to seize entire districts again. Obama changed the US approach. Following a protracted internal debate, he ended up following the advice of Generals David Petraeus and Stanley McCrystal, who were advocating for a counterinsurgency approach to the war.[14] In 2009 and 2010, this new approach targeted "winning the hearts and minds" of the local Afghan population, flooding some key areas with resources, while ignoring others. In many instances, this meant more money for local commanders and corrupt officials, but little for the general population, which also was subject to Marines traipsing through their fields and conducting raids in their homes at night. It also meant more money flowing through contractors who hired local Afghans to fight much of the war for them.

CHAPTER 2

A Contracted War

ON THE FINAL DAY OF A WEEKLONG 2010 BOOTCAMP FOR FUTURE Afghan translators, a US Army officer arrived. The training had been taking place in a dusty compound with hastily constructed plywood classrooms on a base right outside of Kabul. During the entire recruitment, testing, and training process, the officer was the first actual US soldier that Najeeb had seen; all of their trainers had been contractors and other Afghan employees. The US Army officer stood in front of them and said, "If you want this job, you're going to be sent to Kandahar. It's the only place we need translators right now."

The official then passed around a series of documents for each man to sign, stating that they understood the risks and would not hold the US government accountable in any way. They also asked them to put down a phone number of who they could call to come collect their body, if necessary.

Najeeb signed the form.

With that, he joined the ranks of tens of thousands of other young Afghans who were now serving in the US war effort. Unlike the American soldiers they were working alongside of, however, Najeeb was a contractor, working for Aegis Mission Essential Personnel (MEP). This status brought with it a host of risks that were very different from those assumed by the soldiers he would be working alongside.

After finalizing their paperwork, Najeeb and the other translators were then given instructions to report to the large international air base in Kandahar in two weeks' time. Later, recalling the time before he deployed, Najeeb said, "I knew it was dangerous. We had heard of other translators getting killed, but it was a calculated risk. A year, maybe two in Kandahar, and hopefully I could get transferred to someplace in the north where things were safer. Maybe even get transferred to Kabul. I have always been an optimistic person, so I tried to just believe that it would all be fine."

He had reason to worry. Operation Hamkari, which was meant to stabilize the city of Kandahar and the surrounding districts, had just started. The operation name, which means "cooperation" in Dari, was meant to highlight the working together of American and Afghan forces. At that point American soldiers were dying daily in and around Kandahar. Less noted in the international press, Afghans working alongside them were being killed in fights with the Taliban at an even higher rate.

As the war ramped up, the air base in Kandahar became home to tens of thousands of international troops and even more civilian contractors. While the US war strategy in Afghanistan had shifted under Obama, the one consistent trend was the increased reliance on private contractors, particularly Afghans, to do the work that would have been done by soldiers in previous wars. This meant that some contractors were hired to be translators, but others were also hired to build the bases, deliver fuel, maintain the aircrafts, and clean the latrines. There were American contractors hired to do maintenance on aircrafts, Filipino contractors working in the dining hall, and thousands of Afghan contractors, generally doing the worst jobs, including, for example, manning the burn pits that incinerated the trash on bases, producing toxic fumes.[1]

By the time Najeeb arrived at Kandahar Airfield, there were more than one hundred thousand contractors working on Department of Defense contracts alone, and tens of thousands of others working for other government departments ranging from the CIA and DEA to USAID and the State Department. This meant that there was one contractor for every US soldier by Obama's surge in 2010, and later, as troops were withdrawn, the number of contractors dropped more gradually and there were eventually more than three contractors for every US military personnel.[2]

The increased number of contractors was often described as a cost-saving measure, though studies suggest hiring temporary contractors may not save costs in the long run. The costs that the contractors did reduce for American politicians, however, was the political cost of the war. Every dead US soldier was a negative news story for the US administration in power, and when Afghans or other internationals were killed, there was much less media attention. The fact that international and Afghan contractors were considered expendable became immediately apparent as Najeeb signed his contract.

While some of these contractors were American or from other Western countries, over the course of the war, the vast majority of them were Afghans like Najeeb. Many of them signed on because the pay was good, but Najeeb, like many others, believed in the cause: They were working together to help the Americans build a new Afghanistan. This group of Afghans had much in common with Amena, oftentimes able to earn paychecks and get training that allowed them to advance their careers and help their families. They imagined new lives in Afghanistan, but they were exposed to great risk, as well.

When Najeeb signed his contract, the Kabul-Kandahar highway was known by many as the "highway of death," Najeeb said. Taliban fighters routinely stopped buses or taxis and pulled out anyone who appeared to work for the Afghan government. In the best cases, they beat them and stole their belongings, and, in the worst cases, kidnapped or killed them. No US troops were traveling down that road at the time, much less traveling down it unarmed, and yet, the manager from the contracting company said that was exactly what the new Afghan recruits should do.

When Najeeb's family heard this, they protested. It was one thing to go off and join the fight, but another to take a road that could mean death before he even made it to the base to report. They bought him a plane ticket on a commercial carrier that left from Kabul and stopped at the decrepit civilian airport in Kandahar. Najeeb could pay them back from his first paycheck, he decided.

Najeeb joined a couple of other translator recruits who got off in Kandahar. They sat on plastic chairs in the arrivals lounge, because there was no one there at first to meet them. It was Ramazan, the month of fasting, so Najeeb was neither eating nor drinking. It was hot and Najeeb started to feel dehydrated, which gave the entire experience a more surreal feeling. Jets roared past on the runway every few minutes it seemed.

After an hour or so a van pulled up, driven by an American who introduced himself as Dave. He was also a contractor who worked with Mission Essential Personnel to coordinate the translators. Instead of heading out of the airport, the van drove around the long runway and then onto the base that was just across the runway from the civilian airport. As in Kabul, the US military had essentially taken over the Kandahar landing strip, allowing the occasional plane to take off out of the civilian terminal while a sprawling military base grew up across the tarmac, dwarfing the civilian side of the airport.

At that point, the air base was expanding massively, home to approximately twenty thousand soldiers and contractors. It was an operations hub with helicopters coming and going every few minutes, ferrying troops to various smaller outposts that were expanding across the south. In addition to hosting a flow of supplies and people, the base had fast-food restaurants, a hockey rink, and several less-pleasing features such as the "poo pond," a large open pool of human excrement.[3]

Najeeb and his companions were dropped at a tent that housed the Mission Essential Personnel translators who were coming or going from bases around the region. Many parts of the base were restricted, so while they could walk around certain areas, for the most part they were confined to their tent, waiting to be sent out. The more experienced translators seemed to enjoy scaring the new recruits by telling them stories of Taliban ambushes and rocket attacks and showing them their own scars.

The rapid buildup of troops had serious consequences for those like Najeeb who were hired to join the war effort. Obama had announced a surge of troops, but he had also made it clear that he expected those troops to withdraw in approximately two and a half years. This meant the military needed to show success immediately. The emphasis was on speed; troops needed to get out into the field, and, with so much of the war being contracted out to companies supporting the United States, this meant also spending money quickly, and carelessly.

Translators were just one of the aspects of the war that the military was struggling to keep a supply of, leading the military to use a shifting set of companies to find translators for them. After Titan, the contracting company originally supplying translators to the military, struggled to deliver the number of translators they promised, Mission Essential Personnel won a contract to replace them, despite that they had never done anything at this scale before. When MEP won the contract in 2009, it had just $6 million a year in revenue (qualifying it as a "small business" under the Veterans' Benefits Act), but despite its small size, it was offered a contract by the US military for $414 million over five years to provide 1,691 translators.[4] After winning the contract, the company immediately slashed the salaries of the Afghan translators working for it, and it struggled to provide support for the translators they had. (They were also responsible for getting translators to and from the various bases where they were needed.) In some cases, injured translators were fired for "being late," and several outlets reported on MEP abandoning employees once they had been wounded.[5] Najeeb joined the company just after they had been given an extension of another $679 million.

The additional funds did not improve conditions for the translators. In fact, if a translator was injured alongside a soldier, he might receive immediate first aid, just as any soldier would, but after this, many contracting companies were not equipped to provide additional medical care. In some cases, injured contractors were flown out of the country to be treated in cheaper medical facilities.[6] These and other exploitative practices meant that many of these translators and other contractors in places like Kandahar were facing many of the same risks that American soldiers were, but their companies were supplying them with none of the same supports.

Most of the US soldiers Najeeb worked with had no sense of how little the translators were being paid and how poorly they were being treated, but of course the contracting process allowed the military to ignore these practices. After reports of more egregious abuses came to light, clearly trying to distance the military from some of MEP's practices, a US Army spokesperson said that the army "does not have direct oversight of MEP's employees, as this contract is not a Personal Service

Contract. Consequently, MEP's contractual obligations to its employees reside outside the direct government's purview."[7]

Najeeb, like many contractors, knew none of the company's history as he sat in the hot tent in Kandahar and waited to be deployed to one of the outposts in the region. He thought that he would be a part of the unit he was fighting alongside, not understanding that as a contractor, this relationship could be terminated at any minute. His father had served in the Afghan armed forces and Najeeb thought that by serving as a translator, this was a way he could work to improve the country. Growing up in Kabul under the Taliban, Najeeb had been frustrated by the pointlessness of school. It was all religious texts. He was in sixth grade when the US invasion began and at such an impressionable age, he immediately grabbed onto the promises that the soldiers brought with them. He saw the Americans as a "window of hope," he said. Suddenly they could go to movies and walk down the street without worrying about being stopped by a Taliban policeman for being too noisy. The promise was not just of a life with things like movies, but also opportunity. The chance to shape the country he lived in. When the first elections were held in 2004, he joined one of the voter registration drives, which helped get individuals registered to vote and encouraged them to come out on election day.

Like Amena, Najeeb was convinced that school was the best way forward. He wanted to study law and had prepared hard for the Kankor entrance exams. His scores qualified him for a law program in Kapisa, about a two hours' drive north of Kabul, but this was in 2008, and universities outside of the major cities still had few resources. When Najeeb had arrived in Kapisa, much of the college was either crumbling or half finished. The dorms had been rented out to local shops and had become a small bazaar. Few of the professors actually showed up for classes and the other students did not seem serious. After two weeks Najeeb had given up. What was he going to learn in such a place? So he headed back to Kabul, where he heard about the need for translators.

***

A helicopter dropped Najeeb off on a small Forward Operating Base, or FOB, in Kandahar. This was just as the Marines were expanding their footprint rapidly in the south of the country, setting up a necklace of small bases manned by both Afghan and American troops.[8] Najeeb's base was on the road between Kandahar and Helmand, which at that point was increasingly under Taliban control. This meant that Taliban fighters were using the road past the post to move in and out of Helmand, connecting them with the city of Kandahar and Spin Boldak, one of the key border crossings with Pakistan.

The surge had sent 10,000 American, Canadian, and Afghan troops into the rural districts west of Kandahar. They were joined by a growing number of locally recruited Afghan Local Police, who were lightly formalized local militias trained by US Special Forces. With a local population of only 150,000, this was a massive buildup of troops. Yet, as the international troops entered the area, the Taliban shifted away from a strategy of direct attacks and aimed instead to harass these small bases, killing and injuring when they could but largely avoid direct confrontations. This made it hard to eliminate the insurgent fighters and, as one Taliban fighter explained, "Here all the people are Taliban. The Americans cannot put everyone in prison."[9] For those like Najeeb on the base, the result was constant fears of small rocket attacks or roadside bombs, set up right outside their gates. At night Najeeb would look up and watch the tracers of bullets pass over the outpost.

He remembered thinking how much worse it all was than what people realized in Kabul. Some of the news of the fighting was trickling out in Afghan and international media sources, but there just weren't that many journalists willing to come to areas where the fighting was happening. Those who did make it rarely spoke with the local Afghans who were in favor of the Taliban.

Most days he accompanied three missions "outside the wire," meeting with local officials and translating for the Marines. These were tense meetings. The locals were almost always weary. Why cooperate with the US soldiers when they would probably soon leave and they would again be confronted by the Taliban? The locals also viewed Najeeb, an Afghan who had decided to work with the Americans, with suspicion. He was from the city and while they were all Afghans, the elders said, they clearly did not trust him.

This was the height of the "counterinsurgency" approach, when US Marines were asked to go around to small communities in territory that was resistant to the Afghan government and "win hearts and minds." Najeeb and the hundreds of other Afghan translators involved were ultimately the Afghan face of this approach. Serving as the voice of the US military in local council meetings and with groups that potentially supported the Taliban, Najeeb and other translators became increasingly recognizable and targeted by the Taliban for their actions.

When not on patrol, Najeeb was required to sit in a tent and translate Taliban radio conversations as those on the radio plotted attacks on the base that he was sitting in. It was a strange hell having to listen to hours of someone discussing your own death. The Taliban would report the movements of US troops with shocking accuracy as they watched them from a distance. They would then joke about killing them and torturing the Afghans who helped them, knowing that translators like Najeeb were listening.

While US soldiers were often quick to point out the difference between soldiers and contractors, over the course of the war the line became increasingly blurry. For instance, few large bases or international compounds were actually guarded by US soldiers; they were guarded by private security firms. These firms often hired Nepalis who had retired from the military to serve there.

The contracting model also created massive discrepancies in how Afghans and Americans were treated, even as they were side by side. One *Wired* report found that MEP paid "$235,000 per year, plus health benefits and a 401-K, 'analyz[ing] communications' and 'perform[ing] document exploitation' on one of Afghanistan's big, comfortable military bases," while their Afghan counterparts earned $900 a month working on the front lines.[10]

As the surge went on, both international and Afghan contractors were a more and more important part of the war efforts. US officials were eager to draw down troops and "Afghanize" the war. This meant replacing US service personnel with contractors whenever possible. These American policies also impacted the way the Afghan military was supported. So, for instance, in its setup of the Afghan National Army (ANA) and Afghan National Police (ANP), the United States also encouraged Afghan forces to rely on international contractors, which meant that any withdrawal of international contractors from Afghanistan was likely to severely impact the ability to maintain security. This impacted aspects of the war, big and small. For instance, in 2021 only 19 percent of ANA and 7 percent of ANP vehicle maintenance was being done by the ANA, and the rest relied on international contractors.[11] Neither the Americans nor the Afghans were maintaining much of their own equipment. This meant that Afghan forces were not just heavily reliant on US troops for support, but also on the international contractors who came with those troops.

The increased role of contractors in the war meant incentives for fighting were strangely skewed. For soldiers, ending the war meant getting to go home. For contractors, an end to the war meant an end to their contracts and employment. Companies had an incentive for the war to continue and, perhaps unsurprisingly, the war stumbled on.

In the meantime, individual contractors were left to perform tasks they were not trained for. Ultimately, this weighed on Najeeb. In meetings with locals near his base, he explained, "My job was to say who is a good guy and who is a bad guy." If someone pulled up to a convoy on a motorcycle in Afghan dress and an AK-47, it could have been a Taliban attacker or it could have been one of the locals the Special Forces had recruited into a local militia working with the Americans. In a split second Najeeb was asked to make that decision again and again, a decision that could get one of his soldiers or the man on the bike killed before anyone knew what happened. The stress wore him out, day after day.

The most disturbing thing for Najeeb, however, was the feeling that they were all being constantly recycled through the war machine. It soon became clear that Najeeb was replacing a translator who had been killed in action just a few days before. Everyone kept talking about what a nice guy the translator had been. His items were still in the tent, and Najeeb was asked to take his spot in the tent and continue his job, almost as if the other translator had not left. If he was killed, Najeeb wondered, would he be replaced this quickly too?

When Najeeb heard that there was an opening for a translator on a base near Kabul where he would be primarily translating documents, instead of accompanying Marines in the field, he applied immediately.

CHAPTER 3

A Divided Country

As the sun set on the Gobi Desert, Zeinab adjusted the straps of her pack. She had been running in an ultramarathon in Mongolia since that morning. Her legs ached. She was used to that from the marathons she had run previously, but the pack bothered her. As the moon came up, she adjusted the straps and looked around. "I am so privileged to be here," she thought. "There are so many other talented women in Afghanistan, but I am so lucky enough to have been given the opportunity to work hard and leave and see things like this." Thinking back to that night, she concluded quietly, "Sports taught a lot of things to me, but particularly persistence."

Like Amena, Zeinab had been born a refugee in Iran. Her family was originally from Bamiyan, where the famous sixth-century Buddha sculptures were located. Their destruction by the Taliban in March 2001, when Zeinab was five years old, drew international criticism and attention to the harsh rule of the first Taliban era even while much of their abuse of women, torture of prisoners, and other blatant human rights abuses went unremarked on in the international media.[1] During the next twenty years, Bamiyan would actually be one of the safest provinces in the country. The Taliban insurgency that gained traction across the country had no appeal for the Shia Hazara in Bamiyan. Bamiyan also gained fame as the first province with a female governor. Despite this, many of the most peaceful areas in the country were also the ones that received the least international funding, and economic opportunities there were few and far between.

So, instead of returning to Bamiyan, Zeinab's family settled in Herat. Like many returning refugees, they preferred urban areas, because despite their high costs there were more of the resources they had come to enjoy in Iran, like schools and hospitals. It was an escape from the grinding poverty that still pervaded in most rural areas, and the city had begun to rebuild and expand since the US-led invasion. Herat was a big city, but security was far better than in Kabul and there was a peaceful air about the wide boulevards. Her father opened a welding shop to support the family, and they began to adjust to their new lives.

Zeinab was happy to no longer be discriminated against as a refugee, but this was in 2004 and conditions were still difficult. Electricity was unreliable and her house had a well that was a hundred feet deep. They had to drag the water up, bucket by bucket. Often the water had small red and black worms in it, which they tried to pull out. The entire family suffered from bloody diarrhea the first weeks they were back. "I was so dehydrated," Zeinab recalled, "that I could barely walk across the room."

Her first few years of elementary school occurred in a tent. The students had to bring blankets from home and wrap themselves to stay warm in the winter. Unlike Amena's family, Zeinab's father supported Zeinab and her sisters' schooling. "He always treated his sons and daughters the same," Zeinab said. "He is illiterate and does not always understand the things we are studying or what we hope to achieve, but he always tries to be supportive. 'You are free to do whatever you want,' he used to say."

After finishing high school, she did well on the Kankor exam and enrolled initially in the University of Herat, studying literature. It was not her top choice, but based on her Kankor score, it was the best that she could do, and she could study at the University of Herat and continue to help at home.

In 2015, two years into her studies, the American University of Afghanistan set up an outreach program in Herat. The American University of Afghanistan, or AUAF as it was generally called, was founded in 2006 as Afghanistan's first international, liberal arts university. It had quickly become known for the opportunities it provided to young Afghans to work closely with international faculty. Its graduates often went on to work for international NGOs. AUAF was working to bring in more poor, promising female students from other parts of the country to the growing university in Kabul. The funding was provided by USAID, through a program that "strengthens women's participation in civil society, boosts female participation in the economy, increases the number of women in decision making positions within the Afghan government, and helps women gain business and management skills."[2]

The school offered Zeinab a full scholarship, but she initially declined. She and her older sister looked after her younger brothers much of the day and she could not leave them. A year later, however, the university contacted her again, telling her the scholarship was still available if she was interested. She was still reluctant to leave her family and travel on her own, but now, her brothers were a bit older. Discussing it with two friends, however, they insisted that this was an opportunity she could not let pass, and Zeinab agreed.

It was one thing to win a scholarship, but even the logistics of getting to Kabul as a single, unmarried woman were difficult. Traveling by land at that point was dangerous—the Taliban had abducted thirty Hazaras traveling by bus on that road earlier that year. Zeinab also did not have a male relative to accompany her. Rich families could fly, but she didn't have that kind of money. Finally, without telling Zeinab, her father borrowed enough money to get her a one-way ticket. And just like that, she was off to Kabul.[3]

***

In the decade before Zeinab arrived in Kabul, the city had expanded rapidly, reflecting the growing inequality of the country. When Zeinab arrived the city probably had a population of around five million, but no one knew for sure, since there had not been any serious attempts to conduct a census and much of the population was in ever-sprawling, unregistered settlements around the edges. Also, stating a precise population number ignored the fact that Kabul was very much a city in motion: young men from the countryside coming in to work, others looking to migrate abroad, families who lived half their time in the city and half their time working on family farms. Working-class families lived in waterless, powerless dirt homes that crept up the informal land on the city's hills, while professional-class Afghans saved to buy apartments in new buildings that shot up in the residential neighborhoods sprawling out from the center.

It was also an expensive city. The cost of living was drastically higher than in other parts of the country. This made some of the poverty of Kabul all the more shocking.

As Zeinab drove through Pul-e Sokhta, on the way to the AUAF campus, the road was lined by drug addicts. Heroin had long been the drug of choice in Kabul, particularly for young men who had worked abroad in Iran and elsewhere and returned to Kabul unemployed. Now, however, heroin was being challenged by the growing popularity of crystal meth. Drug users, chased away from the sidewalks in front of stores, huddled on the traffic divides, crouched around shared pipes. Others lay collapsed beside them, oblivious to the cars rushing just past them. At night, Zeinab was told, they slept beneath the nearby bridge.

While Kabul was awash in cash from the American war, there were 2.9 million people in the city living in poverty.[4] The campus of the American University, however, was completely different. While the walls were not high, they kept out the noise of the city, and inside was a green courtyard that looked similar to the central quad that you might find on a small New England college campus. There was a cafeteria and students could sit and drink tea and chat after classes.

Zeinab loved the grassy campus, but she was aware of how it highlighted the economic inequalities in a country where a family in the bottom 10 percent earned one-tenth of what a family in the top 10 percent did.[5] The international community brought with them economic growth, but most of the opportunities that came from this were in urban areas and were much more accessible to men than to women. By most employment measures, men in rural areas and men in urban areas had similar levels of unemployment (19 percent compared with 18 percent). For women the difference was much greater: 57 percent of urban women were neither working nor attending school, and 69 percent of rural women were similarly unoccupied.[6] With 70 percent of the population still living in rural areas and 82 percent of them in poverty, this meant that for many women, in particular, education and work were still a dream.[7] For Zeinab, her family may have been supportive, but it was still a fight to imagine a future different from that of her mother or aunts.

In contrast with this, the families who were making money off the international presence grew increasingly wealthy. Caravans of armored cars whisked rich men around the city. They built compounds and villas on prime real estate. They sent their children abroad for schooling. A 2019 investigation by the Bureau of Investigative Journalism found numerous Afghan government officials who had purchased luxury villas and apartments abroad, including parliamentarians, ministers, and close relatives of the former president.[8] Most notoriously, Ahmad Zia Massoud, the former vice president and brother of the jihadi fighter Ahmad Shah Massoud, was said, in a leaked State Department cable, to have flown into the UAE with fifty-two million dollars in undeclared cash.[9]

Below this ultra-wealthy class of elites, there was another group of professionals who worked for the companies they ran or the international organizations that funded them. This was what Arsalan called the USAID generation, and it was between these two worlds that Zeinab was going to find herself pulled.

***

After arriving in Kabul, far from her family, Zeinab had few friends and at first was lonely in the large city. Surprisingly, it was a big rainstorm that seemed to open up opportunities for her. During the rain, Zeinab's dormitory flooded and everyone was moved into new rooms. In the aftermath of the chaotic move, Zeinab immediately clicked with her two new roommates. They were friendly and different from many of the other girls, who tended to talk about marriage and spent most of their time on social media. The other strange thing that they did was they both got up early to run at 4:30 a.m. before classes. This was not a typical thing for a young Afghan woman. Those hours were some of the few times that the streets of Kabul were not blocked by constant traffic and the only time women could run alone in the streets. Zeinab asked if she could join their next run.

When she joined them the next morning, it felt exhilarating to be out on those empty streets. Zeinab enjoyed the dark and the quiet, running past nomads taking their sheep to market and a few shopkeepers unloading their supplies. On that first morning, despite that she had never gone for a run before in her life, Zeinab and the two other women ran six miles. "They said, 'Wow, I can't believe that was your first run, and you didn't stop once,' and I thought, 'Maybe I can do this,'" Zeinab recalled.

Running was considered an odd, if not inappropriate, activity for a woman, and as Zeinab said, "I tried not to talk about it with others, because people were generally critical of women doing things like running, and listening to them would make me feel ashamed. But eventually, more and more girls saw this, and joined us." They set up a club at the university and Zeinab was elected president. Still, they were subject to taunts and, on one occasion, a friend was punched by a man on a bicycle who then simply rode off.

While Zeinab and her friends started by running on their own, they eventually joined up with a group called Free to Run. The group had been set up by a human rights lawyer and runner to encourage women living in conflict zones to find safe places to run. Suddenly having a group to run with was not just encouraging, it also made things safer for them. The group organizers would drive them to safer areas to run or pick them up at the end of longer runs, so they did not need to loop back and attract more attention. "That is when I realized not just that I like to run, but that I really like longer runs," Zeinab said.

In 2015, the group helped organize a marathon in the Bamiyan Valley. The province was chosen deliberately since the climate was good for running, but also because the Hazara minorities who live in the region tend to be more supportive of women being active in public life than other groups in Afghanistan. As the governor told one international reporter covering the event, "Bamiyan is a good place for this. In other places, they would be killed."[10]

Bamiyan was also Zeinab's ancestral home, and when she first went there to run in the marathon, she was overwhelmed by the beauty of the mountains and how welcoming the people were. The stress from the poverty and insecurity of Kabul seemed to melt away. "For me, Bamiyan is like heaven," she recalled.

Zeinab embraced the challenge and set off on her first marathon. Even while most onlookers gaped as she and the other racers ran by, she decided she loved the racing experience. By pushing herself, she was suddenly more aware of what she was capable of, both mentally and physically.

"At first, I just did it for myself, to be healthy, but after running my first marathon, I had the first real sense of accomplishment in my life. I felt that I was strong," Zeinab said.

After Bamiyan, she heard that another Afghan woman had been working with the head of Free to Run, training for an ultramarathon in Mongolia. They asked Zeinab if she was interested. It was 250 kilometers, or 150 miles, over the course of seven days. It was also an opportunity to leave Afghanistan and see a new place and meet participants from all over the world. She signed up and the two Afghan women, along with Taylor Smith, the American director of Free to Run in Afghanistan, made up the three-woman team.

Zeinab had heard the race was through the desert and thought that it would be sand dunes and sun, but she was surprised at how beautiful and varied the rugged terrain was. She was also impressed with the fact that women were competing alongside men equally. In a race over seven days, it was not as much about speed as it was about the ability to persevere day after day.

This was something she knew how to do. In Afghanistan, she had already trained through the month of Ramazan, when they would run having not had anything to eat or drink since before sunrise. She also knew how to deal with the unknown. During the months she spent waiting for a visa, she had had to simply forge ahead believing that it would come eventually. Her support team of fellow Afghan women and inspiring international women runners helped her to believe she could make something like this, something she could have not even imagined a few years ago, come true.

The first day went fairly smoothly, but the race was different from a marathon, and each day they had to meet a certain time to continue on the following day. The runners were also required to carry all their supplies with them over the hilly course. They had trained with packs to simulate this, but actually doing it for miles at a time was much different. They began the second day, Zeinab recalled, a thirty-mile run, already tired and sore. They had to get to the end of stage two by 4:00 p.m. or risk being disqualified. As the afternoon progressed, the road stretched out ahead of them and they could see far off into the distance, but they still couldn't see the finish line. At 3:30 they started to feel some panic. Where was the end? Would this be it? They kept pushing. "We were crying and running all at the same time." Finally, they saw the volunteers at the end, "and we crossed the finish line exactly at 4:00 p.m.," Zeinab said. That night they decided they needed to throw out some of their food and other supplies to cut down on weight.

Unfortunately, two days later, the other Afghan competitor injured her ankle. It was so swollen that there was no way she would be able to run. It meant the end of their team effort, since all members of the team needed to complete the race. "It was so sad," said Zeinab. They discussed, and she and Taylor decided that they still needed to finish the race as individuals, so that someone from Afghanistan might finish the race. She felt a new responsibility as the race continued.

The longest stage was fifty miles, and they ran through both the day and the night. Zeinab invented games to keep her mind off the pain. It began to rain and lightning, and while it was difficult, it was also beautiful. "I felt so lucky to be there." She finished that stage at 2:00 a.m., and in the final miles before the finish line, she remembers thinking, "This is not for me, it is for me to represent my country and the women of my country. That was my motivation. Even if I must crawl at the end, I need to finish this. Other girls and women in our country are looking at me. I felt responsible."

Returning to Kabul, she also began to work for Free to Run, organizing some of their activities for other women, taking them on runs and long hikes that they could never have done just on their own. Working with the women, Zeinab said, "helped them learn about communications, conflict resolution, leadership skills, and nutrition. Afghan students are taught nothing about nutrition in schools and nutrition is so important. We taught them about vitamins, proteins, carbohydrates, everything about nutrition."

As she raced longer and longer distances, training became more difficult. There simply weren't enough places around Kabul where she could easily go off for a two-hour run. Free to Run worked with various expatriates to try to find spaces where they could run. Some of the few places that were spacious enough were military bases.

The runners got permission to run every other Friday on the base that housed the International Security Assistance Forces (ISAF) headquarters, right in the center of town. This base, however, like many in Kabul, had strict security regulations when it came to any visitors. Anyone who was visiting the base had to have an escort with them at all times. This made jogging somewhat tricky, and to get around the regulations, every single Afghan runner with Free to Run had to be paired with someone working at ISAF headquarters who was technically escorting them as they ran along. This is how Zeinab met Jackie Faye.

Jackie had first come to Afghanistan in 2015. She had just graduated journalism school at Columbia and had gotten an email out of the blue asking if she was interested in a job in Kabul. She was excited by the idea of going to Afghanistan to "help Afghans," she said. Before continuing her story, she added, "I realize now just how naive that sounds." Her first job left her confined on a compound, rarely working with Afghans, but it gave her the experience to get a series of more interesting jobs. By this point, unfortunately, much of the international community in Kabul had rather limited interactions with Afghans; they lived in high walled compounds and rarely spoke with Afghans other than those few English speakers on their staff. This was one of the reasons Jackie was excited when she met Zeinab in 2018.

At that point, Zeinab's English was good, but not great, and the pair had to speak slowly, but that seemed to suit their running pace. For Jackie, it was also her first opportunity to have a real conversation with an Afghan woman, not just the formal conversations that she had with the few Afghans who were allowed on military bases. And Zeinab was willing to discuss everything, from family to sex to running, to what it meant to be a woman in Afghanistan. Jackie also found that Zeinab persisted. She had been paired with other Afghan women who would ask to walk every few minutes. With Zeinab, however, she said, "I would ask, 'Do you need a water break?' And the answer was always, 'No, let's keep going.'"

These bases, however, were also strange worlds, removed from the everyday life of Afghanistan. Here Zeinab could forget about the everyday pressures of school and family. Everything that made Kabul so difficult: the poverty, the pollution and the drugs. Here, men and women interacted differently, and everyone seemed to have money and had come from all over the world having achieved amazing things.

Jackie had long been an endurance athlete, and in 2018 she finished six different Ironman triathlons on six different continents all in one year. As she had spent years planning and training for this, she expected that by the time she was done she would feel some sort of accomplishment. But when she finished it and went back to Afghanistan, instead, she said, she "went from feeling 'I'm special,' to, 'of course I did this, I'm an American woman.'" At that point, she decided that while running the triathlons might not have been transformative for her, it would certainly be transformative for an Afghan woman. So, working with some of the organizers from Free to Run, she started looking for some Afghan women who might be interested.

"Look at the women and men in the C-suite, 80 percent of them played sports," Jackie said, when explaining why she was so drawn to sports. "Sports show you what you are capable of." Women did not have enough opportunities to do that in Afghanistan, she thought.

At first, Zeinab said, it was odd hearing about Ironman triathlons. Why would you race in three different ways for such a long time? How did it work to change into a swimming suit? It was all a little strange. Zeinab had owned a bike when she lived as a refugee but had not been on one since. And she had never swum. In fact, she had once fallen into a lake and had been nervous about being around water ever since.

Determined to spread the empowerment that she felt came to women competing in triathlons, Jackie began to raise money and set up an organization she called She Can Tri. Unlike many other international organizations, the focus of this group was incredibly specific: to support an Afghan woman to complete an Ironman triathlon. And so, Zeinab signed up.

Part II

A Growing Distance

ARSALAN—SEPTEMBER 8, 2021:

People don't dare to go out now, particularly women. They are afraid of this new "Taliban 2.0," as my friends have been calling them. They are afraid of their outfits, their features, and their odd behavior. The young fighters are all strange, even for those of us who can remember the Taliban the first time they were here. They are more confrontational. They clearly think that their key enemy are women, particularly educated women, and they single them out on the streets, harassing them. Women seem to be the real target now.

I was stopped at one checkpoint by a Taliban fighter who could not have been more than eighteen years old. In Afghanistan, honorifics are important, so normally we would call an officer "saheb," or sir. But for a religious man, you would refer to him as "mullah," and an educated man would be called "engineer" or "ustad," teacher. But what do you call a young Taliban fighter? He was the authority now, so I should have been respectful, but I didn't know how to address him or even make sense of the situation. I stumbled in my greetings to him.

He didn't seem to know what to do either. Asking me gruffly for my identity card, looking at my beardless face suspiciously, but also seeming to struggle to understand my formal Dari. Here is a young man, who grew up fighting in the hills, now asked to be a police officer in an enormous city. It must be a change for him as well.

So many of those who worked with the international community have now fled, particularly those who could secure visas or had a Western passport of some kind. Those who had spent time abroad before seemed to have the easiest time leaving. Some of my friends had received scholarships to study in Europe or the United States. My family was not as well connected, but each year there was a competition for scholarships for universities in Turkey. In later years, a lot of these scholarship programs were corrupt and just the sons and daughters of commanders, warlords, or high-ranking political figures seemed to be selected. But back in those days the competitions were still pretty fair. I applied to it in 2006 but wasn't selected. I applied again in late 2007, and this time I was lucky enough to win one of these awards. Studying in Turkey was not as glamorous as some of the stories my friends told me about studying in Germany or the United Kingdom. The Turkish government, to save money, did not fly us commercially to Turkey. Instead, they waited until there was space available on one of their military transport planes. We were never certain exactly when the flight would leave and worried that we might not make it for the start of classes.

But I enjoyed living in Turkey. It did not feel as far from Afghanistan as some of those other countries and the food was good. It was my first time living away from home on my own. Over the next few years, I received my BA and then applied for my MA, returning each summer to Afghanistan to work with Noah, conducting research.

Still, my BA and MA were looked upon differently by many of those Afghans who managed to spend time in the West. There was a hierarchy within Kabul, particularly among young professionals, that was not just about how rich you or your family was, but also how well-connected you were to the West and international organizations. They called these the "USAID generation," not because they all worked for USAID, but because they wanted you to know how Western they were, by their clothes, their haircuts, their makeup, and even the way they spoke.

You could feel this when you walked into certain offices.

A few years ago, I had one project that I was working on that was supposed to be supporting the Afghan Children Read Project (ACR). This was a $70 million project that USAID had given to the contracting company Creative Associates. They would then hire smaller companies and NGOs like mine to do the actual work of implementation. Our company was primarily involved in conducting research for them. The Afghans who worked at

Creative Associates would then oversee these contracts and make sure we were following their orders.

Their office was like an entirely different planet. Their employees drove up in private SUVs and big cars. Some even appeared armored. They would drive through these big gates, past multiple layers of security. Maybe the security was there to protect some of them, but it was also there to let you know how important they were, and even the guards treated normal people in a condescending way. When we came for meetings, they would make us wait outside in the street for someone to come get us. Even when we were there for a previously scheduled appointment, they would always make us wait at least a few minutes and sometimes we would have to sit outside for half an hour in the sun.

Inside, all the Afghan men were dressed in Western outfits, no one had the traditional Afghan dress. The women were wearing pants, and these offices always seemed to have coffee everywhere. I do not know exactly, because I have not been to the United States, but these offices seemed to me as if they were actually in the United States and had just been dropped into Kabul.

Even when the meeting was just Afghans, some would speak in English just to show off. When they were speaking Dari, they would insert all sorts of English words, like "outcomes" or "capacity-building," just to show you that they were well-connected. If you were wearing traditional dress or even had a beard, they were even more likely to do this and speak to you dismissively. Even though I was a vice president at my organization, they would speak down to me too, and these people were supposed to be implementing projects in rural Afghanistan, meeting with local communities. If they were to go out into the poorer communities in Kabul, people would just stare at them with their strange clothes and hairstyles.

One of our field team leaders had a large beard, and in his community he was respected and treated like an elder, even though he was still fairly young. We hired him because he was very smart and knew a lot of local communities very well. He was running one of these projects for a contracting company and we had a meeting to report on the progress of the work to the company. When we arrived, it was me, my Australian boss, and the field team leader with the beard. My boss and I went through the security checkpoint, but then they didn't let the field team leader through, even though he was the one giving the *presentation on the work that we had been doing. They asked my boss, "Who is this? Your security guard? He should stay outside."*

It was very insulting, but it also wasn't surprising. There were several projects with USAID, the UN, and others where I was running the entire project and had all the information, and yet, the officials at USAID did not want to meet with me unless my Australian boss was there, and he didn't know much about some of these projects.

Afghan officials were the same way. In one case, we were supposed to interview the governor of Logar on aid effectiveness. I was working with another Afghan running the project with the assistance of an outside consultant from Canada helping with some of the research. My Afghan coworker and I went all the way to Logar to meet with the governor and when we arrived, he asked, "Where is your Canadian colleague?" He wouldn't talk to us since he was expecting an international. It was this type of thing that turned many ordinary Afghans away from the government and the international community.

There were also always rumors about the women who worked in these international organization offices. To criticize their work, more conservative people would gossip and say that these organizations were corrupting women, turning them into prostitutes. This, of course, was not true, but it was a way to spread rumors, and many who ended up supporting the Taliban said they did so because these foreigners did not act respectfully with women. Often foreigners did not realize that they were even doing this. Something simple, like a male foreigner sitting in the backseat of a car with an Afghan woman, could seem like nothing to them, but would lead Afghans to question the woman's reputation.

I returned to Afghanistan full time in 2013 and started working at my current research firm, which had just been set up. One of the things I liked about it was that we largely had managed to avoid some of the mistakes of those companies that felt so isolated from the real world of Afghanistan. We had our challenges, but since so much of our staff was in the field, conducting interviews and running surveys, we had to stay connected to local communities. We had a lot of female researchers since we worked on projects around health and other issues that required interviews with Afghan women, but we were careful not to appear to be one of those international firms that were bringing in Western values.

For instance, in more conservative parts of the country, our female researchers often travel with a mahram, or male relative, as an escort. Even in Kabul, we tried to make sure women had their own space in our offices and encouraged them to take private transportation rather than riding the city buses. Still, professional women in Kabul were often harassed for being too Westernized. For instance, we used to have taxis wait outside our office and once I hopped in one, and the driver shooed me out, telling me, "I am waiting to give a ride to one of the fashionable women who work in your office."

I'm not sure what they imagined was going on inside our offices or what some of our female staff thought of them, but you could feel the divide growing. Ordinary Afghans were suspicious not just of the American military, but all those international organizations that had come with them. They were not bringing stability or economic growth to the country, it seemed, so clearly they must be there for some other reason. And, if you listened to those who supported the Taliban, it often came back to how they treated women. At our office we worked to avoid this, but as the 2010s moved on and the number of American troops in the country started to decrease, people became more and more skeptical of the international presence and fewer and fewer ordinary Afghans were on the side of the government and the international community that supported it.

CHAPTER 4

Young Politics

EVEN AS NAJEEB AND OTHERS WHO HAD FOUGHT WITH THE AMERI-cans were being targeted, the early years of the 2010s were still a hopeful time for certain sections of the population. Many of the groups that suffered the most under the initial Taliban regime made strides in the first decade of the American intervention. This was true of Hazara groups and women in particular, as in the case of Amena, but another group that benefited was young people.

In his Ted Talk in Kabul in 2013, Lotfullah Najafizada walked onto the stage and, giving a slight smile, opened with, "I wish that this is not too boring, given the fact that I have ten minutes and food is waiting."[1] An apologetic opening is typical for young Afghans, who are taught from an early age to be deferential to their elders, but Lotfullah's youthful cheerfulness and young age hid his real power and charisma. Named one of *Forbes'* "30 under 30 Asia Influencers in Media," Lotfullah worked briefly for the media office at NATO before joining the independent TOLO television channel, part of the Moby Media group.

"I am more optimistic because of the levels of interaction and engagement we see in society, and the level of maturity we see in society, especially among the youth . . . they are coming with ideas, with plans to further strengthen the national dialogue."

Looking ahead to the upcoming election and the potential first peaceful transfer of power in Afghanistan in half a century, Lotfullah continued, "The youth have a critical role to engage in a national conversation, to make wise decisions. . . . So, with the elections in 120 days, exactly from today, I think that it is going to be the first-time voters, or the youth, or the kids who went to school in 2004 and are voting in 2014 for the first time, are changing the political landscape and the political calculations in our country. . . . We have a responsibility as a generation to work harder.

"It is important for the youth to get together, to build networks . . . to discuss how we can change things, simply, how we can influence policies, how we can influence big decisions made by the government and the international community.

"The government and the international community should hear the voice of the youth," he concludes. "I am very hopeful . . . that youth will show the world a different Afghanistan."

And, for a brief moment, as Karzai transitioned out of power, replaced by the thoughtful academic and former World Banker Ashraf Ghani, there was hope that as the US troops declined, a technocratic state, powered by newly educated young people, could show Afghans a way forward that was neither blindly following the West nor reverting to Taliban rule.

***

By 2014, over half the population of Afghanistan was below the age of twenty, which meant that they had little to no memory of the Soviet period in the 1980s or the Civil War in the 1990s, and they were just children during the Taliban period in the late 1990s. As this new generation came of age, many who were lucky enough to go to school and learn English, particularly in Kabul, found themselves in high demand as the rapidly expanding NGO and development sector snapped up these educated individuals.

Many of these young people were particularly hostile toward the corruption and nepotism they saw in the older generation of politicians who ruled the country, even while many benefited by coming from these same well-connected families. Some reports point to the parliamentary elections of 2010s as a turning point when the corruption of many of the old-guard type of politicians became even more visible.[2]

This was also just as smartphones were becoming more and more available, particularly for younger Afghans. Previously the internet had been available, but this was largely in city cafes. These cafes were dominated by young men playing video games and were not very appealing for others to visit. With the rise of smartphones, all of a sudden, many Afghans had access to the internet and Facebook in their pockets. This revolutionized communication and organizing for young people. Now news was not just coming from a couple of independent Afghan TV stations and Western sources, but people were putting up posts about everything from family to politics. In places where it was considered illicit for unrelated men and women to speak with each other, these new devices opened up entirely new social worlds and networks.[3]

As technology and educational opportunities for young people expanded in urban areas, it became increasingly common for young people to set up groups and social clubs of varying levels of formality and organizational structure. At the more informal end, Arsalan and some of his friends started pooling funds each year to support a student from a rural area to attend university in Kabul. At first, this was just an act of collective charity, but as more and more of their friends contributed, they started a formal selection process to determine which students would receive the funds. On a more formal level, USAID and other international sponsors set up youth programs that were designed to give young people certain skills, but they also encouraged networking between young people from different areas and ethnicities. This meant that, for example, the alumni network of Afghans who had received Fulbright scholarships, which met monthly for meals and conversation, became increasingly strong.

Still, most of these efforts were small and few attempted to reshape politics at a national level. This changed in 2012, when a network of young activists, politicians, and leaders set up a group called "Afghanistan 1400." (In the Afghan calendar, the year 1400 would be ten years later in the Gregorian year 2021, suggesting that politics in Afghanistan needed to have longer horizons.) Young civil society leaders came together and made a series of demands aimed at giving young people more influence in politics nationally. That they were not connected to any other political parties gave them the independence that they craved, but this also meant they were criticized by many in the mainstream political establishment. Interestingly, then-president Karzai came out strongly, urging young people and university students, in particular, to stay out of politics. While this seemed to be a reference to the student movements of the 1960s and 1970s, which contributed to some of the divisions in the country that eventually led to the war between the Communist government and the Islamist mujahideen, this was seen by some youth as a typical response from an establishment that was still dominated by the generation of leaders that had overseen the past thirty years of conflict.

Despite this, these young aspiring politicians quickly became media darlings, making visits to various Western embassies who wanted to see political change of some kind. The same year, USAID published a report entitled "Youth in Development in Policy: Realizing Demographic Opportunity," and funds increased for programs that appeared to be targeting young people. The next year many of Afghanistan 1400's leaders were taken on a trip to the United States to meet with American politicians. A decade later, many of the young people who participated in these programs were exactly the type of Afghan who were in danger of being targeted by the Taliban for their connections to the West, but who lacked the credentials or time served to receive a Special Immigrant Visa (SIV). However, in 2012, while the political impact of the group at first appeared negligible, it was clear that they were inspiring other young Afghans to think differently about their roles in politics.

Even for Afghans from the poorest and most rural backgrounds, hard work, a good knowledge of English, and the willingness to work their connections allowed for upward mobility into a class of young urbanites, who drank coffee in Kabul's new cafes, spoke of democracy and human rights, and became increasingly disconnected from the rest of Afghan society.

Twelve years before he was to climb on a plane with twenty-eight unaccompanied children, Munir was one of these young Afghans, hopeful about the future of the country and the place that the younger generation could have in it all.

***

Munir has a warm but shy smile and a tendency to look off into the distance when he is thinking. The youngest of seven children, he had a gentle way of speaking until he comes to a point, and then he furrows his brow and becomes sterner. It was clear as he spoke to us of his youth that the images were clear in his mind, but also seemed far off.

Munir was born in a rural part of Wardak, not far from Kabul, but a very different world. It is fertile area and known for its orchards and apples. His village had *karezs*, underground irrigation channels that were a centuries-old feat of engineering and community cooperation. They used to be common around Afghanistan, but Genghis Khan destroyed many during his invasion of Afghanistan, and the technique of destroying irrigation systems to punish local communities has been used ever since.

The majority of those living in the province were Wardaki Pashtuns, and most Afghans meeting Munir for the first time would assume that he too was Pashtun; however, his village were Sadats, sometimes referred to as Sayyids, who are well-known for being descended from the Prophet Mohommad and were said to be descended from Arabs who had settled in Afghanistan centuries before.

They were a small village of about thirty-five families, or three hundred people. During times of peace, the Sadats lived easily alongside their Pashtun neighbors and were given special respect because of their religious connections and reputation for being well-educated. Due to their high education levels, despite living in a rural area, the community produced more than their fair share of engineers, teachers, and, of course, government officials. During times of conflict, resentment from neighboring Pashtun villages over the status of the Sadats could turn into violence. All the villages around Munir's used the same karez system for irrigation. This heightened tensions because it was simple for a village upstream to cut off flow to their downstream neighbors. The livelihoods of everyone in these communities were tied together in a complex web, and when fighting got worse in the area, the village suffered.

Afghanistan is an incredibly ethnically diverse country, and this means that many of these patterns of villages and communities working together during times of peace but then becoming more distrustful during times of war are common across the country.[4] This also contributes to the rapid scaling up of violence in certain moments.

Munir's father was killed during the chaotic Civil War period of the late 1980s and early 1990s when his store was looted by a militia. Munir and his six siblings were left without a father and needed to largely fend for themselves. As the youngest of his four brothers, Munir was responsible for the family cow and their goats while his older brothers looked after the family land. Munir particularly looked up to his eldest brother, who was deaf, but who was known in town as incredibly strong and hardworking. His second brother had gone to university, but he returned to the village to help look after the family.

"It was because of them, I could go to school," Munir said. "It was a hard life for the family without our father, but it was also happy, I now realize, because the simpler things are, the happier they are."

His village was conservative and when he was growing up, it had a couple of radios, but no televisions. The only outside news source they ever heard was BBC Persian and Voice of America. Their school was supported by an Arab NGO from Saudi Arabia, and the first time Munir ever saw a television was when he was nine years old and the NGO brought a television to his village school to show a documentary on animals from Africa.

"Between the animals that we had never heard of and the magic of the TV screen, we were all amazed," he recalled.

This made Munir eager to learn more about the world beyond Wardak, but this was during the Taliban-controlled era in the 1990s, and it was several years before he even saw a television again. Most of his school courses were on religious topics or Arabic language classes, and he was frustrated by the seeming pointlessness of the rote memorization that was demanded. With the collapse of the first Taliban government, schools suddenly were able to teach other things and Munir jumped at every opportunity he had. He spent time reading English books and studied Dari as well. Since everyone in his village spoke Pashto, however, by the time he attended university, Munir could read and write fairly well in English and Dari, but, as he put it, "not speak a word," since he had never heard English spoken and conversed only rarely in Dari.

Even under the new Karzai government, not everyone embraced the Western message about liberalism. Munir started studying at the University of Jalalabad in 2005, which was one of the largest and best-known government universities. Still, many of the professors at the school were active supporters of the Hizbe Islami party, a group that was not allied with the Taliban but which did share many of their conservation beliefs. This made the university a place where it was common to hear anti-Western and, at times, anti-government sentiment, even though it was technically a government university. Still, he was hopeful that a degree could get him ahead and allow him to help support his family. The day he graduated from university, he went with his brother to the local internet cafe and wrote their resumes, preparing for their next big step.

Munir moved to Kabul in part because this was where most of the jobs for young people were at that time, but also because the Taliban were gaining influence in the villages around his home in Wardak. In fact, by the late 2000s, much of the province was controlled by the Taliban and there was a shadow governor appointed by the Taliban as strong as the actual governor. This made life in his village even more difficult. There were American drone attacks regularly, not to mention night raids targeting supporters of the Taliban insurgency. The drone attacks were particularly terrifying since there was no warning, just a sudden explosion as a missile took out a car or whatever its target was. The drone attacks also had devastating impacts on the fabric of the community. Whenever there was an attack, there were immediately questions afterward: Why had that family been targeted? Who benefited from the attack? Who had given them information?

Some family members and other Sadats in Munir's village were being targeted by the Taliban since many had family members like Munir, working in Kabul. They assumed those in the big city must have connections to the international community and the government. Former warlords who essentially ran criminal gangs took advantage of both the Taliban presence and the mistrust between communities. Uncertainty and lawlessness were helpful for them since they profited from the lack of clear political control, extorting protection money and land from the weak.

Munir realized it was safer for his family to stop visiting his home.

In the meantime, the first job he got in Kabul was for an Afghan NGO that did advocacy work, promoting the participation of women and people with disabilities in politics. After gaining some experience, he then moved up, applying for a job at the Afghan Research and Evaluation Unit (AREU), one of Afghanistan's most important independent research organizations. At AREU Munir worked alongside an array of young international researchers, as well as Afghans who had been educated abroad and returned home. They had some of the Western ideals that the bigger contracting companies did, but as an independent research group, AREU did not pay as well as the international contracting companies that were increasingly hiring young, educated Afghans, like Munir. So Munir started looking for a better paying job with one of the international contractors.

***

While the United States outsourced much of its military work to contractors like Najeeb, the development funds that came from US and other Western sources similarly poured into NGOs and private contractors that were building schools, running training programs, running elections, and facilitating the disorganized international approach to state-building that was particularly well-funded during the surge years.

All this meant jobs for young, urban, and educated Afghans, like Munir, but it also meant a growing disconnect between the urban areas where there was real belief that positive change was possible and the rural areas that were bearing the brunt of the war. Perhaps no one embodied this urban optimism more than Ashraf Ghani.

After leaving his post as a professor at Johns Hopkins, he had worked at the World Bank and written a book entitled *Fixing Failed States*. He served initially as an advisor to Hamid Karzai and later as finance minister, before running against Karzai in 2009. In 2009, he received only approximately 3 percent of the vote, despite, or perhaps because of, the fact that he had the backing of the US embassy.[5] Many in those days said that Ghani was a *kharaji*, or a foreigner, since he had lived in the United States for many years. Five years later, however, with funds from the international community dwindling, there was a sense that perhaps his connections to the international community could keep some of those fundings coming in. The young professional class in Kabul particularly embraced his candidacy.

One of Zeinab's friends remembered, "In 2013, Ashraf Ghani and his wife came to our school to discuss his plans for the future, especially how he would include the voices of young people. It was so inspiring. Later, when I was a student leader at Kabul University, I got to meet him in person. That made me feel so good about the future of Afghanistan, especially the promises he made about creating job opportunities for graduates in Afghanistan and how he was encouraging Afghans educated abroad to return to the country."

By combining the support of this young professional class along with a strong voting machine in the Pashtun areas, Ghani was able to win the highest percentage of the vote in the 2014 election. However, the winner needed more than 50 percent of the vote cast, and the vote count descended into chaos and violence as supporters of Ghani and second-place vote getter, Abdullah Abdullah, clashed. After a protracted set of negotiations, John Kerry helped negotiate a deal between the two where Ghani would be president and Abdullah Abdullah would be chief executive officer—a position that did not exist under Afghan law. They also evenly divided the appointment of governors and ministers, and in the process of the negotiations, most of the key warlords and politicians managed to retain positions of power.

Still, for young people like Munir, the election of Ashraf Ghani presented opportunities for his generation. The administration brought in younger Afghans, many who had been educated abroad. There were significant attempts made to professionalize the civil service and lower rungs of the government. It was not rare to see young technocrats working in the presidential palace, a shift from earlier administrations that had favored older politicians who were more embedded in the political system. This too gave Munir hope. The "USAID generation," in particular, was represented within the administration by figures such as Hamdullah

Mohib, who had been the head of information technology at AUAF before working on the Ghani campaign. Mohib, who was educated in the United Kingdom, was brought into the Ghani administration first as deputy chief of staff.

Mohib had written in a 2011 *Foreign Policy* article that the problem with Afghan politics was, "Too many of those who made it to the parliament are not truly representative of their constituencies, but instead are often warlords and regional strongmen whose power has been bolstered through their strong political ties and bribery." He argued that if the national government connected with the grassroot democracy found in local village councils and among leaders like local *maliks* and other elders, a more Afghan-style democracy would emerge. Afghanistan, he concluded, "is not ready for a centralized Western-style democracy."[6] Ghani, he suggested, was the type of leader who could circumvent the warlords and bring grassroots democracy to the people of Afghanistan. It was the type of argument that many of those involved in youth politics were making, and the polished Mohib rose through the ranks quickly. He was appointed ambassador to the United States and then national security advisor.

He was also on the helicopter that Ghani used to flee the country in 2022.

While things during the early years of the Ghani administration went well professionally for Munir and many of those other young people living in the city, the security situation in his village was worsening. The Taliban were particularly attacking families who worked for the government or the *kaffirs*, infidels, as they said. It didn't feel safe to keep his family there, so even though Kabul was expensive, he moved the rest of his immediate family to the city in 2010, joining the ranks of people displaced by the war. That was the last time he saw the village that he was born in.

Chapter 5

Special Immigrants

In 2014, Amena, in addition to her other duties, was assigned to work with a private university to help develop their medical school. She went twice a week to have meetings with a team of administrators and discuss their curriculum. One of the young men who sat in on those meetings was Murtaza. During these weekly meetings, the two became friendly, and six months later they were engaged. A week after that, they married.

While so-called love matches were becoming more and more common in Kabul among educated young people, family pressure still often played a significant role, and the brief length of the engagement was surprising. In Afghanistan, engagements can stretch on for months as the two families visit each other and exchange gifts. Murtaza's family, however, was leaving shortly to immigrate to the United States, and it was improper for the young man to be engaged with no family to watch over the relationship, so the engagement was only a week. Still, Amena was happy that she had been able to choose her husband unlike many other women, and now she could make her own decisions about her career and life. This was a welcomed change.

At the same time, the quick wedding was stressful. The ceremony had to be rushed because Murtaza's father, a lawyer, had been receiving death threats, and his family decided they needed to flee, but Murtaza was not able to go with them. To understand why the family was splitting up, we need to dive into the tangled bureaucratic web of the US immigration process.

Murtaza was the eldest of four children. While Amena and Murtaza were from different provinces in Afghanistan, they had both spent time in Iran. Murtaza's father, Ismaeil Hakimi, had spent his early years in Ghazni, a mountainous province in the middle of the country. He, like many in his village, had moved to Iran with his family during the Soviet period in the 1980s when he was a teenager. Ismaeil went to school there and received his law degree after spending ten years studying Islamic jurisprudence in Qom. One of his brothers was still there, but Ismaeil had returned to Afghanistan with his family early during the Karzai period.

When Ismaeil returned to Afghanistan in 2002, the drafting of the new constitution had just begun, and Afghans with legal experience were needed to support the process. He did this for a year but eventually got hired by a contractor funded by the US State Department to support the judicial sector. This made Ismaeil an advisor to the Ministry of Justice, even while he was technically working for the contractor Pacific Architects and Engineers, or PAE, as it was more commonly known. PAE assisted the US government with "logistics" and provided expert consultants on a range of projects, including legal experts.

Ismaeil worked in an office at the Ministry of Justice headquarters. There were rumors that the construction of this building was poor, and the library had to be moved because the floors could not support the weight of the books. The building also lacked security measures, like steel safety doors, that were built into many other, newer government buildings.

The decrepit state of the building went from a joke to a real issue on February 11, 2009. On that day, five men armed with guns and suicide vests killed the guards at the gate of the ministry and broke into the building. Their goal appeared to be assassinating the minister. Ismaeil's office was on the third floor of the building, one level below the minister's. When he heard the explosion and the shooting, he and his other three colleagues quickly pushed a table and a small refrigerator in front of their office door. Ismaeil was not optimistic that it would slow the attackers much, but it made them feel like they had at least done something.

They considered jumping out the window, but the drop was steep and it was concrete below. Even if they could fashion some sort of rope, it seemed likely that they would break bones while falling or would get shot, so instead they sat and listened to the shooting get closer, echoing through the halls along with the muffled crying of some of their coworkers in the office next door.

The police guarding the building mostly fled, but luckily, the minister was present that day and had a personal security team that was better trained than typical Afghan police officers. The security team was able to shoot down the stairwell at the attackers, killing three of them and slowing the progress of the others, while military units started responding to the attack.

The assault on the ministry building was one of the first of many coordinated and complex attacks that Kabul would live through—attacks in which suicide bombers targeted key buildings and were accompanied by a series of shooters aiming to create additional danger and chaos to slow rescuers and kill security forces. Later attacks would be even more deadly and well-planned out, but Ismaeil still sat in his office for two and a half hours in terror, hoping that they would not target his hallway. Finally, a group of Afghan soldiers banged on the office door and told them they should run out, but to avoid the bodies of the dead fighters since they still had grenades strapped to their chests that they worried might explode.

The attack was later said to be organized by the Haqqani network in revenge for the killing of several Haqqani-affiliated prisoners at Pul-e-Charkhi Prison. According to media reports, the attackers killed twenty and wounded another fifty-seven.[1] In the days that followed, Ismaeil was unsettled. He had heard of colleagues in other departments who had used the Special Immigrant Visa (SIV) program to go to the United States, but this seemed like a drastic move. Things were going well for the family. He had a good job and the children were in school. Working on the Constitutional Commission felt like he was really doing something to advance the legal future of the country, and while his current contracting job was less dynamic, it still felt good to be working alongside both Afghan and international legal experts.

Just the year before, Ismaeil had begun construction on a home, and they were making progress on the ground floor. They had plans to put on a second floor once the first was done. When his children married there would be space in the house for their families as well. Ismaeil particularly dreamed of buying a small plot of land outside of Kabul where the family could plant an orchard and visit on weekends and holidays. He was very happy when he moved to the house he owned for the first time. They were feeling settled for once.

At the same time, however, news from Ismaeil's home province of Ghazni was not good. The Pashtun parts of the province were almost completely under the control of the Taliban. The Taliban were relentlessly attacking Hazara communities there and, particularly, as someone who worked for the government and was now considered urban, Ismaeil would surely be targeted on the road. It pained him not to be able to visit his extended family, but his security situation was difficult.

Attacks like the one Ismaeil survived had an odd psychological impact, he said. You don't always feel the shock and the fear right away. During the attack, he said, one of his colleagues had called his mom and told her in a completely normal tone of voice, "I am in my office and the Taliban has just attacked the ministry, but everything is fine." Ismaeil asked why he would tell her that he was in the building that the Taliban was attacking and that he was "fine" when clearly they were not. His colleague replied, "My mom watches a lot of news on the television, and if I don't call her and she sees some report on the attack, she will assume that I have been killed already. This is much better."

As the months passed, Ismaeil continued to think about the attack, and as these incidents became more frequent in Kabul, particularly targeting Hazaras and those working with the international community, Ismaeil decided he could not wait any longer to leave the country. It was a drastic step, but a necessary one.

***

The SIV program was initially set up in 2006 to protect Iraqi translators after one who had been working with the US embassy was kidnapped and killed. The US ambassador wanted to set aside visas for those translators who were at risk for the work they had done for the American government. It was set up to be a small program, just for the few Iraqis who seemed to be at the greatest risk.

The program was extended to Afghanistan in 2007 and was initially capped at fifty visas per year. One of the issues, however, was that the number of foreign translators working for the US government was expanding rapidly. During the early years of the wars in Iraq and Afghanistan, the government had decided to rely primarily on native speakers for translation, rather than ramping up language training for US officials.[2] This meant first pulling from the Afghan-American population, who already spoke Dari or Pashto, but eventually relying much more on local Afghans who had learned English on their own, like Najeeb. Eventually, Afghan translators far outnumbered Afghan-American translators, particularly since they were still far cheaper than their Afghan-American counterparts—even though they were well-paid for Afghans. But the job was dangerous and as the Taliban started targeting both translators and their families more and more, the government started to rely on the SIV program to get these Afghans out of the country.

As a result, it soon became clear that the number of visas was insufficient, and the Afghan Allies Protection Act of 2009 expanded the number of visas to 1,500 and opened the application process to all those who, for more than a year, were "employed by," or "on behalf of," the US government, including the US Armed Forces in Iraq and Afghanistan, granting successful applicants status as US Lawful Permanent Residents. In addition to military interpreters, embassy employees and other Afghans working on US-sponsored programs were now applying for SIVs. (In part because of the overwhelming number of applicants, the length of the required employment service was extended to two years in 2016.) This made the typical applicant more urban, educated, and upper-middle class than they had been previously, when the program was just for translators.

As the case numbers increased, the number of SIV recipients became an increasingly higher percentage of the total refugees resettling in the United States. In 2008, the number was just 1 percent of all refugees. This increased to 9 percent in 2015 and jumped all the way up to 26 percent in 2017 when the Trump administration lowered the overall number of refugees admitted into the country.[3]

The problem was, the SIV application process was poorly designed from the beginning and as applications numbers increased, things only got worse. In total, the application process has fourteen steps. Applicants had to fill out a complicated application packet, which was sent back and forth between the National Visa Center, the US embassy, and the Department of Homeland Security. The application was entirely paper based, transmitted as PDFs, instead of as a web-based electronic application. Later in the process, the applicant was called to the US embassy for an interview.

The State Department was aware of the challenges the program had, however, since no one agency had authority over the entire process, a delay at one of these three aforementioned agencies could stall the process indefinitely. The interviews at the US embassy in particular took time to arrange and also meant that applicants, many of whom were under threat, were required to return to Kabul—a place that was often more dangerous than their home villages. During this time, applicants received very little information on the status of their application. Some of these applications could be processed in a matter of months, others took years. This led many applicants to complain that the application process was either corrupt or at least biased. Certainly, the United States was providing favors to certain ethnic groups? Or perhaps just those who worked at the embassy? What else could account for these delays?

The lack of clarity was difficult for someone like Amena's new father-in-law, Ismaeil. After submitting his application he wondered, should he prepare to leave for the United States? Should he consider selling his house? There was no way to know how long the process might take. In the early years, many applications were completed in six months, but as the number of applications increased, the wait time jumped. By the end of the 2010s, it took three to six years for an application to be approved.

Ismaeil was lucky. His situation was dangerous, but he felt he could wait for the visa to be processed. Others in more immediate danger, however, were faced with difficult decisions. Should they continue to wait, in danger, in Kabul, attempt to flee across the border, or hide out someplace else until their visa was processed?

Over the next years, the number of visas handed out increased, but so did the backlog and the time it took to process the applications: In 2008, 705 visas were issued to 371 Afghans who had worked with the US government and their families. In 2014, 10,681 visas were issued to 3,876 Afghans and their family members. But the numbers of visas issued peaked in 2017 and actually started to decline, even while the number of applicants increased.[4]

The problems with the SIV process, however, were not just about wait time. Many applicants, for instance, struggled to secure all the documents that were required. In particular, candidates must submit "a letter of recommendation or evaluation from your direct US citizen supervisor or the person currently occupying that position or a more senior person."[5] In the long war in Afghanistan, internationals were generally on short deployments and positions had high turnover rates. This meant that in most instances, supervisors were no longer posted in Afghanistan and had moved on to other positions and often other companies. Some didn't respond to emails at all, and SIV applicants spent hours scouring Facebook trying to find former bosses and convince them to write them letters. Even if they could get these letters, many were then sent back to applicants if they were not precisely worded, causing further delays.

The application process had other rules that felt capricious to many applicants and could alter families permanently. For example, those who received the Iraqi SIV could bring all their dependents with them to the United States, but a slight change in the wording of the law setting up the Afghan version of the program meant that dependents older than age eighteen did not qualify. For Ismaeil, this was a crucial problem. When he applied, his three youngest children were teenagers, but his eldest son, Murtaza, was just over eighteen. If his application was approved, he would be able to bring his wife and youngest children, but Murtaza would have to stay in Kabul, alone. Since they would arrive in the United States and apply for status as Legal Permanent Residents, it would be years before they could even apply for a visa for Murtaza to come and visit them.

By the time Ismaeil applied, processing times were already more than a year, which felt long to him at the time, but would be incredibly quick compared to those who applied a few years later. He submitted his application in the summer of 2013. On October 3, 2013, the National Visa Center completed the process of his application and forwarded it to the US embassy. Then, he waited for eight months, unsure of his status. In May 2014, the embassy asked him to turn in his passport. Finally, on June 1, 2014, he received the visa. The family was torn about leaving, but with attacks increasing in Kabul, Ismaeil felt they had to go. Better, however, to make sure that Murtaza had married before they left, since they would not be able to return later for a wedding. So, they celebrated the happy couple, all while packing their most precious belongings.

And, just like that, Ismaeil, his wife, and three of their four children arrived in San Diego on September 16, 2014. It would be years before they saw Murtaza again. This was the way that the SIV process worked—for many it was a lifeline, but a lifeline that reconfigured families and altered lives forever.

***

Now back in Kabul, Najeeb's new job was primarily translating intelligence documents. The work was not the most exciting, but it was far better than accompanying Marines out in the field in Kandahar, and it led to other opportunities. He found that the American University of Afghanistan was offering evening classes, so he applied, was accepted, and enrolled. He started studying political science there and thought that perhaps he was back on his way to potentially being a lawyer.

However, Najeeb also began to realize just how much the US military's reliance on contractors threatened the very people who did much of the work of the American effort. Particularly in urban areas, Afghans working for the US government were very rarely allowed to live at the installations they worked at. The reasoning here was often financial, but it was also linked to fears of so-called "green on blue," or insider, attacks, where Afghans working with the international military had been recruited by the Taliban to attack their colleagues.

While this may have made the Americans inside feel safer, the Afghans who worked there were then forced to go in and out of the compound every day via gates that were often the targets of suicide bombers. They often had to wait in long lines and go through slow and invasive searches. Sometimes, just getting onto the compound could take more than an hour. The irony of much of the violence against international troops in Afghanistan was that most international compounds in Kabul were guarded first by a group of Afghan police and often after that checkpoint there was a group of Nepali private security contractors. The Western soldiers were only at the innermost security checkpoints and were, thus, the least likely to be injured or killed in an attack on the gate. At the same time, Najeeb and the other Afghans he worked with were forced to come and go regularly by that same gate. This led some American soldiers inside the compounds to refer to these Afghans and Nepalis as their "flak jackets" or "bait" for suicide bombers.[6]

Also, as Taliban intelligence became more sophisticated and their networks of informants in the city grew, these Afghans could be easily followed as they left work, and it was not just the Taliban they were worried about. Organized criminal groups in Kabul had grown rapidly, oftentimes working together with anti-government groups. Anyone working for the internationals was assumed to be making a good salary, and thus became a target of for-profit kidnappers.

Najeeb had several friends who were forced to live with distant relatives or rent second homes to keep their families safe. For Afghans like these, it was a difficult cycle to get out of: If they quit the jobs that were putting them in danger, they could no longer afford the second apartment or the car they had purchased to keep them safe, but the longer they worked there the more danger they were in. Even if they left, it was not guaranteed that these groups would stop targeting them as someone who had worked for the foreigners. Sure, Najeeb thought a lot of the American soldiers were putting their lives at risk while in Afghanistan, but at the end of their tours they could go home.

Not long after returning to Kabul, Najeeb started receiving death threats. Najeeb had been facilitating meetings with groups of elders and political elites. Many of these same leaders were on the fence as to whether they should be supporting the Afghan government or the anti-government forces. Reports made their way back to the Taliban quickly, and soon Najeeb was receiving threats with specific details from these meetings to let him know that they were watching him in particular. Najeeb started varying the routes he took to work. He stopped going anywhere but home, work, and school. He began wearing a scarf over his head as he entered and left work.

As the threats grew, Najeeb realized he would need to leave.

Najeeb first applied for the SIV program at the end of 2012. His supervisor, a retired Army officer, sent him a letter of recommendation to include in the packet. The application was more than twenty pages long, and if any of the boxes were not filled out correctly, you had to do the entire thing again.

He sent his application off and, a few weeks later, they sent it back to be corrected. He filled it all out again. This time he waited for three months, only to get a letter saying that it had been denied by the National Visa Center. The letter said that his supervisor in his letter had not mentioned a "specific enough" threat, but it didn't give any details about what they meant or what a specific threat was.

He worked with several other Afghans who were responsible for intelligence at their base and asked them for advice. They suggested that he needed to put more details into his threat statement and gave him some intelligence reports to back up his claims. Najeeb was not hopeful that resubmitting his application would change the result, but then one of the other Afghan translators he was working with received an email that his visa was being processed. Suddenly all the other translators he worked with were more optimistic that the process might actually work.

This pattern repeated itself in other organizations and places like the American embassy. The SIV process, particularly in the early days, was so confusing and confounding, many were reluctant to apply. The FAQ page gave strangely worded information and many believed the entire process was some type of scam, until, of course, someone they knew received a visa. As a result, those who were successful shared tips with their colleagues and helped them fill in their applications. The sense among translators, Najeeb said, was "the only way to actually get a visa is to have a coworker who was already successful help you."

Najeeb spent a month rewriting his application. This time, he waited six months after submitting it before hearing that he had been approved for an interview at the embassy, the twelfth of the fourteen steps. For many contractors, particularly those from poorer and less-educated backgrounds, the interview process was by far the most intimidating step. First you had to wait outside the high walls of the embassy, passing through multiple layers of security when your name was called. Once inside, the consular officer hooked you up to a polygraph machine and asked you a series of questions. Applicants shared notes and tips. Some thought there were trick questions and you had to look for certain cues from the interviewer. One man allegedly heard if your heart rate was high the entire time, they could not detect a lie, so he drank two cans of Red Bull just before the interview.

There were some good reasons, however, for applicants to be skeptical of the interview process. For instance, the interviewers asked applicants if they had any ties with the Taliban and other insurgent groups, but, as Najeeb pointed out, while he didn't have any close connections with them, by 2014, every Afghan, just about, had a distant relative or an old friend who had sympathies in line with one militant group or the other. That didn't make them a threat, Najeeb concluded, but it wasn't clear whether the polygraph would then say you were lying if you said you had "no connections to the Taliban."

There were other issues with the process: In some cases every applicant from specific companies was being denied. This seemed to coincide with instances when a senior executive at a company had been convicted of a crime. Yet even if those working below them had nothing to do with the issue, they were still being rejected, regardless of the risks they faced, as if this was somehow punishing the executives at the top of the company.

Najeeb felt more prepared than some of the other applicants. His friend had recently gone through the interview process and was able to give him a sense of what the questions might be. He practiced describing the threats and making sure it lined up with the statement he had put into his application. When the interview day arrived, he was nervous, but as they went through more and more questions, he started to feel better. He had heard from other interpreters who had been rejected that the consular officers told them straight away that their documentation was not good enough, so after the woman who was interviewing him did not push him on his documents, he started to think that perhaps his case would be accepted. Still, he said, sitting in the room, he realized that everything was in her hands: If she said yes, he would be on a plane soon, if she said no, he would have to start preparing for a life in constant danger in Afghanistan or perhaps elsewhere.

The interview, unfortunately, was not the end of the process.

Perhaps the most ambiguous step is number thirteen, after the interview, which is called "Processing." A friend of Najeeb's had gotten stuck in "Processing" for four years, with no communication from the embassy. The days after Najeeb's interview were painful. It could be a few weeks or a few years before he heard anything.

Luckily, Najeeb's processing took about three months. Then he received an email saying that he needed to get a medical exam and submit some final personal details. Finally, they told him to return to the embassy and the officer handed him a packet that included his visa and also information about settling in the United States.

Once he had the visa, Najeeb felt again conflicted. He did not like the idea of his family potentially being targeted for the work that he had done, and it seemed unfair that, as a single man, the program did not allow any of his family members to come with him. At the same time, he reasoned, they would probably be safer without him there. It would be best for them all. And so, he boarded a plane headed to Dubai with a connection on to Texas.

***

For Munir, the SIV process was even less forgiving. Based on his work experience with the Afghanistan Research and Evaluation Unit (AREU), Munir ended up with a job working for the Bureau of International Narcotics and Law Enforcement Affairs (INL), a branch of the State Department. A major component of INL's work in Afghanistan was in prison reform. Prisons were a contentious issue. The Obama State Department appeared terrified of any prison scandal that might draw parallels with the Abu Ghraib torture in Iraq, but at the same time, the conditions in Afghan prisons were horrid. They were overcrowded with criminals arrested for murder and robbery, but also, anyone the US forces had picked up on the battlefield, ranging from those who had been discovered planting car bombs to others who just happened to be in the wrong place when a raid occurred. Many of the prisons were simply large rooms where the prisoners maintained their own order. Cell phones, weapons, drugs, and other contraband were available in many of these prisons, and criminal leaders and terrorists alike were said to still be able to run their operations from behind bars.

Munir traveled to prisons in several different provinces. His job was to collect information on various prisoners. Much of his work was in Pul-e-Charkhi, the largest and most notorious prison in Afghanistan, located just outside of Kabul. The prison housed more than five thousand prisoners, and in both 2006 and 2008, rioting prisoners had taken over large sections of the facility for days at a time. The issue of prisoners in these facilities was contentious. Hamid Karzai had taken to complaining about the United States' indiscriminate approach to arrests, ignoring that it was his administration that was overseeing their imprisonment. As a result, President Karzai was given to granting amnesty to long lists of prisoners, particularly on holidays. Prisoners were anxious to get other political leaders to lobby the president's office on their behalf to get them released.

Munir interviewed a range of prisoners. He found that the murderers and robbers were not anything to worry about, since they were common criminals. Even the suicide bombers were not particularly dangerous, since, as Munir concluded, they were all "brainwashed" and didn't make any sense in their interviews. The prisoners he worried about were those accused of drug trafficking and smuggling.

Those involved in drugs and smuggling had powerful connections. The transportation industry was one of the most corrupt in Afghanistan. Many of the companies had legitimate contracts to supply goods to US military bases, but it was common for these companies to also have connections with the Taliban, since they often had to pay off anti-government groups to allow them to pass through disputed territory. The INL was involved, in part, because there were also a high number of individuals convicted of smuggling who were set up to take the fall for corrupt officials (who were actually profiting from the smuggling themselves). It was Munir's job to interview prisoners and update their classification files, which could then be used by officials to include prisoners in presidential amnesty lists.

In some instances, he was asked to interview the same prisoner two or three times. As Munir described it, "After one time, they might not remember you and your face, but you can be sure after two or three times they will."

Munir also conducted interviews in Wardak, his home province. When he was there some of the prisoners recognized him and assumed that he had connections that could help them get released. Soon he was getting harassing phone calls from relatives of these prisoners, people he barely knew, telling him that his family would be harmed if he did not get specific prisoners released. Munir complained to his international bosses, but there seemed to be little they could or at least were willing to do to help him with his security.

After eight months of working in the prison, Munir quit. He felt the work was too dangerous. Who knows when one of these prisoners might have been released and tracked him down? Of course, he had no way of knowing that eventually the prisons would be completely emptied when the Taliban seized power and opened the gates. At the time he quit he also did not realize that the SIV program required twelve months of service to qualify for a visa.

"If only I had known that then," he lamented, "I would have worked the four more months." Even after he left his job, the harassment continued. First, he just changed his phone number, but that provided only a temporary respite. Eventually he and his family had to move to a new neighborhood, even though they had already fled from Wardak to Kabul.

Even still, in 2016 and 2017, when security was not good, Munir still hoped that things would improve. He got a new job for UNICEF that focused on providing legal support for children accused of crimes and for those who were imprisoned, giving them some education. This felt much safer than interviewing drug smugglers. In his new job, there was some international travel. He went to Germany, Italy, and Belgium. In each of these places he could have stayed and applied for asylum, but he never did. He truly thought things might improve, and he knew if he applied for asylum, it could be years before he saw his children again. Having grown up without his father, he didn't want to make them go through the same thing.

Munir did not apply for the SIV at first because he had not worked for long enough at a US-based organization. The eight months of service he did interviewing prisoners was far less than the two years of service the SIV program required before 2021. Even when the number of months was reduced to twelve, he was still four months short. None of this made any sense to him, he said, since the Taliban was not going to make distinctions between those who worked four months, or seven months, or a hundred months. If you had worked for the Americans, you had worked for the Americans.

Later, however, as the security situation worsened, he started to gather his documents, just in case. Describing what the process was like, Munir said, "I went looking for my supervisor online since his email address was no longer working, but could not find any trace of him. It had been almost ten years since I last worked there and I emailed almost a hundred people from the company, and almost no one responded to my messages."

No one he emailed seemed to understand just how urgent the situation was going to become.

CHAPTER 6

Willful Ignorance

"THERE WERE NO WOMEN AT THE COMMUNITY MEETING," NOAH TOLD the World Bank official.

"No, that is not possible," he replied.

"I'm not sure I understand. It's not whether it's possible or not possible, it's just that there were no women there."

"But it is very clear in the manual that every meeting must have women or that the women must be at a parallel meeting. There must have been a mistake."

"Maybe," Noah replied, "but we've now found at least a dozen communities in our sample where there is no female participation, so if it's a mistake, it's a common one."

"Well, perhaps the report should just focus on the bigger land conflicts and you can leave those other pieces out of the report," the official kindly suggested.

***

How was it that so many did not see the collapse of the Afghan government coming? In the 2010s, there were analysts on both the security and the development fronts who warned of the growing strength of the Taliban and the increasing ineffectiveness of the Afghan national government. Yet, these voices were in the minority. Also, with so many programs having already invested money in either the "stabilization" or "development" of Afghanistan, whether it was building schools or recruiting Afghan Army soldiers, those who oversaw much of the policy in Afghanistan were highly invested in promoting the perception that, even if there were challenges, things were at least improving. Perhaps unsurprisingly, many then went to great lengths to ignore, or at least reframe, reality.

In 2011, Noah spent time interviewing several Navy SEALs, trying to get a sense of how they understood the conflict from the ground up. There were a lot of lessons from these conversations, but one of the most jarring was how much emphasis there was for the SEAL officers on making sure they were "briefing better," rather than engage with the population better or more effectively target the Taliban. Yes, there was planning and tactics that were considered, but there was also much time spent creating narratives about various attacks. If there was an incident, one officer explained, he would do a write-up of the event and send it to his commanding officer. After some back-and-forth, often the commanding officer would edit it, just giving it a slightly more positive spin to make everyone look better, and send it up the ladder, where again it would be changed just slightly. The final result, however, was that those at the top often had a distorted view of the experience of those below.[1]

This was not a problem confined to the US military in Afghanistan. When Arsalan's research firm was hired to write a report, it was common practice for the donor to read an initial draft and then ask for revisions. At times, these revisions had something to do with the methodology of the report, but it was much more common that the revisions were aimed at making the report more positive or portraying the work of whoever commissioned the report in a more positive light. The report would then be sent to higher-ups in Washington, London, or Brussels, who had little idea they were receiving, at times, a very edited version of the original report. This contributed to a pattern in which, as the decades of intervention went on, those working in Kabul, including Afghan staff, but particularly internationals, were disconnected from the realities of daily life on the ground for Afghans in more rural areas.

Given the rapid collapse of the top of the Afghan government in August 2021, it's also worth looking at what happened to those members of the government closer to the ground, the district governors, the provincial council members, and other officials who were the ones who the majority of Afghans interacted with on a day-to-day basis, bringing them their disputes over land, concerns about crime, and other highly local issues.

Early in the 2000s, the international community (and the United States in particular) became increasingly frustrated with Hamid Karzai's government and corruption at the national level. One of the ideas was to send more and more funding directly to local officials through a series of programs aimed at building the state from the ground up. In fact, over the two decades of US involvement, more than two billion dollars was allocated to supporting local governance.[2]

One of the reasons this happened was because the US military often undercut these local officials by spending money haphazardly, trying to "win hearts and minds." As Frances Z. Brown, an expert on local governance in Afghanistan, argued, "The huge injection of external money undermined any accountability between the state and citizens, effectively turning district-level administrations into . . . ministates."[3] International troops and money that supported these government outposts, including the so-called Provincial Reconstruction Teams (PRTs), which housed many of the NATO troops supporting the growing Afghan state, ended up generating more violence. Ashley Jackson summarized this as, "The more troops NATO deployed and the more operations they conducted, the more they were targeted by the Taliban. The more PRTs tried to cultivate local support, the more the Taliban targeted civilians who co-operated with the PRTs."[4]

The end result was that much of the funding in Afghanistan bypassed the national government and actually tended to create more violence.[5] This opened up opportunities for corruption and, in other cases, money might go directly to Taliban leaders who were actually in control of many areas.

This was not true in most of the rest of the country. The village in Wardak that Munir came from and the village in Ghazni that Ismaeil came from were now all far from the reach of the government. And while there were some international organizations that were attempting to run projects there, these were happening only with local negotiations with the Taliban, sometimes with those running the projects back in

Kabul not even fully aware how involved the Taliban were. As Ashley Jackson summarized in her 2021 study of the relationship between local communities and the Taliban: "The majority of Afghans live in rural areas, but they have seen fewer post-2001 benefits than those living in urban areas (i.e., standard of living improvements, access to opportunities). Afghans in largely government-controlled urban areas, by contrast tend to be more educated, wealthier (thanks in part to the aid economy) and more connected, through media and internet, to the outside world. . . . The Taliban remains an insurgency rooted in the mentality and beliefs of Afghanistan's more conservative countryside, which has given them leverage with the rural population."[6]

As a result, by the end of the 2010s, for all the attempts by the Afghan government and international donors, few government officials in rural areas had local legitimacy. When the Taliban arrived in local districts, some of these officials simply fled. The savvier actually cut deals to avoid bloodshed, giving Taliban leaders de facto control of areas that often appeared to have a government presence.

We, too, had to adjust to this reality in the various districts we were studying and working in, where the farther from Kabul you were and the bigger the international program was working in the area, the more the picture became blurry and distorted.

***

In the final years of the Afghan Republic there was probably no program as celebrated in Afghan government and donor circles as the Citizens' Charter Afghanistan program. This was a nationwide program that was meant to blend grassroots democratization and development, by having communities come together in democratically elected councils to assess the needs of the community and prioritize development projects. In total, the World Bank allocated $717 million to the project to be spent between 2016 and 2022, with the promise that more money would be on the way after that.[7]

The project was expected to build off of the National Solidarity Program (NSP), which for the three years beginning in 2003, gave small grants to communities to do infrastructure projects like building irrigation channels, while allowing them to largely determine what shape the project would have. The NSP was overseen by Ghani, who was finance minister at the time, and, despite criticism from certain sectors, it was considered by most development experts one of the more successful large, internationally sponsored projects of the early years of the intervention. The program was built off of many of the themes in Ghani's book, *Fixing Failed States*, and Ghani was fiercely protective of the program. He often pointed to it as one of the few successes during the early years of the intervention. "I think it was a huge gamble that a billion dollars has gone to the Afghan villages [and] I think has been much more efficiently spent than any other billion dollars spent in this country," he said.[8]

He also often implied that if the government and international donors had only funded further phases of the NSP, perhaps the Taliban would not have gained the momentum that they had in the late 2000s. He lamented, "Of course the other part, which is unfortunate, I designed National Solidarity in phases and they're stuck in phase one."[9]

Ghani was not the only one who was evangelical about this approach of intertwining development and funding. Scott Guggenheim, Ghani's presidential advisor and longtime friend, was often cited as the intellectual architect of the program. In an interview about his design of the program, he asked, "Is the Parliament of Afghanistan really representative of the country, or is it a bunch of warlords dividing up national rent? This is what American foreign policy in Afghanistan has created. The institutions they built up are deeply corrupt. They do have elections, but in terms of power structure, it is a deeply flawed version of democracy."[10]

The message was clear. Democratization on the national level had largely failed. What was needed instead was grassroots democracy to help drive local development. The program could revolutionize Afghanistan. In theory.

The Citizens' Charter project was an ambitious follow-up that massively expanded the approach initiated by NSP, starting with an injection of half a billion dollars from the World Bank, stating explicitly that it was meant to be an experiment in community-driven development, or CDCs as they were more commonly referred to. The Citizens' Charter Afghanistan Project, or CCAP, as it was called, was primarily run by the Ministry of Rural Rehabilitation and Development (MRRD), but as with the war and most development in the country, it was actually outsourced to a series of NGOs that did all the work, reporting back to MRRD and ultimately the World Bank.[11]

One of the things that was compelling about the design of the project was that it gave communities the ability to select how funds were spent locally. This is not as simple as it sounds, however. To solicit community input, the World Bank decided to try to build democracy from the ground up using a community mobilization process. This involved a series of workshops that were run by a variety of NGOs, which brought the community together to discuss their needs and challenges. The community collectively made a map of resources in the area and charted out the planting and growing seasons to see when and where resources might be most helpful. In some cases, perhaps this was an expansion of the irrigation system. In others, it was perhaps a road to better get produce to market. Either way, it was expected that the community would decide.

But how do you determine that "the community" decided, as opposed to having a local commander pressure the area to do a project that would support just his family? How do you ensure that the NGO running the program didn't just set up the program that was most convenient for them? The theory was that each community would hold a local election to select a group of men and an equal number of women to make the decisions for the community, free from the pressure of local commanders or others. Ballots were collected, and photos were taken of them and sent back to the offices in Kabul, but, as we came to see, there were all sorts of ways to manipulate these local elections to make sure that certain groups continued to determine how the funds would be distributed.

***

Shortly after the program was rolled out in October 2016, we were asked to do a study of the project and how it was impacting conflict locally. We visited a series of community mobilization events and watched the election process. When we visited a community mobilization session in Wardak, we sat with the men as they gathered at the local mosque. About thirty of them arrived and sat on the floor, joking with each other. Then the NGO worker in charge of mobilizing the community stood up and explained how the program would be built upon their discussions. As is the case in meetings like this, most of the young men sat towards the back, while some older men stared wearily closer to the front. Following this, a couple of other men stood up and expressed their gratitude to the NGO worker who was leading the meeting.

Since Noah was there, it seemed, the community members seemed particularly enthusiastic to demonstrate that the program was working. Several made speeches about how important it was to generate consensus and particularly how if they were given more resources the program would be even more successful. They discussed the needs of the community and seemed in agreement that they needed the roads paved and help with agricultural production. There was no debate, however, and the entire process felt like a performance for the visiting NGO officials and Noah.

We then went outside to point to some areas where the projects would run. While we stood outside the mosque, it became clear that another group of men had gathered just across the street, sitting on the steps of a couple of shops. There were as many there as were gathered at the mosque. The men at the mosque ignored them. When Noah asked one of the men standing towards the back about them, he said, "Oh, they live here, but they are not a part of the community."

The other problem: Where were the women? All mobilization was supposed to happen with women as well. In most of the country this could happen in two simultaneous segregated meetings, but they were supposed to happen simultaneously. So, as we were preparing to leave, Arsalan asked when the women were going to have their mobilization meeting. The NGO worker said, "Later." Arsalan pushed a little harder, "This week? Next week? Soon?"

"Yes, soon," the NGO worker said with little conviction in his voice.

As we visited other communities and had researchers report back to us from other provinces, this was a pattern we heard again and again. The women's aspect of the mobilization was either not happening, or, most commonly perhaps, it was happening, but only involving three or four women who were usually the close relatives of the leading men in the village. We went through lists of those women who had been "elected" to be a part of the CCAP councils. In many cases, it turned out that the women elected were the spouses of the men who had been elected. There was little evidence of these women actually meeting or participating in the discussions about how funds were to be spent.

In other instances, NGO officials confessed privately that the community had no interest in elections for the men or the women, and so they essentially worked with some of the key elders to select representatives and then moved ahead with the work. They were scared, however, to report the truth to World Bank officials in Kabul, since they worried that this would mean cuts to their funding. The reports back to Kabul all said that the elections were taking place as they should be, but really, what was happening on the ground was more of a negotiation between the NGO workers and the leaders of the local community.

This was not exactly grassroots democracy. At the same time, of course, for the Afghans living in the villages impacted, this was not the most important aspect of the program. It was the roads, the irrigation channels, and the other infrastructure that the program was supporting that really mattered. Surely, if the program were delivering these valuable projects to the community, the fact that the councils were not working as they were designed to do should have been a secondary matter.

So, when we wrote up our initial reports for the World Bank, we mentioned that women were not being represented in the manner that program documents outlined, but the report focused much more on the infrastructure and services that were being delivered. The response we got back, however, was strong. First our methods were questioned. Perhaps we were misunderstanding what we were being told in interviews, but then they were more direct: The report had to be corrected to downplay all the issues with women's participation on the councils. If they weren't participating, the World Bank did not want anyone to know about it.

What was odd about all the resistance we received was that in many ways it echoed the World Bank's own assessments of the work if you dug into their reports carefully. One of the key World Bank assessments of the NSP concluded that "the National Solidarity Program had a positive effect on access to drinking water and electricity, acceptance of democratic processes, perceptions of economic well-being, and attitudes toward women. Effects on perceptions of local and national government performance and material economic outcomes were, however, more limited or short-lived."[12]

Despite this, the World Bank and Afghan government officials continued to emphasize the democracy-building aspects of the program that simply did not exist in reality on the ground. As late as 2022, the CCAP website was still claiming that "50 percent" of CCAP members were women, when in reality, women made up a tiny fraction of these councils.[13] Yet, the participation of 50 percent of women was something that experts in Kabul, Washington, and elsewhere wanted to see, and Afghan government officials realized that in order to continue receiving funds, they needed to perpetuate such images. As a result, the distorted picture of life outside of the major cities in Afghanistan became truth for many of those supposedly working in the country.

In the meantime, the World Bank and the Afghan government worked to carefully craft a narrative about the success of the program in other venues. A World Bank article on the initial work the project had done included pre-highlighted passages to make it easy for the reader to tweet things like, "A key feature of the approach is the democratically elected Community Development Councils (CDCs), which lead inclusive development processes and ensure poor and vulnerable people are included in initiatives and activities."[14]

By 2020, it was not only that criticism of the program was being suppressed, but the World Bank and Afghan government were even thinking about expanding its work to include reconciliation and to bring the Taliban into government through participation in the CDCs.[15] This of course ignores the fact that the CDCs were already working closely with the Taliban in many parts of the country and, in fact, were often paying money directly to them.

As one report summarized, one of the lessons for the international community from its experience in Afghanistan was that "agencies should update their monitoring and evaluation (M&E) and learning systems to ensure they are positioned to adapt policies and programs in response to fast-evolving political dynamics in fragile states."[16] To translate this out of development speak: The international community needs a better sense of what is actually happening on the ground. The irony is that the jargon of the development world just makes it all the more difficult for the organizations that fund these projects to actually communicate effectively with those working on the ground on carrying them out.

For internationals working in Kabul, there was less and less sense of what was actually happening outside of the cities. In many ways, their Afghan counterparts and those in the government might have had slightly more information, but it often was not in their best interest to point out that reality. And so, by the end of the 2010s, for many, Afghanistan was not what they thought it was, and this would make things even more dangerous for those working with the international community.

PART III

THE SECOND COMING OF THE TALIBAN

ARSALAN—OCTOBER 12, 2021:
The first days that the Taliban were in Kabul were disorienting. Most of the fighters came from rural areas and did not seem to understand how to navigate the city. They were asking for directions and taking selfies in front of various buildings.

Now things have settled somewhat, but there is still this issue that the Taliban leaders are ruling a Kabul that is very different from when they were here last time. Certain people seem to be taking advantage of the situation, trying to work with the new Taliban, or at least make themselves safer or even make some money off the fact that so much remains unclear. These people have been able to change allegiances quickly or convince the Taliban that they are useful.

My family and I are taking the wait-and-see approach. It's true that I was working with internationals, but since it was with an Afghan company, so far, we're hoping we can stay in the country without being targeted. I keep hearing from friends who were in more dangerous positions who are moving between safe houses and still searching for a way out of the country. More often, however, they simply disappear. They stop posting on Facebook and their phones get switched off. Sometimes they then pop back on with a photo of themselves in Istanbul or even Paris, always with big smiles, showing that they made it out.

At the same time, there is a smaller, surprising group that actually seems to be benefitting from the Taliban presence. Part of this is that the Taliban don't seem to have much experience running a country. While they care about making religious decrees, they seem less interested or able to do things like paving roads or keeping schools open. So, while the real elites have all fled, some of those politicians, businessmen, and brokers who were one step down the hierarchy have moved in to fill the void.

One of my colleague's uncles, Zabi, is a good example. Since it's been dangerous going into our office in the center of the city, my colleague has been using his office to get work done and, since it's not too far from his home, I've visited him there a few times in the past weeks.

I knew Zabi before but hadn't spent much time with him. He's friendly and seems to know everyone. Part of the reason his office is so safe is that Zabi and his brother are, like many families that have been successful in the past twenty years, well-connected to a lot of different groups. Even though he is a supporter of the Northern Alliance, from Baghlan, one of the northern provinces that has resisted the Taliban most strongly, he has managed to also make connections with the new Taliban government, and in some cases he has worked with both sides simultaneously.

Last month, his friends even paid some members of the Taliban to help deliver supplies to the Northern Alliance to fight against other Taliban troops! When I asked him how he managed this, he said, "We need to make sure all channels are open to us, to the Taliban, to the former government, to everyone."

It helps that the Taliban themselves are divided and not all wanted to see them attack the resistance group in Baghlan, Panjshir, and elsewhere in the north small pockets of anti-Taliban fighters remain. So, by approaching one of these more moderate groups of Taliban, he was able to convince them to transport the supplies, for a price, of course.

While he is now rich, his family was not wealthy originally, and he is not from one of those families that has been ruling Afghanistan for generations, like many of our leaders. His brother had worked as a laborer in Iran for years, and Zabi had gotten a job working for a relief agency in the 1990s. Recently, we sat and drank tea and he reflected back on those times. His first job, he said, paid seventy dollars a month, and he moved between several agencies providing relief during the civil war. These various positions helped him grow his network and by the time the United States invaded, he joined with a few friends to invest in a construction firm in 2002. As business grew, he went out and set up his own company and started to make a steady income working on smaller projects.

He told me about his first contract with the US government, laughing about how inexperienced he had been. In 2006, he submitted a bid to paint some of the ministries that were being built. Not a particularly big job, but still one that required hiring a good number of low-wage workers for a variety of sites. His company got the contract and went about doing the painting. When the job was complete, he went to pick up the payment from the American overseeing the work. Back then, the banking system was a mess and payments like this were still often made in cash, and when he walked into the office the man handed him a bag of bills. He was startled. Surely this was not what they agreed on, and he said, "This is too much." The American said, "Oh, you're funny. Take this and get out of here." So, he did and when he got back to the office, he checked the contract and realized they had made a mistake in the contract and instead of 2.5 million Afghanis or about $25,000, they had put down 25 million Afghanis or $250,000, and they had paid the full amount!

After this, he said, their business really took off. He got more and more contracts for bigger and bigger construction projects. To pull these off, he and his brother needed to build their networks not only with the US military, but also with the commanders and businessmen who were so important in accessing them. In particular they worked closely with the minister of the interior, as well as a powerful parliamentarian who represented the area around Bagram Air Base and who had a lot of connections with those inside the base. Most of these connections were with these Northern Alliance politicians who supported the government.

As their businesses grew, they also realized that a position in the government would be good for them. So, Zabi's younger brother ran for provincial council in 2018, with Zabi organizing his campaign. The campaign was well-organized, and they used their business and political connections to get voters to come to rallies. He ended up winning easily.

Since their businesses had to work in both government- and Taliban-controlled areas, Zabi learned how to create contacts on both sides. His brother would work the government side and he would reach out to members of various anti-government groups. This was mostly done by contacting local commanders who could be convinced to work with him, and some of their building projects and their work delivering supplies was being done in areas where the Taliban had a lot of control, so they had made a lot of deals with low-level Taliban guys to make sure that their business could keep working. They knew how to work the system. I had seen lots of other cases of this, even some NGOs doing it, but with business guys like these, it was always easier.

The brothers also owned a lot of properties around Kabul, including two large private compounds that they had built up with walls and watchtowers, complete with a private security team that looked like the military. These compounds were then rented out to some international NGOs who did not have their own militaries to protect them.

In the days before the Taliban took Kabul, there was a lot of talk about resistance. Since their primary contracts were with the international community, Zabi and his brother certainly preferred to see the Ghani government stay in power. They even went so far as to move some of their construction equipment to the north so that they could build military facilities and dig trenches to help the fight against the Taliban. But then, for the most part, the Baghlanis, Panjshiris, and other Northern groups did not fight the Taliban, and the brothers soon realized that the resistance would be minimal at least initially.

The brothers quickly changed course and talked with some of their Taliban contacts and got them to allow them to bring their equipment back from Baghlan to Kabul. Essentially, this meant driving heavy equipment back across battlelines during a very tense time. Somehow, they had enough connections on both sides to make it work.

A couple weeks later they were already using the equipment to work on projects sponsored by the Taliban government. These are the types of things that money and good connections can get you.

Still, not everything is good between the Taliban and the brothers. One of the contracts they had was supplying fuel to the Afghan Police and they had thousands and thousands of gallons of fuel in reserve waiting to be delivered. When the Taliban took Kabul, they seized the supply. Zabi is still hoping to get it back, but I'm not so sure that he will. They are biding their time and trying to figure out how to work with these new Taliban, as just about everyone else *who has not fled must do. Listening to him talk about his business, I wonder if I and my family will be able to make compromises like this to stay afloat.*

For the most part, we have adjusted some of the things we do on a daily basis. I've started carrying a second phone. I leave my own phone with all my contacts at home and carry an old phone with me, in case I get stopped in the street and searched. This is annoying because at work I now don't have my contacts with me. It's like a reminder almost every minute that the Taliban are here.

Still, it's not like I didn't know people with connections to the Taliban in certain areas before. To run a successful research firm like ours, you had to be in almost constant contact with whoever is in control of different communities, particularly if you want to collect data in areas where the government had limited power. In recent years, that meant much of the data we were collecting was from areas where the Taliban had at least some strong influence. Working in Taliban areas previously mostly meant working through local elders to identify the most important Taliban leader in the area. Then we would use these contacts to negotiate permission to conduct research in the area. Dealing with Taliban leaders from a distance and on the phone, however, is very different from Kabul, where these same leaders are now in charge of everything.

When the Taliban first returned in August, I was at first a bit careless, assuming that these Taliban knew nothing and wouldn't try to stop me from going about my work. The religious ones were mostly interested in making sure women were wearing a burqa, and the corrupt ones seemed to be mostly interested in taking money from the rich and looting vehicles. I became more cautious as I started to hear more stories. A friend of mine had a music video on his phone and he was stopped at a checkpoint. They dragged him out of his car and beat him with a pipe. He couldn't sit up for days after. When I heard about that, I stopped acting so recklessly.

Things are also becoming more dangerous in other ways, and not always directly because of the Taliban. It's like there is no law, or perhaps more accurately, you have to guess what the law is and who has the power to enforce it. For example, a year ago, my company had taken over a contract monitoring and evaluating some construction projects that had been run by a large British company, the type that gets lots of contractors in Afghanistan and rarely understands the local people at all. Part of the deal, however, was that we needed to keep on the same architects who had worked for the previous contractor. These architects, however, had worked for years for this company and were used to the lack of oversight from the company itself. Almost immediately, it was clear that the architects were a part of the problem: The best of them were lazy and did not go out into the fields to get data for their reports, and the worst were clearly taking bribes to approve poorly done work.

We had to fire them all. This might not have seemed like a big deal in other places—we had clear evidence and cause, but in Afghanistan, this was the type of attack on a man's honor that could result in a revenge killing. The architects were also particularly mad at me, because, as the most senior Afghan, I was the one who had to inform them that they were fired. Why couldn't I just take a cut of the bribes they were collecting like their previous boss had, they wanted to know. Some of the men after they had been fired came around the office and told other employees that they were going to get even in some way. For the most part we ignored them, but with the Taliban in power now, if they go to the new government and tell them that we are corrupt and were working closely with foreigners, this could cause a real problem for us. Since my boss has left the country, I am the one who they will probably go after. I worry about that.

One of the big things that has helped us continue to operate has been our informal relationships with the Taliban. While we might not have been as well-connected as Zabi, I did realize we needed some better contacts with the Taliban.

About two years ago we were working on a survey project that required us to travel to a lot of areas in Wardak where the Taliban were active. I had met with several local elders who we asked to explain to the local Taliban leaders in the area the work we were doing and how it was aimed at assessing the needs of local communities. These types of things could be real hassles, constantly meeting with elders and trying to secure permission from the Taliban, but it could save our researchers from getting kidnapped, so we went through all the steps.

After several of these meetings, I got a call from an unknown number on my phone. The voice asked me if I was Arsalan, and I said yes. He said that his name was Kabir and he had gotten my number from some of the local Taliban in Wardak. Kabir explained that he, himself, was not a Taliban member, and in fact, he worked at one of the ministries in Kabul as a government official. He, however, did have deep connections with Taliban leadership and he could *serve as an intermediary between those leaders and myself, instead of me needing to contact a large number of officials at the local level every time we did a study. Besides, he said, somewhat matter of factly, if the Taliban come back to power, you'll want to have some contacts with them.*

Kabir had been working in the Ministry of Trade and Commerce and had good ties with officials in the Pakistani government, working on a series of trade deals. But he also had personal connections with the Taliban. One of his cousins had married an influential Taliban commander in Pakistan. Since we were working in almost every province in the country, as the Taliban grew more powerful, it made sense to have a contact who could help us work with them.

And so, just after August 15, I found myself calling Kabir to ask for his help in making sure that the Taliban would not raid our office or shut down our work.

In these early days, as the Taliban have been setting up their government, we have watched how some government officials, who perhaps were sympathetic to some Taliban ideas or had Taliban connections, were able to quickly rebrand themselves as loyal to the Taliban. Almost all of the top level of government, the ministers and cabinet, were forced to flee, but in many cases those directly below them were able to stay on. This was the case with Kabir, who was now calling himself our "consultant."

While Kabir had previously worn a suit and tie, he now wears traditional Afghan robes. He's also taken to conspicuously carrying a pistol with him. I'm still worried that the Taliban might come and shut down our office, but when I called him, he was reassuring. He said, "Don't worry, if they give you any issues just give me a call." Then he paused. "Maybe we should invite them for lunch."

CHAPTER 7

Insecurity and Failed Diplomacy

BETWEEN RUNNING WITH OTHER MEMBERS OF HER ATHLETIC CLUB AND taking classes, Zeinab started to feel like she was finding her place at AUAF, even while she missed her family in Herat. Kabul became less daunting as a city, in part because she felt she knew the streets from her runs. It was also easy on AUAF's pleasant green campus to forget the threat of attacks and the poverty of the rapidly expanding city.

That all shifted in July 2016, when two of the professors at AUAF were kidnapped in a daring attack in broad daylight. Zeinab was not taking courses with either of the faculty members, but many of her friends were, and the entire episode rattled the community. Each day, they paused what they were doing to pray for the two men. For a while, all people could discuss was the latest news on the case, arguing about whether there had been armed guards with the professors or not, discussing whether it was the Haqqani network that grabbed the professors, and speculating about whether the school was negotiating with the kidnappers.

When Noah taught there in 2010, there had been armed security that would check the badges of everyone entering, but the check was perfunctory and the guards joked with the students as they passed through. The campus still had a rather open feeling to it, with faculty and students coming and going regularly. After the kidnappings that July, new security restrictions were put in place, like more rigorous searches as students came and went from campus. These were meant to make them safer, but ultimately made them even more isolated from the world outside.

Since the attack on the Ministry of Justice that Ismaeil had survived, attacks in Kabul had become increasingly frequent and sophisticated. A January 2010 downtown bombing killed 10 and injured more than 70. A month later another attack targeting an international guesthouse killed 18. A 2013 bombing of the Supreme Court killed 13, a 2014 bombing killed 7 soldiers, and a coordinated truck and suicide bomber killed more than 50 on August 7, 2015.

While these were often targets associated with Westerners, like an attack on a Lebanese restaurant popular with expats and the two luxury hotels that housed most visiting diplomats who did not live inside embassies, it was often Afghans who worked in these places who ended up getting killed. Walls around the buildings that were seen as most vulnerable were built higher, with additional barriers built out into the streets of many of the main roads in Kabul, blocking traffic.

In response, attacks became more sophisticated. Now attacks regularly relied on multiple suicide bombers and shooters working in a coordinated manner. In 2011, a suicide bomber and nine gunmen laid siege to the Intercontinental Hotel. It took most of the night for Afghan and international troops to clear the building. In 2015 the Park Palace guesthouse, popular with long-term international development workers, was attacked, killing fourteen, including Munir's former boss at AREU, Paula Kantor.

What's more, for ordinary Afghans, these attacks and crime more generally had become a part of daily life. If you had a good job, you tried not to let your neighbors know out of fear that you might be targeted or your children kidnapped. Kabul, a city that had been relatively safe in terms of crime in the early 2000s, was now filled with private citizens in armored cars and CCTV cameras outside of homes.

On the idyllic AUAF campus, it was almost possible to forget all of this. With a dozen buildings that had sprung up around its small green quad in the center, the campus felt cozy, said Zeinab. One of the things that she liked most about it was that there was always someone she knew there to greet and chat with.

But then, on August 24, just a little more than a month after the two professors were abducted, Zeinab was taking a break after her IT class.

It was a peaceful early summer evening. She and some friends went to the cafeteria at the center of campus and ordered food. They brought it outside with them to sit on the lawn. Some of the others who were there with them went off to do their evening prayers. There were five of them remaining on the grass, three girls and two boys.

Suddenly they heard four quick cracks. Such noises weren't that uncommon in Kabul, and the boys reassured the girls that it was probably just firecrackers. But then, there was a huge explosion just across the small grassy area from them. "It was like being in a movie," Zeinab recalled. "It was all so unreal that I could not believe that it was me that these things were happening to. It felt like I was watching it all from a distance."

The explosion shook the ground they were sitting on and the dim evening was suddenly blazing white with light. Zeinab could feel a wave of heat. When recalling the events, she said she was not sure exactly what happened next. Had she gotten up on her own? Or had someone pulled her? They had done evacuation drills before and maybe that helped, but the next thing she knew, she and her friends were running toward an emergency gate that opened into the compound next door. One of the girls stumbled and one of the boys had grabbed her by her arm. Zeinab dropped her phone. She turned back to pick it up and she could see several men with guns running towards them, scanning for targets. She turned and ran faster.

The shooting seemed louder as they got closer to the gate. Glass started breaking all around her and she could hear bullets thudding into the wall she was running by. There was screaming and shoving as people tried to push past.

Instead of attacking the main gate of the compound, which was heavily fortified, the attackers had gone through the less well-guarded compound next door, which was a school for the blind, unassociated with the university. Once inside that compound, they had detonated a bomb that had blown a hole in the wall that separated the two compounds, giving the shooters who came in afterward free access. In the chaos and panic that followed, the shooters had time to position themselves around the compound. When the Afghan Special Forces in charge of responding to such terrorist attacks arrived, they found they had to work their way through the large compound room by room, unsure which were filled with students hiding under desks and which might have shooters in them.

In the meantime, Zeinab and her friends in the initial minutes of the attack had rushed into the compound next door, which held some UN offices. They were concerned that the attackers might somehow find their way into that compound next, but they also worried, what if there were more suicide bombers out on the street? There had been cases where follow-up bombers had targeted the police and ambulances responding to such attacks. The consensus seemed to be that they were more at risk staying in the compound, and the crowd of students gathered in the UN offices rushed out and into the street. They stood there for a moment, trying to figure out what to do. Several of the women were weeping loudly and everyone seemed to be gasping for breath. They tried to figure out who of their friends was accounted for and who was still missing. Some people tried to tell the students to go back to their dorms, but Zeinab's roommate was convinced that there might be Taliban attackers there as well. If they made it onto the main campus, maybe they were inside the dorms too.

Finally, a friend who lived in Kabul, not far away, suggested they all go to his house.

Back on the campus, the remaining students barricaded themselves into classrooms and offices. Two hundred of Zeinab's classmates and faculty remained inside as the entire attack played out publicly, in part because it happened just off a busy thoroughfare right as many Kabulis were returning home from work, but also because trapped students were sending text messages and tweets to those on the outside. Afghan Special Forces had some international assistance, but the process of clearing the compound was slow and the shooters continued to fire on those coming into the compound.

At their friend's house, they were close enough to still hear these shots, and every time a gun was fired, they wondered if it had killed someone they knew. They tried to sleep, but no one could, so they just kept texting friends and checking in with each other. Finally, around dawn, they heard the campus was cleared of attackers, but by then it felt like it was too late to sleep.

***

In Afghanistan, there is the expectation that you go and visit the family of someone who dies as soon as you can. This meant the next morning, before any of them had had a chance to really sleep or change their clothes, she and her friends went to the homes of the students they knew who had been killed just hours before. Zeinab was still in shock, but they tried to put on a brave face for the families of the dead, who appeared even more dazed. Their friends, like most AUAF students, had been so hopeful, and their parents had been so proud of their ambitions. In the end, the attackers killed thirteen people, including seven students and one young professor: Naqib Ahmad Khpulwak, who had previously been a Fulbright scholar in the United States and a visiting fellow at Stanford Law School.

From there, they went to visit some of their classmates who were in the hospital. Some had been shot and left for dead by the attackers. Others had injured themselves while jumping from windows in the rush to escape.

In the days that followed, the school announced that it would close at least temporarily, and Zeinab feared that she would have to return home to Herat. Some of her friends transferred to other universities. Her father encouraged her to do the same, but she couldn't bring herself to do this, since she loved the school so much. She decided to wait to see if they reopened as promised. She stayed in Kabul and found a job at an insurance agency doing clerical work. It helped distract her from the memories of the attack, but the trauma stayed with her. Every time someone came to the office and rang the doorbell, she couldn't help but jump up. Some nights she couldn't sleep at all.

Eight months later, AUAF reopened. They had built a new, fortress-like campus just across the street from the smaller campus where the attack had taken place. The new campus "felt like a prison or a military base," Zeinab said, with bomb-sniffing dogs and multiple checkpoints that you had to pass through to gain access to the campus.

Once you were inside the thick walls with looming guard towers, it felt like you were no longer in Kabul. Still, Zeinab concluded, the students were happy to be back and the new campus was "safer than anywhere else, and inside, no one from the outside could judge them for what they were doing." Even better, inside the high-walled, spacious compound, it was even easier for her to run.

***

The election of Donald Trump was as shocking to most in Kabul as it was to many Americans. Many did not want to see the return of Hillary Clinton, who they associated with many of the mistakes made during the Obama presidency, but at the same time, Trump was an unknown quantity. For those Afghans who had already immigrated to the United States, like Ismaeil, Trump's prejudices were even clearer. His Muslim ban combined with his zealous support for the state of Israel meant that many Afghan-Americans, even those who had supported the Republican party, were wary of him.

"It just seems like he doesn't listen to anyone else," Ismaeil concluded.

In that sense, he seemed to embody the worst of American leadership in Afghanistan: a lack of understanding of the on-the-ground realities and a desire to commit as few resources as possible to the war and development efforts. Beyond this, however, it quickly became clear that Trump treated his role as the commander in chief overseeing the US war efforts differently from any of his predecessors. Unlike other recent US presidents, Trump seemed far more interested in military parades in Washington than he was in overseeing the war in Afghanistan. He did not visit Afghanistan at all until Thanksgiving of 2019, almost three years into his presidency, and then, he stayed for only three and a half hours on a visit to Bagram Air Base. President Ghani had to fly to Bagram to meet him at the US base, an embarrassing demand to make on the president of the country he was visiting, many Afghans noted.[1]

At the same time, despite Trump's claims of being an outsider president, in fact, many of his appointments were from the D.C. circuit. Many of the generals he promoted within the national security apparatus had deep experience in Afghanistan and were committed to continuing the war in the same way it had been fought for the past decade. David Petraeus, Trump's CIA director, had been the commander of both International Security Assistance Forces (ISAF) and US troops in Afghanistan, and H. R. MacMasters, Trump's national security advisor, had been deputy commander of ISAF. With the careers of so many tied to US success in Afghanistan, it is perhaps unsurprising that when the administration ran its first review of the war, Trump was ultimately convinced to send more troops to the country, like his predecessor Obama had. Still, Trump made it clear that his priority was to get US soldiers out of Afghanistan, and that sped up and ultimately undermined the diplomatic negotiation process that had slowly been gaining momentum.

The Taliban had already been in informal talks with US counterparts during the Obama administration, and a Taliban office had been open in Doha since 2012 to facilitate diplomacy. Still, there was little trust on either side, and it was not until the second year of the Trump presidency that it seemed like talks could lead to some sort of peace deal.

In early 2018, Ashraf Ghani made calls asking the Taliban to come to the negotiating table, offering them official recognition, something they had not had in the past eighteen years of the conflict, and something many perceived as an important first step. The Taliban, however, did not respond publicly, with many believing that since they had military momentum, it would be better to wait.

At first, for those on the ground in Afghanistan, there were some signs that pressure might be building on leaders from both sides to end the fighting. After a car bombing in March 2018 at a soccer stadium killed sixteen in Lashkar Gah Helmand, the families of some of the victims set up tents near the site demanding all sides work for peace. Such protests had arisen before, but when this group of the protesters decided to walk four hundred miles to Kabul to meet with government officials and others, the movement gained attention on social media.[2] The country watched the protesters head north despite 100-degree heat, getting updates on their position on the nightly news. In the meantime, camps of peace protesters in tents were set up in Herat, Sherberghan, Wardak, and dozens of other provinces to show their support for the marchers. The group started with eight marchers and eventually grew to one hundred by the time they reached Kabul thirty-eight days later on June 18.[3] There the group presented their demands to both Afghan government officials, including Ghani, and representatives of the Taliban.

The movement was notable for several reasons. First it managed to expand rapidly into both Pashtun and non-Pashtun areas and it remained decentralized. There was an advisory council, apparently of twenty members, but the focus was really on the protesters themselves. Unlike the earlier youth movement, composed of mostly middle- and upper-class educated young people, this movement was more rural, composed of farmers and laborers. The protest was also notable because it remained critical of both the Afghan government and their international sponsors, as well as the Taliban.[4]

The marchers were making news at the start of the Eid ul-Fitr holiday, a time when Afghans traditionally visit family and friends, often returning to their villages of origin if they live in the city. Ghani used the moment to call for a cease-fire despite recent ongoing clashes between government forces and the Taliban. While the Taliban had dismissed the marchers as sympathizers with the government, Ghani's announcement put pressure on the Taliban to join the cease-fire. The Taliban leadership made no formal announcement, but for the next three days, hundreds of Taliban fighters returned to their homes, and pictures of them embracing members of the Afghan National Army (ANA) and Afghan National Police (ANP) and visiting with government officials spread across the internet. As with the peace march, it was a moment for social media with selfies posted of Taliban fighters with ANA soldiers, and other instances of the sides praying together and sharing a meal. For a moment, many Afghans could imagine for the first time what reconciliation might look like.

Unfortunately, this was just about as close as Afghanistan was to come to peace between the government and the Taliban.

The day after the holiday ended, the Taliban assassinated a district governor in Nangarhar and there were attacks reported in nine different provinces. Ghani called for a continuation of the cease-fire, telling Taliban soldiers to come to the cities for treatment if they were wounded and allowing the families of imprisoned fighters to visit their relatives.

The Taliban response, which would set the tone for the rest of the peace negotiations, was to insist that the United States withdraw all troops, and only then would they negotiate with the Afghan government.[5]

The United States, without ever explicitly saying so, agreed to this approach: Instead of the grassroots cooperation of the peace marchers and working together with the Afghan government, Trump's administration gave the go-ahead for talks in the Sheraton Grand in Doha starting the next month in July 2019. These talks largely excluded anyone from the Afghan government. It also included only the very top Taliban officials, who were the most ideologically extreme and hardened by years of being hunted by American soldiers. None of those local voices, the ones who really wanted peace, were included. Instead, US officials and the Taliban both agreed that they needed to reach an accord, and neither seemed particularly concerned if the Afghan government or anyone from local communities where the fighting was happening were not involved.

As a part of the renewed peace talks, Trump appointed Zalmay Khalilzad as special representative for Afghanistan reconciliation, a position formerly held by the legendary diplomat Richard Holbrooke under Obama. Khalilzad had been the US ambassador to Afghanistan and Iraq, and later, ambassador to the United Nations under Bush. He was also born and raised in Afghanistan. During the first Taliban period he had worked for Unocal, an oil company attempting to negotiate a pipeline through western Afghanistan.[6] This history meant that particularly during the early years of the US war in Afghanistan, there was the perception among many Afghans that Khalilzad was meddling and trying to twist negotiations, particularly to favor Pashtuns, the group that he came from.

Between Khalilzad's neocon politics and the rumors of his interference in Afghan politics, the Obama administration avoided working with him. The diplomatic gossip in Kabul and Washington that Khalilzad was considering running for Afghan president in 2009 strengthened this sentiment. The Trump administration had fewer qualms about being perceived as meddling in Afghan politics, and it saw Khalilzad as the US diplomat who could best negotiate US troops out of Afghanistan quickly.

Khalilzad could put an Afghan face on negotiations that were largely excluding any Afghans other than the Taliban.

Unsurprisingly, Khalilzad's appointment further alienated many in the Afghan government, making it even more difficult for the United States to negotiate a truce that involved all three key parties. Mohib, who by 2019 was national security advisor, lashed out at Khalilzad during a press conference in Washington, expressing the frustration of many in the Afghan government, saying that Khalilzad was angling for a position like a "viceroy." He argued that Khalilzad had "his own personal history—he has ambitions in Afghanistan. He was wanting to run for president twice."[7] In response, the United States cut contact with Mohib, who at that point was the highest-ranking security official in the Afghan government—a strange move considering the fact the United States was still actively fighting a war in support of Mohib's government.

There were also concerns about Khalilzad within the Trump administration, and, according to Bolton, Trump had once said of Khalilzad, "I hear he's a con man, although you need a con man for this."[8] Others at the Pentagon and State Department complained that Khalilzad did not share information about the talks widely enough and was prone to having private conversations, in person or on WhatsApp chats, with members of the Taliban negotiating team, without alerting members of his own team.

None of this gave Afghan leaders or those living in Kabul and elsewhere much faith in the talks. What was the United States doing speaking with the same men they had been fighting against for twenty years, but excluding the democratically elected president? Repeatedly, the US government stated that their goal was intra-Afghan talks between the Taliban and the government, but these kept hitting roadblocks, and the United States never insisted to the Taliban that they speak with the Afghan government in a timely manner.[9]

In September 2019 news leaked out that the United States and Taliban were apparently close to a deal that would lead to the withdrawal of all remaining US troops, along with the startling revelation that Trump had invited Taliban leaders to Camp David. A bombing in Kabul, however, killed a US soldier and Trump pulled out of the talks.[10] Later that winter, talks continued close to where they left off. In November the two AUAF professors who were kidnapped just before the 2016 AUAF attack that Zeinab had survived were released, something that many interpreted as a sign that the Taliban were serious about an agreement with the US government, even while they refused to negotiate with the Ghani government.

That deal, between the United States and the Taliban, was finalized in Doha on February 29, 2020. The US negotiators had pushed for a comprehensive cease-fire between all parties, but the Taliban rejected this again and again. Instead, they agreed to stop attacking US troops but resisted any compromise with the Afghan government, promising only that they would negotiate a cease-fire with the government once all US troops departed. Finally, the United States backed off its call for an immediate cease-fire, essentially allowing the Taliban to continue its full-scale war against the government as US troops were being pulled out of the country.[11] The persistence on the Taliban's part and the willingness of US negotiators to back away from their demands paved the way for the Taliban's return eighteen months later.

This might not have been self-evident at the time, but the first clauses of the agreement made clear the two main priorities of the two sides: that the Taliban "will prevent the use of the soil of Afghanistan by any group or individual against the security of the United States and its allies" and that the United States would completely withdraw its troops. The final clause ended up being the most problematic: "A permanent and comprehensive cease-fire will be an item on the agenda of the intra-Afghan dialogue and negotiations. The participants of intra-Afghan negotiations will discuss the date and modalities of a permanent and comprehensive cease-fire, including joint implementation mechanisms, which will be announced along with the completion and agreement over the future political roadmap of Afghanistan."[12]

The agreement essentially undercut the Ghani government and allowed the Taliban, if anything, to build on their military momentum against the government. The result was, over the course of the rest of the year, only 11 US service personnel were killed in Afghanistan, while 3,035 Afghan civilians were killed and another 5,785 injured.[13] As

Afghans on the ground could see, this peace settlement was certainly not bringing peace to them.

The other major component that was damaging to government morale and ultimately undermined real peace efforts was the references to Taliban prisoners. The initial agreement between the Taliban and the US government called on the Ghani administration to release 5,000 Taliban prisoners, 150 of whom had actually been sentenced to death. Of course, the fact that the Afghan government was not actually a part of the negotiations that finalized the agreement created significant resentment among Afghan government officials. These prisoners had been sentenced in Afghan courts, under Afghan laws; who were the Taliban and the US government to say that they should be unilaterally released?

Many were also concerned that these prisoners would immediately rejoin the Taliban on the battlefield, but the larger issue was the ways in which this issue undermined the legitimacy of Ghani's government.[14] There were also voices inside the US government opposed to the prisoner release, which included more than a dozen individuals who had been involved in insider attacks, killing US military personnel. By this point, however, it was clear that the Trump administration's top priority was finalizing some sort of deal that would allow them to get out of the conflict, and so despite some internal complaints, the administration continued to apply pressure on the Ghani government to release the prisoners.[15]

Eventually Ghani released 4,600 of the prisoners in stages during the spring of 2020 but hesitated with the final 400, who were considered the most important. He called together a shura of 3,000 leaders in August to consider their fate, and hopefully secure some political coverage. In a speech to the group, Ghani made clear the link between the prisoner release and the peace process: "The Taliban have said that if the 400 prisoners are released the direct talks between our negotiating team and the Taliban will start three days later. In the meantime, they have threatened that if they are not released, not only will they continue their war and violence but they will escalate it." The group eventually called for the release of the final 400, but not without some strong dissenting voices pointing to the unconstitutional nature of the move and some even calling it treason.[16]

Now, hardened Taliban fighters were walking out of Afghan government prisons, while negotiations between the Taliban and the Afghan government remained stalled. While the Taliban's lack of genuine interest in peace was the major factor here, with a presidential election in 2019, some felt that Ghani was also intentionally delaying talks until after his reelection. When Ghani did announce his negotiation team in March of 2020, the month after the United States and the Taliban reached their deal, Khalilzad stated, magnanimously in a tweet, "I want to congratulate Afghan government, political & civil society leaders for coming together. They've forged an inclusive negotiating team for talks with the Taliban. The Islamic Republic delegation reflects the true tapestry of the nation and the instrumental role of women."[17]

The reality, however, was that while the team might have seemed to check certain demographic boxes—it included five women and members of most major ethnic groups, many in Afghanistan felt the group was largely made up of government cronies who would not have the political muscle to really push the Taliban to negotiate. When talks did finally begin in September, the Taliban negotiators dragged their heels, spending weeks on procedural points. Often the Taliban negotiators would simply not show up to talks for several days at a time, frustrating the government negotiating team.[18]

In the meantime, towards the end of 2020, the Taliban continued to gain momentum militarily. In early 2021, as the Biden team took over, Biden announced that the Doha Agreement was "perhaps not what I would have negotiated myself" but that he would stick with it and remove all US troops before the anniversary of the September 11 attacks. Khalilzad made one last effort to convince the Taliban to come to a summit in Turkey in order to discuss forming a transitional government. They refused, essentially ending the final real attempt by the United States to broker a deal between the Taliban and the Afghan government.[19]

This left the Afghan government in a precarious state. Ghani had been elected, in part, because of his close ties to the Americans and the international community more broadly, but now they had turned their backs on him, and he never had the local power base of other Afghan politicians who had fought during the Civil War. It was said that Ghani was isolating himself and listening only to the opinions of those who were close to him and who agreed with his approach to politics. Much of the criticism focused on Mohib and Fazel Fazly, the head of the administrative office of the president. In the final days of the presidency, Mohib and Fazly increasingly were the only conduits of information to the president. Some referred to the two young advisors and Ghani as "a republic of three."[20]

Ghani lashed out at media criticism and shut down peaceful protests against the government. As one analyst concluded: "Many had expected that the erudite president, who has a doctorate in anthropology and had worked for the World Bank, would rule as a technocrat. Yet his behavior was more authoritarian than democratic."[21] Even some of his closest allies were defecting, and a local news agency had been pressured not to print a story stating that out of twenty-seven ministers in Ghani's cabinet, only two had family living in Afghanistan. All the others had already moved their families abroad. Even these members of his cabinet were preparing for a government collapse.[22]

The entire process of the US negotiating with the Taliban delegitimized and hollowed out the Afghan government. It also ensured that when the United States left, the Afghan government and military it left behind would struggle to stand on their own. The elites realized this and moved money and family members to the Gulf and elsewhere. But for Arsalan, Munir, Amena, and the hundreds of thousands of other urban, educated Afghans who had supported the United States but did not make millions of dollars off their presence, the situation was going to be much more difficult.

After Biden announced in April 2021 that he planned to remove all US military personnel from the country by the anniversary of the September 11 attacks, the situation became even more desperate, particularly for those who did not have international networks. And, even if they could make it out, what was waiting for them in new countries where they had no jobs or connections?

CHAPTER 8

The Challenges of Resettlement

NAJEEB ARRIVED IN TEXAS IN THE MIDDLE OF THE NIGHT. HE HAD NO friends or family there and when, the next morning, he stepped out of his temporary accommodation and could finally see where he was, he felt both exhilaration and a sense of dread. Being able to walk down the wide concrete sidewalks without a scarf pulled over his head to hide himself from the Taliban was liberating. It was as if that fear had simply vanished now that he was half a world away from everything he knew and was familiar with. At the same time, all he had was five hundred dollars in his wallet and he knew that with no friends or family, he was, for the first time, entirely alone. There were few Afghans in Dallas at that point and, unlike parts of the United States with established Afghan communities, no Afghan mosque to gather in to meet friends and family, celebrate holidays, and mourn during funerals.

"Wherever you live in Afghanistan," he said, "you live with your family and you know your neighbors. Even in Kabul, you see people out on the street by your home and they greet you and you greet them. Everyone knows everyone. But in America, you can't just go up to someone and ask them about their personal lives. Really, in a lot of ways, it's very lonely," he said, thinking back on those days.

It was also difficult because he knew his family at home was still in some danger because of his job. Everyone knew he had worked with the military and it was possible that his family would be targeted instead. Now he was safe, but it did not make him feel better about his family.

When Noah conducted research among other Afghan immigrants who had received an SIV, he visited Afghans who were living across the country, in the Bay Area, Washington, D.C., Florida, and Washington State. Despite the very different places they ended up, the stories were similar: Even though many were well-qualified professionals in Afghanistan, almost all were finding it hard to adjust both economically and socially to starting over with so little in America.

The Special Immigrant Visa, it might be necessary to point out, is just a visa. It does not come with special benefits or any real means for assisting Afghans settling into their new lives in America. For the first ninety days, very basic benefits are provided, as they are to all refugees, but little more in terms of assistance. Savings from work in Afghanistan did not last long in the United States, particularly if you had a large family to feed. Relying on food stamps was a shock for many of the better-educated arrivals. The fact that they received some material aid like this was nice, but there was little help on some of the more important areas, like education and health care. Even though some had been injured alongside US troops, they did not qualify for VA benefits.

For Najeeb, like most SIV recipients, his first priority was finding a position that would pay him quickly. He did not have time to be picky or find a job that might fit with his skills. As a result, his first job was working the graveyard shift until 3:00 a.m. at a window and door factory. It was exhausting work and gave him little time to do anything else. "How was I going to advance, working a minimum wage job that barely paid the bills?" he asked later. He had some friends who were earning more working for Uber, but he decided, "If I start working for Uber, I'll just be doing that for the rest of my life. I need to study."

It was a blow to his ego. "In Afghanistan, I had worked with colonels and officers in senior leadership positions. I had worked with the Special Forces. Everyone there was treated with a lot of respect, but now I'm in a job where my boss is yelling at me if I'm not working fast enough. It's heartbreaking."

So he went over to Dallas County Community College to see what courses he might be able to take. He was disappointed initially when they told him that they would not accept any of his credits from Afghanistan, not even the credits from the American University there, except for one single English class. He would have to start all over again. So he did.[1]

Now, studying during the day, Najeeb got a job working as a security guard at a large warehouse. While it was not the most prestigious job, it was still an improvement since he could use some of that time to study. When his boss found out he was working on his degree, he kindly switched his post to one of the quieter areas in the building, so that he would have time to get his work done.

Over the next few years, several of the translators he had worked with on the base in Kabul also applied for the SIV. Najeeb helped them with the applications, prepped them for the interview, and, when they were successful, several of them immigrated to Dallas since Najeeb had already paved the way for them. They all moved in together and shared rent on two nearby apartments. This cut down on costs, plus it felt almost like he had family around, even though the rest of his family was still in Afghanistan. Three years after immigrating, he also had filed the paperwork to become a US citizen.

Through all this, however, Najeeb's primary focus remained on his education. This is the way to get ahead, he kept telling himself. After finishing his associates degree at Dallas County Community College, he transferred to the University of Texas at Arlington and began to study political science just as he had at the American University in Kabul. Two years later, he graduated and began prepping for the LSATs to apply to law schools. He did well and was accepted at five different schools, but he ultimately decided to stay in the area and attend Texas A&M University. It was an up-and-coming school it seemed, plus it was close to home and the Afghan friends he was living with.

***

In some ways, the choices Najeeb had to make were simpler, because he traveled on his own and did not have a family to support. When Ismaeil arrived, he was traveling with his wife and three of his children. With them, they carried all their most valuable possessions. This was more typical of Afghan migrants who preferred to at least keep as much of their family together as they could.

When No One Left Behind (NOLB), an NGO focused on helping former translators, conducted a survey in 2020 of SIV applicants, it found that out of 129 who responded, only 11 immigrated as single individuals, like Najeeb. Families were much more common, with 24 responding they had arrived as a family of four, 32 arrived as a family of five, and 20 arrived as a family of six. Four had even arrived as a family of nine. Ninety-six percent of SIV recipients were male and 91 percent were between 25 and 44 years old.[2]

Ismaeil had hoped to settle in Fremont, California, a town called Little Kabul because of its large Afghan population. He and some colleagues who had also applied for the SIV had discussed buying a gas station or small shop together as a way to get their start. But because he had no strong connections with anyone in the United States, especially in Fremont, the International Organization for Migration (IOM), a UN agency that helps facilitate refugee resettlement, told them they would be placed instead in San Diego. Ismaeil was concerned about moving to a city where he didn't know anyone, and he heard that as a border city, there might be more racism and issues with recent immigrants, but he also didn't feel like they had time to lose.

They arrived in the afternoon to Los Angeles International Airport, where they were met by a driver from IOM, who loaded them and all their belongings into a van. He drove them south two and a half hours to the San Diego airport and upon arriving at the terminal said, "Here you go."

Ismaeil looked at him. "What do you mean here you go? I thought you were taking us to an apartment or some place to stay."

"This is where they told me to take you," the driver said unhelpfully. "I was supposed to drive you from LA to San Diego."

Ismaeil was not sure what or where LA was, and by now, it had become night and Ismaeil looked around at the traffic coming and going and at all the luggage piled in the van. "We can't get out here," he said. "They said someone would meet us and show us where we are going to live."

"I don't know about that," the driver said, "but you need to get out of the van."

There was nothing that Ismaeil could see around them that gave him any hope, just cars driving by and a terminal with passengers streaming out. "Can you take us to a hotel or a motel or someplace we can spend the night?" he asked. The thought of them just sitting there with their luggage on the side of the road was paralyzing.

By this point, an airport police officer had noticed them arguing and had walked over. He seemed more sympathetic to the refugees, who at this point had barely been in the country four hours. He asked them what was going on.

"I'm just doing my job," the driver said. "They told me to drive them here from LA, and here we are."

"What is LA?" asked Ismaeil.

"LA is Los Angeles. That's where he picked you up, right?" the police officer asked. Then the officer asked, "Who are you driving them for?"

The driver gave the number of the resettlement agency manager, and the officer took out a phone and called the agency, eventually reaching the director. As Ismaeil listened, the director said he would call the caseworker. Finally, he called back and said that the caseworker was on his way.

Still, with some reluctance, Ismaeil and his family got out of the van. "It's going to be fine," said the police officer. "The caseworker will be here soon."

Coming from Afghanistan, where police are often more of a hindrance, asking for bribes or issuing tickets, Ismaeil was grateful for the officer's help, though he also realized that he was lucky: His English was good and he had some idea of what to expect.

"I have lived in Iran, traveled to India with my family, and gone to the UAE and Malaysia for conferences, so I have some experience with traveling internationally, but imagine what it is like for a family coming from rural Paktika or some other remote part of Afghanistan. They would have just been left there by the side of the road. I remember when I went to Malaysia and I saw a crosswalk light for the first time and I thought, 'Look. How is it that people who are walking are making the cars stop for them?' For someone from the rural parts of Afghanistan, life in America is a shock like this."

The caseworker eventually drove them to the apartment they had been assigned, and the family tried to settle in.

***

There are nine federally approved resettlement agencies that are funded to help refugees upon their arrival, but things often did not work out as described on the websites of these organizations. Many of these agencies are accustomed to helping refugees from other parts of the world, who are poorer and coming from much worse conditions. The "employment assistance" they receive, for instance, is often just a list of jobs paying minimum wage doing things like landscaping or cleaning hotels.

In some cases, the SIV recipients complained that the caseworkers for the resettlement agencies either intentionally or unintentionally took advantage of the new arrivals. Resettlement groups usually moved Afghans into subsidized housing in run-down neighborhoods. Unscrupulous landlords, with the help of some of those working for resettlement agencies, convinced the new arrivals to rent moldy apartments with long-term leases. Rarely did they know exactly what else was available, and since most SIV recipients had no credit score or rental history, they were often forced to take whatever the settlement agency made available.

Many of the agencies also did not take into consideration the unique circumstances of each family. In one instance, a man whom Noah interviewed had eight children and was settled in a suburban part of San Diego without a car, where there was little public transportation. How could he get his family around anywhere, he asked? The bus came to his neighborhood only a couple of times a day, and they didn't have the money to buy a van large enough for all of them.

Before coming to the United States, Ismaeil had been a refugee before, but when he had moved to Iran, it was with other people from his village and they had joined a Hazara community there. Similarly, he had known some people when he moved back to Kabul. At that moment, sitting in that van with all his belongings, he realized that there was no one in San Diego that he knew.

Luckily for Ismaeil and others, while some of the staff at the resettlement agencies did not always seem compassionate and competent, some of the local volunteers were much more helpful. While the first days were difficult, Ismaeil was pleasantly surprised when one of the volunteers who worked to help the refugees settle in stopped by. The volunteer was a pastor.

"'What is your ethnicity?' the pastor asked," Ismaeil recounted. "I was surprised. 'Do you know the different ethnic groups in Afghanistan?'"

"'Sure,' he said. 'There are Pashtuns, Tajiks, Uzbeks, Hazaras. Tell me which group you are and I can introduce you to others.'"

Ismaeil told him that they were Hazara, and two days later, the pastor took them to meet some of the Hazaras living closer to the coast. Ismaeil was surprised to find out that there were almost forty of them and was even more surprised at how welcoming they were. Several members of the community showed up at their apartment with gifts to help them with initial furnishings. One person they met offered them a ride to the mosque whenever they needed it. Another helped his daughter to get a job. One even helped them buy a car later on.

Despite this support, San Diego was expensive and it was difficult to find work for recent Afghan arrivals. A Government Accountability Office study surveying SIV recipients found that ninety days after arrival, 60 percent were still unemployed.[3] Notably, 65 percent of those with a post-secondary education were unemployed, suggesting that those with more education struggle even more to find work that fits with their skills.

This was certainly true in Ismaeil's case. At first, he could find only offers that paid little and required few skills, like working as a convenience store clerk. The whole family pitched in and soon his younger son, Ahmad, had gotten a job working at a grocery store owned by a family from India. He was also finishing high school and was considering joining the military. He was interested in math and astrophysics, but higher education was so expensive, he felt it might be better to serve in the military and then receive his education through the GI Bill.

The inability to find jobs that allowed for advancement was a common trend with SIV recipients and their families who worked in low-wage jobs often in the gig economy. One survey found that 40 percent of SIV recipients worked for Uber or Lyft.[4] There were not a lot of good jobs for individuals with little or no employment history. Uber might get you some quick funds, but there is no insurance or other benefits and very little stability. (Only 27 percent of respondents had a job that provided them with health insurance, for instance.) During COVID, this type of work dried up overnight. Recent arrivals were left to scramble looking for other jobs, but with nothing on their resume other than Uber, they found they were not much better off than when they started.

What makes these wasted opportunities all the more painful is that most of these new arrivals were well educated, with plenty of experience and skills working for Western companies or the US military itself. Of the 129 surveyed by NOLB, only 3 had not completed high school and 55 had a BA or a BA plus a graduate degree. Forty-eight percent thought the thing they needed most was help securing an appropriate job. Next was help paying rent, 28 percent, or a loan, 10 percent.

Noah later interviewed several people who worked for one of the few organizations set up to help Afghan immigrants. After describing the lack of resources that many of the resettlement agencies devoted to Afghan immigrants and bureaucracy that prevented many of these Afghans from getting real help, he concluded with a sigh, "If you really want to help an arrivee from Afghanistan, just buy them a car. At least that way they can go out and find a job. . . . These agencies often leave recent arrivals stuck in the neighborhoods they are settled in. Plus, with a car, it's easy to get quick work driving for Uber or Lyft."

Najeeb agreed. "A car can open many other doors. Particularly in a place like Dallas, a bus might take you two hours to get somewhere while with a car you could be there in twenty minutes. With a car, you can stand on your own two feet."

After the evacuation in 2021, some of this would change. The national attention brought to the challenges of resettlement for Afghans led to a great deal of generosity and better options for many of those who arrived after August 2021. But even then, most Afghans struggled.

Debt or the cultural adjustment could be too much. In several cases, the Afghans had actually returned to Afghanistan despite the threat to them. More common were the cases where the male SIV recipient would stay in the United States long enough to secure his green card and would then return to Afghanistan to work for a contractor on a military compound, while leaving his family in the United States. In these cases, the families wanted the safety of living in America but had decided that there was just no way to make it work financially.

***

Others, after years of work, slowly began to find their footing.

Ismaeil found a better position as an assistant teacher in a middle school. It was still far below his level of education, but he discovered that his degrees from Iran did not count for much in America. At least this allowed him to start taking classes that would count on his resume.

In other ways, adapting to life in the United States was challenging. Ismaeil's wife particularly missed Murtaza and Amena, and her extended family. Her English was not as good as the rest of the family, which made it difficult for her to make new friends.

The other reality the family faced was that life was simply too expensive in San Diego. Rent was high, you needed a car, and while there were some other Afghans in the area, the Afghan community was not as integrated as it was in other places. So they made a list of potential places, mostly areas that they had heard of other Afghans settling: Texas, Colorado, Washington State, Pennsylvania, Northern California, and Utah. Each of them got busy researching. They called acquaintances and researched the cost of living and property taxes. His biggest complaints, Ismaeil said, was that there was no way they would ever be able to buy a house in San Diego since costs were so high, and "Afghans don't like living in apartments. You need to own a house to feel like you have a place in the world."

After a long call with a friend who lived in Salt Lake City, in December 2017, three years after arriving in San Diego, Ismaeil decided to fly to Utah to see what it was like. The day he arrived it had just snowed, and everything was incredibly picturesque, with the mountains looking down on the city just as they did in Kabul. Even though it was cold, Ismaeil said, he and his family liked this type of weather. It was not that different from the weather in either Kabul or Qom, where they had lived in Iran. And, most importantly, prices seemed reasonable compared to California.

So the family packed their things and moved from a two-bedroom apartment in San Diego to a bigger and less expensive three-bedroom apartment in Salt Lake City. His oldest daughter was working for Target and got her position transferred to a location nearby, and his son got a job quickly at the airport. His son and his younger daughter both went to school, and within a year the family had enough money for a down payment on a house.

Perhaps the best development, however, was that Ismaeil got hired by the library at the University of Utah. While curating the Middle Eastern collection was not exactly in line with his training as a legal scholar, it at least seemed to build on some of his research skills and it put him in an academic community where he felt his knowledge was respected. Additionally, after three years, he was able to start his children taking courses at the university for reduced tuition.

Still, it was difficult to feel truly resettled when his eldest son remained behind and Murtaza and Amena were still living in their old house in Kabul. That distance felt even further when Amena gave birth to her first child, Ismaeil's first grandchild.

CHAPTER 9

Lawyers, Travel Agents, and Traffickers

THE SIV PROCESS FELT ARBITRARY AND UNFAIR FOR MOST OF THOSE who applied for the visa, but the worst part of it, according to many we interviewed, was the uncertainty of the application process. It took applicants, who had been successful professionals in many cases, and put them into an indefinite limbo. And in that limbo, many became desperate and started to look for other ways out.

Amena left her job for several months after the birth of her first child. After returning to work, she was given the task of overseeing several projects in Farah and Ghor, two of Afghanistan's more remote provinces, where it was very uncommon to see a woman doctor. This is when the harassment started. At first it was just threatening phone calls and Amena would block those numbers. Later, however, she started being followed, and at one point, when she was walking toward her office, someone released a dog that attacked her. During this period, as the Taliban gained more territory, crime also increased in Kabul and other Afghan cities. There were kidnappings and robberies, particularly targeting those who were wealthy enough to be envied, but not wealthy enough to live in fortified compounds.

In rural areas with few outsiders, rumors also spread fast. This was a particular problem in Ghor, where some of those who saw the work Amena was doing assumed that she was working for foreigners, not the Ministry of Public Health. That the clinics she was overseeing were distributing birth control, among many other items, gave credence to the idea that she was trying to lead women away from their duties as mothers. At one point, while driving to a meeting, someone fired a series of bullets at her car. No one was hurt in the attack, but the authorities also didn't catch the person who had done it or figure out how they had known where Amena would be.

While women working publicly in Afghanistan have often faced challenges, in 2015 debate about the role of women in public spaces became more sensitive. In March, Farkhunda Malikzada, a twenty-seven-year-old teacher, was accused by a mullah in the center of the old city of Kabul of burning a Koran. An angry mob then lynched her in public while hundreds watched. This all happened within a mile of the presidential palace and the US embassy.

In the months that followed, Amena said, men seemed emboldened and less hesitant to be seen harassing women on the street. Amena, for instance, described how not long after the lynching she was walking to work and heard some men yelling insults at her. She kept walking, trying to ignore them, but they then began throwing rocks. As they bounced off of her, she stumbled but kept walking until she reached the gate of the office she had been approaching. Looking back, if that gate had been a little farther away, Amena wondered if she would have made it.

"I kept asking my husband during the night to check our house's main door to make sure it was locked. After he did so, I would doubt that he had actually done it and I would go myself to check it as well." The tension inside her grew and grew, and she struggled to sleep.

Finally, the family got a visa to fly to Turkey, where they were planning on applying for refugee status from the United Nations High Commissioner for Refugees, or UNHCR. For many in Afghanistan who were hoping to receive an SIV, this seemed like a good second option. To qualify, they had to show that they were "fleeing the risk of persecution or serious harm, including human rights violations, armed conflict, or persecution," and that returning to Afghanistan would cause them harm.[1] If their case was accepted, they could settle somewhere in Western Europe. If it was rejected, they'd be deported back to Afghanistan.

In Istanbul, the family submitted evidence of the harassment they had suffered and were left to wait for an interview while their case was being processed. Amena had Afghan friends who had been waiting for more than five years in Turkey just to receive an interview, so she was somewhat encouraged when they were called for an interview after just five months—they must have seen how at risk we were, she thought. To their great disappointment, however, their case was rejected. They received a letter that allowed them to remain in Turkey for one more month to organize their affairs, but then they were sent back to Afghanistan.

This process was psychologically taxing on Amena. She had trouble focusing and sleeping. When they returned, at first, they didn't experience any renewed threats, but, Amena concluded, this was probably because no one realized they were back yet. Her husband encouraged her not to work and to take at least a year off to recover, but this didn't seem like the right thing to do. She was offered a new position at MSH, but she also heard about a job at a smaller organization working more directly to counter violence against women.

The NGO, which had German government funding, worked with a series of shelters for women, providing counseling and legal support for the women there. As Amena described, she had experienced so much physical and psychological violence as a young woman that working to help others avoid this experience felt like the right thing to do. Despite receiving some funds, the NGO was not as well-connected to the German government and other international donors as MSH had been, but that didn't seem particularly important to Amena at the time. Those international donors brought their own ideas about how to help women in Afghanistan, which felt patronizing. The big donors, of course, also brought some of the resources and political connections that were important during the days of the evacuation as well, though that was still several months off, and it was not something Amena could have known at the time.

One focus of several women's rights groups during this period was to work on changing perceptions about virginity tests—a common tool still used by the police and families in cases of sexual assault. Many of the women bringing cases to Amena's organization had been told by the courts that if they wanted to proceed with a rape case, they needed to first take a virginity test. This test was considered particularly problematic for unmarried women and served as a major deterrent, leading many women to simply drop their cases. The practice was also, technically, illegal, but no one was taking action to stop it.

Amena had met with the UN and other women's rights groups to advocate for adherence to legal procedures, particularly in rape cases. Such work, however, was slow, and with worsening security conditions, corrupt police, and a government filled with leaders who were focused partially on fighting an insurgency, but more on filling their own pockets, there was no real support from official channels for their work. Three of their support centers in outlying provinces closed because of threats against them. As American troops began to withdraw more rapidly, Amena started wondering, who would continue to support this work when the international troops are gone? Would women's rights organizations continue their work or would they all be forced to close?

Recounting this period, Amena continued, crying softly, "Every time I leave home, I hug my kids tightly, because I do not know if I will return. I have already been a migrant twice, first coming to Kabul and then going to Turkey, and every time you go, you must start again from zero. I don't want to go through that again, but it's the only way I know to save my life and the life of my children."

Since her father-in-law, Ismaeil, was already a US citizen, she hoped that they could still, in some way, make it to America. Even with these plans, however, she was still firmly committed to the Afghan women she was working with. She had already looked into the necessary steps to getting her medical license in the United States and hoped that if she got there, she could then work from America on a program that would send resources back to Afghanistan that women badly needed. Despite being rejected by UNHCR, she held out hope that her work for MSH and in the public health sector might make a difference in the application process.

***

Since MSH worked for the US government, Amena thought she had a good chance at getting an SIV. When she applied, however, she was told that since she was a contractor and not a permanent employee, she had not done enough "service" to the US government to qualify.

This was a common refrain from rejected applicants we spoke with. The SIV process was defined by two terms, neither of which were clearly explained to applicants: "service" and "threat." In theory, if you had performed a "service" and were now under "threat," you should get a visa to protect you, but how were these terms defined?

For service, the government stated initially that 12 months working for the US government or being an employee of a US government contractor qualified you for a visa. Later that 12-month requirement was increased to 24 months, only to again be decreased in 2020 to 12 again. Beyond this, however, there was a lot of confusion around what type of contractors qualified for visas and what type did not: In most of the cases we gathered, employees working directly for the US government were granted SIVs, but contractors on US government projects, as was the case with Arsalan and Amena, were often, but not always, rejected. (Translators were technically contractors as well, in almost all instances, and they were far more successful at receiving visas than contractors on development projects or in more labor-intensive military contracts, even if they happened in the same area. Those contractors working at the US embassy also seemed far more likely to receive an SIV in a timely manner than other contractors.) There was resentment between some of those Afghans, like translators, who had served in combat zones, risking their lives on patrol each day, and those who worked in safer (and higher paid) positions at the US embassy or elsewhere in Kabul. Many felt that this service, since it was particularly taxing, should count in the applicant's favor.[2] For most applicants the system felt arbitrary at best and entirely rigged at worst. What was it about 12 months as opposed to 11 months that qualified you? Was there something specific about the last month? And, for the most part, if you worked for 6 months for four different US agencies, it seems like your application was still being rejected.

While service was a difficult term to define and assess, "threat" was even harder. What constituted a "threat" that made an applicant worthy of a visa? This was one of the most confusing steps in the application process, and the instructions did not clarify much.

The website's description stated: "Section 1219 of the National Defense Authorization Act (NDAA) for FY 2015 (Public Law 113–66) provides that a credible sworn statement depicting dangerous country conditions, together with official evidence of such country conditions from the US government should be considered as a factor in a determination of whether an applicant has experienced or is experiencing an ongoing serious threat as a consequence of employment by the US government."This confusing, bureaucratic language was challenging, particularly for those applicants who did not speak English well.[3] Interviews with both those who went through the process and those who worked to support their cases suggested that those who wrote these threat statements and could then support them with Taliban "Night Letters" were more likely to be successful in meeting these requirements.

Night Letters were typically documents left on a person's home instructing them not to cooperate with the government or the Americans or to cease some other activity that was considered against the Taliban cause. Often these letters were very official-looking proclamations from the Taliban shadow government, and in some of our research we found letters in 2010 that were being used to summon Afghans living in government-controlled territory to Taliban courts to discuss issues as mundane as property disputes.

More common, however, were the letters that essentially demanded that an individual stop working with both international organizations and the Afghan government. In many cases, these demands were still vague and general. An example Night Letter, for instance, that the Combating Terrorism Center at West Point posted stated that those in Paktia Province should not visit government buildings or attend government schools and that: "Any kinds of work such as construction, engineering or road work are prohibited. You are even prohibited from leasing your tractor or car to the government. If we capture any government employee, we will punish him severely. Helping the foreign companies or getting help from them is absolutely prohibited."[4]

The problem was that the SIV process seemed to assume that some precise documentation of threat was available to most Afghans, when in fact it was not. In most cases, threats were not this clear cut. They were often made verbally to family members by neighbors who had connections with the Taliban.

What was Amena to do in a case where people threw rocks at her and called her names on her way to work? How could she "prove" that this was a "direct specific threat"? Even when her car had been shot up, it was not as if the Afghan police were likely to write her a police report— they were more likely to have cooperated with the attackers who were probably from the area. Amena was an outsider there. And if she did get a report, how could she prove it was specifically aimed at her and not just one of Afghanistan's random instances of violence?

Even worse, when applicants like Amena submitted documents that did not meet all the specific criteria as defined by the strict terms of the State Department, it was not as if the State Department quickly alerted them that their cases were not considered serious enough. Instead, applicants often waited for years, hoping to get their visas, only then to be disappointed.

In the United States, as the number of Afghans waiting to hear if their SIV applications had been accepted increased, advocates for these Afghans grew increasingly impatient. One of the main constituencies supporting these applications were the veterans and other Americans who had worked alongside Afghans in Afghanistan. No One Left Behind and a series of other veteran-organized groups were set up and would be key players in the evacuation, but much of the initial advocacy was done by legal groups.

For instance, the International Refugee Assistance Project (IRAP) organizes a group of pro bono lawyers and law school students to support legal and human rights for displaced people. While much of their work is on a case-by-case basis, they do file lawsuits both in individual and class-action cases when they see recurring challenges in the refugees and displaced people they are working with. This led them to file a class-action lawsuit against the State Department in June 2018 in which they represented a series of Afghans and Iraqis who claimed the State Department had "failed to process and adjudicate their SIV applications within a reasonable time."[5] The law that set up the SIV program said that the State Department should process applications within nine months. Of course, by this point, it was taking more than three years in most cases.

Fourteen months later, the court issued a decision that said the State Department needed to start completing specific aspects of the SIV applicant review process within prescribed amounts of time. The decision set up an adjudication plan in which "the government committed to time-frames for promptly processing approximately 10,000 SIV applications and to report on its progress."[6] Such rulings gave some of those watching the system hope, but they did little to reassure those in Afghanistan waiting for visas. Many, as a result, started seeking help anywhere they could find it, particularly those who claimed they could help guide them through the application process.

Initially, around 2010, a lot of applicants would apply from internet cafes, and it was possible to find small signs advertising assistance in the application process. As certain people gained a reputation as being particularly good at assisting with these cases, a small industry of "travel agents" were set up, offering help applying for the SIV program, as well as study visas in Australia and other pathways out of the country. For a fee, these offices provided advice and help with forms and, in some cases, even helped facilitate bribes.

Others looked for help from more mystical sources. Arsalan's mother's uncle was a well-known religious healer who gave people who visited his shrine protective amulets and other charms. When Arsalan's cousin was at risk of being deported from the United Kingdom, the healer had given his mother a prayer on a piece of paper to send to him. The healer told the man to burn it behind the courthouse in Britain and that it would protect him during the hearing. The man won his case, and soon others came to the holy man for religious help with the immigration process. For a small donation to the shrine, the man would write a prayer for you to wear in an amulet around your neck and your case would be processed faster.

When we conducted a study of some of the more formal "travel" agencies in 2016, we found that many typically charged $50 to $80 to help with the application, which included filling out the form, but also help writing their threat statements and providing documentation such as Taliban Night Letters. Even for those with legitimate applications, there was often a sense that having a Night Letter to accompany it was almost required. One forger, who spoke to the Associated Press, claimed, "Of the threat letters now being presented to European authorities by Afghans, I'd say only 1 percent are real and 99 percent are phony."[7] He was charging up to $1,000 for a forged Night Letter, though we found many cheaper. In total, however, if an applicant wanted help with the interview and potentially forged Taliban letters, the price could increase to $500 to $800 for a family of four. And it certainly seemed business was good: The offices we visited were busy and one had a list of around two hundred applicants who they were currently helping.

The increased number of forgers and brokers assisting with the process only frustrated applicants further. One applicant told us that he had recently visited a forger who had a reputation for being very skilled with Photoshop and could give you a Night Letter on Taliban letterhead. The forger complained that several of his clients had received their SIVs, but his own application had still not gone through: "My friend worked in a cell phone repair shop. He had no connection to the internationals," he lamented. "And yet, now he is living in America and he has recently gotten visas for his extended family members as well."

Of course, many of those visiting these "travel agents" weren't just applying for SIVs. They were also looking to get visas to other Western countries or take more dangerous and less legal ways to the West, overland through Iran, Turkey, and Greece, or perhaps by boat to Australia.[8] Unsurprisingly, these places became immigration hubs and could put applicants in touch with the gangs of human traffickers who offered various services. Oftentimes an SIV applicant in serious danger would submit an application, but if the process was taking too long, they might then go on and take one of the illegal trafficking routes to Turkey or elsewhere.

As time went by there were more and more applicants stuck in this same limbo, waiting for visas to be processed. More and more began taking dangerous routes out of the country. The price rose and fell rapidly depending upon border conditions, but generally a smuggler charged around ten thousand dollars to get an Afghan to Europe, though this could be a little more or a little less depending upon destination and what types of forged documents or IDs might be provided.

Just making it to Europe, however, did not guarantee safety, as Amena knew from her experience in Istanbul. Once there, asylum cases were often denied, and several European countries ramped up deportations back to Afghanistan. In 2017, Germany announced it would be deporting 11,900 Afghans who had entered the country without visas, and between 2008 and 2020, more than 70,000 Afghans were deported from the European Union and the United Kingdom.[9] These deportations continued up through the final days of the Republic. In fact, just ten days before the government collapsed, the governments of Austria, Denmark, Belgium, the Netherlands, Greece, and Germany sent a joint letter to the European Union encouraging members to continue sending Afghans back in order to not "send the wrong signal" to potential migrants.[10]

In many instances these Afghans returned home to face the same threats they had fled from originally, but now they were in debt to the smugglers who had brought them out of Afghanistan. Sometimes they were in even more danger since criminal groups would sometimes target those returning from abroad because it was assumed that they had made money while working outside of the country. By the end of the 2010s, everyone in Afghanistan knew some friend or family member who had made it out of Afghanistan, and leaving became more and more of something to be considered for many young Afghans. For Zeinab, it was also becoming clear that her competitiveness and athleticism were opening potential doors for her.

**

Zeinab was one of four women selected by She Can Tri, the NGO her friend Jackie had set up, to help Afghan women get into triathlons. They started training together, aiming at competing in the Dubai triathlon. The Dubai triathlon seemed the best suited for the novice Afghan competitors: The course was flat, it was not too difficult for Afghans to secure visas to the Emirates, and travel would be easier than for other triathlons farther afield.

They began their training but were hampered by numerous obstacles. First, there were only two swimming pools for women in all of Kabul, a city of five million. Particularly during the warmer months, the pools were packed with women and kids cooling off and chatting, not at all the type of pool one could swim laps in. She Can Tri gave the women a stipend to cover transportation costs and also to allow them to rent time at one of the pools for their training. But there was also the fact that Jackie was not allowed to leave the military base she was living on except for official trips. This meant that they were on their own to teach themselves to swim. And so, Zeinab went to YouTube and started streaming videos that taught you how to swim.

The cycling portion was somewhat easier but still challenging. There were no high-quality road bikes available in Afghanistan, and once Zeinab did get a bike that was good enough to train on, she was constantly afraid someone would rob her while she was riding it. Kabul roads were filled with potholes, security barriers, and checkpoints, which made riding for long stretches difficult. She returned to her practice of training before dawn, when most of the city was still asleep. She Can Tri eventually raised funds so that Zeinab and two other women could travel to Spain for a week of training camp. There she swam in open water for the first time. A few months after, they went to Abu Dhabi for another week of swimming and cycling training.

By now Zeinab was a senior at AUAF. Her life looked completely different than it had when she had first arrived in Kabul. She was still working at the insurance company while training in three separate sports and taking classes, and she often found herself wishing her days had more than twenty-four hours. She had traveled to half a dozen countries and was thinking about ways of further empowering other women who had not had the opportunities she had. She remained in close contact with her family in Herat, but now, she was traveling outside the country, meeting new people, and running new races. Looking back, she was amazed at how far she had come and how she was able to travel to these different countries when so many others were not able to.

Part IV

The Final Days of the American Occupation

ARSALAN—NOVEMBER 20, 2021:

Already our old lives seem like the distant past. Winter is setting in and everyone in the country is worried about food and fuel to stay warm. We are doing what we can for family members, but Afghans have large families and I have dozens of cousins and aunts and uncles, all of whom have their own families that they are worried about.

Just last year we had all gathered for my wedding. There was a good bit of excitement because I am the oldest son and I had waited a long time by Afghan standards to get married. I wanted to make sure I had completed my studies and had established my own career before I got married, though that didn't stop my mother from pushing me. After I returned from Turkey, whenever my mother saw a baby on the street, she would say, "Our house is too quiet. It would be nice to have some grandkids around."

Marrying in Afghanistan is complicated. You need to find someone who you like, but the families also need to get along and have similar values. While I was building my career, it was difficult to concentrate on all that.

Then, however, my younger sister said she knew someone from university. Her name was Farah, and my sister was certain she would be a good match. She was a good student and beautiful, but also had a sense of humor, she said. I asked around about her family since they were not from the same tribe as we are. Everyone said they were well respected and successful, while still maintaining Afghan values. This was very similar to my family and my mother particularly liked her. Of course, at the same time, her family was asking around about my family and how good my job was. I met with her brothers first, and it was almost like a job interview, as they grilled me, asking about my career prospects. They were concerned, since their family usually married only within their tribe. They even went to my father's home village to ask about our family's history.

The first time Farah and I met in person, we went out to dinner with our families and did some shopping since she was about to travel to India. The meeting went surprisingly well. Usually there is intense pressure on the couple at this moment and our conversation started very formally, but it became natural and warm very soon.

We invited 600 people to the wedding, but many guests brought other friends and family members with them. I later heard that when my brother paid the bill, the wedding hall said there had been 1,100 people there. Most were Afghan, but some of my international colleagues came as well. Everyone was dressed in their best and had come with fresh haircuts, trimmed beards, and new clothes, ready for a celebration.

At most weddings, the dancing doesn't start until later in the night, but we had professional musicians from the very beginning. They played what we call an attan. This is a traditional dance that includes a large dohl, or double-headed drum, and flute. Even when the food was served the dancing continued and it lasted late into the night. This happens only at the most joyful of weddings.

But things change quickly. Now weddings have no music. People just sit and eat. It's an instant reminder of just how different things are from a year ago.

***

During the spring following our wedding, in 2021, news was gloomy. Between COVID and increased attacks around the country, things did not feel great, but at the same time, everyone had lived through years of war. Some years were better, some years were worse.

The election of Joe Biden had at least given many of us some hope. Many of Trump's statements about the Taliban leaders had just seemed so naive and out of touch, like he had no interest in this war that he was commander in chief of. We couldn't believe it when we heard he had invited the Taliban to the presidential camp in the United States. But he also seemed mostly uninterested in the war really, leaving it up to the generals. Biden had been Obama's vice president, and for all the faults of the Obama administration, there seemed to be at least a clear policy and a sense of purpose to what the international community was doing here.

There were continued reports of the Taliban pushing into new rural areas, but this was something that we had heard to a greater or lesser extent for the past fifteen years: In the spring, fighting would resume and the Taliban footprint would creep outward. Over the summer, the ANA with help from US troops would try to push them back.

It was about a week before the fifteenth of August that things started to feel particularly different. For the first time the Taliban started to seize and hold entire provinces, not just large rural areas. Every day it seemed another province had collapsed and people were wondering what might happen next. There were rumors that maybe there would be another deal between the United States and the Taliban, but everyone wondered whether Ghani and his close advisors were involved. We all watched television, but we got even more information from Twitter and Facebook, where, unfortunately, it was often difficult to tell the difference between truth and fiction.

On August 13, two days before the Taliban arrived, Herat and Mazar-e Sharif fell to the Taliban. I stayed at the office late that night, listening to the news with colleagues as we debated what the government response would be. As we drank tea, we asked:

"What will Ghani say about all this? What were the plans to take back these provinces? Or at least keep the current ones safe?"

Most of us thought that he would step aside and an interim government would be put into place. This was the future that seemed the most plausible to all of us. The Taliban weren't prepared to just take over the country, and many of Ghani's allies seemed prepared to abandon him. Surely there was a compromise group that could set up some sort of transitional government, and we just wondered who might be involved. Others were sure that Khalilzad would take power. Everyone expected that the United States would pause its withdrawal and force the two sides to negotiate. In recent days, even to ordinary Afghans, *it was clear, however, that Ghani's inner circle had gotten smaller and smaller, and it was difficult to predict what they might do next.*

I scrolled through Twitter looking for reports from Balkh or Herat, places with few journalists where we knew the fighting had been intense. I kept hoping for good news.

The palace had sent out a tweet saying that Ghani would give a speech addressing the nation soon. Another tweet from someone claiming to have contacts within the palace said that the video had been prerecorded and that Ghani would announce that he was stepping down and forming a coalition government. The coalition, it was said, would involve the Taliban, though they would not lead it. Others said that the United States was pressuring Ghani to launch new efforts at negotiations. Some thought that Pakistani agents were secretly working inside the government to hasten the collapse. Of course, we thought, with US troops in the country, America still had a lot of leverage. They could push to make sure there was some type of solution.

But none of that happened.

At that point, my family wasn't talking about trying to leave, since surely, the government and the American forces could keep Kabul safe from the Taliban. Instead, my organization had research teams all across the country, so we were worrying about how we might continue our work in those provinces where the Taliban had newly arrived. At that point, we thought, the Taliban were a rumble of thunder in the distance, not a storm that was about to break.

For the most part, my family went about their daily lives. My brother, wife, and I all kept going to work. My mother would go out and do the shopping.

We were worried about my cousin who was working in the governor's office in Herat. We had received regular updates from him about the territory that the government was losing to the Taliban. In most cases his reports were slightly more alarming and dramatic in terms of the government losses than what we were hearing from the media. We were also increasingly worried, frankly, for the rest of his family living in his home in Kabul. More and more suicide bombers were targeting high-ranking officials in their homes.

On August 13, the entire Afghan military and government in Herat had surrendered that day to the Taliban. For several hours we couldn't get through to my cousin by phone, and I was constantly calling his family and other contacts to see if we could locate him. We had heard about the Taliban executing prisoners who had surrendered just the week before, and those hours were difficult. But then we heard that the Taliban had released many of the key Afghan government officials and that my cousin was on a plane heading back to Kabul along with the deputy minister of the interior. He was safe, for the time being.

The next day, one of my bosses heard from a contact that one of the major international newspapers had chartered a flight to get some of their staff out and that there were fifteen empty seats on the flight. We still did not feel that much urgency, but I called my uncle and two of my friends who I knew were looking to leave the country to see if they were interested. They hurried to get ready, but two hours later, the seats were already claimed and the plane was gone. Even this felt like something of a strange experience. I certainly did not think things were urgent and I didn't consider leaving on the plane myself. It was as if we were numb to the violence and the political turmoil.

The week before, a massive car bomb detonated at the minister of defense's house, which was just down the street from our office. The police and the other attackers traded gunfire for an hour. I had left only fifteen minutes before the gun battle started. Returning to the office the next morning, I saw the explosion had blown out all the windows in our office and made a real mess. So we directed our staff to work from home for the next few days. Our IT guys had helped make sure everyone could get online and, in many ways, this ended up helping us since we were already set up to work almost entirely remotely.

On August 15, only a few staff were in the office. I was there and joined my Australian boss and our operations manager to discuss resuming on-site work after the windows could be repaired. We also had a handful of other employees who were helping us reopen, including some women. We heard about the Taliban advance, but still, the rumor was that they were setting up camps in neighboring areas and would spend some time amassing troops before they actually entered the city.

Then there were reports that the Taliban were not just outside the city, but that they had actually driven in.

My brother, Yousuf, called and said he was heading home. People started forwarding voice messages around on WhatsApp. One was from a Taliban official saying that they would be landing soon at the airport and would then proceed to the palace to negotiate the next steps. Another clip went around *from the defense minister telling everyone to remain calm. A third was from a former parliamentarian, claiming that the Taliban had appointed him police chief of Kabul and saying that he was going to maintain order. We couldn't tell if these were real or fake, but we listened to them again and again, debating what they meant.*

Through all this, we still felt as if the transition would be orderly and that an interim government would be created. Then a post appeared that Ghani had fled the country.

Surely this was a joke, I thought. And then another confirmed it, and another, and that, I guess is when I finally realized that everything had changed.

Through all this my mother, father, and wife kept sending me messages. When was I going to be home? Why hadn't I come yet? As it got darker, we started to hear rumors of cars being stopped and robbed. Not by the Taliban, but ordinary criminals taking advantage of the chaos. I left my car at the office since it was a 4X4 that was only a few years old and there were some rumors that people were stealing any car that appeared to be in good condition or looked like it might belong to a government official.

When I got home, the electricity kept going out and we had to turn on our backup generator, but outages still made the neighborhood go dark, making it feel even more like we were on an island, alone. We sat there watching TV and scrolling through our phones. All the local channels had switched over to pre-recorded programming and we didn't know what that meant, but assumed it was bad. So, we had to watch CNN, which made my father annoyed since his English is not great and all it showed were American planes taking off from the airport. We kept waiting for some change, for some good news. But nothing. And then, close to dawn, the photos on CNN changed and we saw pictures of the Taliban in the president's office.

CHAPTER 10

Why Wasn't It Fixed?

BY THE TIME JOE BIDEN WAS ELECTED US PRESIDENT IN THE FALL OF 2020, Najeeb was in his first year of law school at Texas A&M. This was not exactly where he expected to be when, ten years before, he had first set out to study law in Kapisa. While compared to many other immigrants, this was a real feat, it also felt in some ways that he had spent the last six years starting over. He didn't want other Afghans who were fleeing to feel the same way.

Two years before, in 2018, Najeeb attended a talk at the University of Texas by two veterans who worked for No One Left Behind. The organization had been set up in 2013 and started rather small. In recent years, however, it had expanded. The two veterans took Najeeb out for a coffee at Starbucks after the talk and outlined some of their plans for expanding the networks of support for recent SIV arrivals.

Najeeb started volunteering for them during his free time. A lot of this was social networking of the type that he enjoyed anyway, and he contacted each new SIV arrival in the Dallas area. Texas was an increasingly popular place for Afghan immigrants—it was warm and the cost of living was reasonable—and the work took up more and more of his time. In 2020, NOLB started an "ambassadors program" that paid a few SIV recipients to liaise with new arrivals and help them through the settlement process. In this role, Najeeb distributed an intake form to new arrivals that was sent around through the network of Afghans living in Dallas. The form was meant to connect these immigrantss with resources that they might not have from the basic package that resettlement agencies were required to hand out. This could range from some initial groceries to emergency rent support for those who had no cash. As the Afghan community in Dallas grew, so did the networks of mutual aid that new arrivals could rely on. Some of these were fairly creative. One man who had attended a software bootcamp and gotten a good paying programming job as a result started offering computer lessons to other new arrivals, some of whom had also secured jobs.

Just as important for the new arrivals, Najeeb explained, was that he tried to encourage them by talking about his own success after years of struggle. "They need to find things to make them happy, to connect with a community," he said. The Afghans who didn't often struggled most and Najeeb knew how lonely it could be. Still, the number of Afghans actually receiving SIVs was little more than a trickle, and even with these low numbers, it was difficult to help each new family.

Najeeb also wished these organizations could do more for Afghan SIV applicants who were still in Afghanistan. There were strict regulations about how money could be distributed in Afghanistan, and organizations had, in the past, inadvertently provided money to individuals who were then linked to anti-government groups. While there were very few actual cases of this, the US government's ensuing red tape made it more and more difficult to actually help Afghans in Afghanistan. "It's quite annoying actually that the people that need the most help are in Afghanistan, not the SIVs here. But it's difficult for the organization to spend money in Afghanistan, since there was no way to ensure the people they were sending money to were not associated with any bad guys," Najeeb said.

Part of the issue for those still stuck in Afghanistan was the pure bureaucratic morass of the SIV process. For instance, each applicant had to submit biometric data including retinal scans and fingerprints. Yet, as one NOLB representative pointed out to Noah, this is information the military routinely gathered for anyone contracting with them, as did the US embassy and many of the other organizations the US government funded in Afghanistan. Certainly sharing this type of data between government offices is not simple, yet, by demanding that the applicants come to the embassy for both interviews and biometric data submission (not to mention also visiting the one clinic authorized to give US embassy-approved medical exams), the embassy was essentially asking those Afghans most at risk, many of whom were hiding far from Kabul, to come to one of the most dangerous places for them to submit information that the US government already had.

Other issues appeared to be linked to the nature of the staffing. In 2019, for instance, the State Department had only one employee doing all the security checks on SIV applicants, despite the fact that there was a backlog of 18,000 submitted applications, and while the process was set up to be overseen by a senior coordinating official, that position had been left unfilled from January 2017 until 2019.[1] In the meantime, for the staff at the US embassy involved in the process, employees rarely were in positions for more than a year, and the high turnover rate meant a steep learning curve and that those actually processing the visas had little experience with Afghanistan or the reality these applicants were living in.

This led to applications being "disqualified for ridiculous reasons" as one lawyer for the International Refugee Assistance Project (IRAP) described to us. In one case, the employer who signed the employment verification letter for an applicant was kidnapped, and the State Department was working to rescue the man, but they then rejected an applicant's application because they could not verify his employment with the man who was at that point kidnapped.

While most of these issues predated the Trump administration, after 2016 other aspects of the slowing of the process were clearly caused by deliberate attempts to undermine the US immigration system more broadly. While the Trump administration's vocal opposition to immigration rarely directly targeted the SIV program, perhaps out of fear of receiving backlash from veterans groups, the policies of the administration slowed down the SIV process even further. In the first two years of the Trump presidency, the number of SIVs issued dropped by 45 percent.[2] The administration did this in part by imposing new regulations on applicants, requiring them to provide twenty-five years of historic data about employment and family, whereas previously they had only been required to provide ten years. As the head of No One Left Behind concluded in an email: "This is just one example of several new policies we believe make it virtually impossible any applicant can ever make it through the vetting and processing procedures."

There were also massive delays in processing of applications. As one government audit found: "SIV applicant emails had not been opened in the approximately 30 days after they were received."[3] In 2016, the processing time for the State Department to complete its review of applications was 293 days. By early 2020 it was taking them 658 days to review the same application.[4] This meant that the number of visas actually available to Afghans but not given out actually increased between 2016 and 2020, and in 2020 there were more than 8,000 visas available but not distributed.[5] The backlog of 18,000 applications was greater than the number of Afghans who had actually received visas in the twenty years since the United States invaded. This was just the time that it took the State Department to deal with the application and did not include the time it took the applicant to submit the application or set up the interview, for instance.

Still, as the election of Joe Biden demonstrated, it was not just a question of foot dragging by the Trump administration that had slowed the processing time of visas. There were still serious flaws in the design of the program even as the Biden administration took over. Congress again increased the number of SIVs for Afghan applicants by another four thousand in December 2020, but this was still not enough to cover a quarter of those who had already submitted applications. By this point, however, the backlog of applications for the SIV program was so long that the system had almost completely broken down.

At this point who was going to wait five years for a visa?

The answer we found was primarily applicants who were not in immediate danger. Many of those we spoke with who were technically eligible for an SIV either had not applied since they felt there was no possibility of receiving the visa in time or, in some cases, had submitted an application and then used smugglers to leave the country and were planning on potentially returning just to pick up their visas, if necessary.

In fact, a NOLB survey in 2020 found SIV applicants living in thirty different countries, waiting to hear about their visas. What this meant was that most of the applicants who had been in touch with NOLB while waiting for a visa for the United States had actually already fled Afghanistan to another country.

Something had to change, and in early 2020, it seemed like there might actually be some shifts ahead.

CHAPTER 11

Priority 2

BY EARLY 2021, WHAT THE *NEW YORK TIMES* REFERRED TO AS A "SLOW creeping siege" of Afghanistan's cities had sped up, and while not one provincial capital was technically under Taliban control, one analysis categorized 15 of Afghanistan's 34 provincial capitals as being "effectively surrounded by Taliban-controlled areas."[1] This was a sharp break from the first twenty years of the war: The Taliban had only briefly taken the provincial capital of Kunduz in 2015 and held it for fifteen days but, other than that the Afghan government, with the support of international forces, had been able to maintain control of all provincial centers.[2] Even this episode in Kunduz was more of a ransacking than an actual attempt to hold the city: During the time the Taliban held the city, they destroyed government buildings and released prisoners. Other than this, during the two decades of war, the rule of thumb was that the Taliban could successfully operate in many rural areas, but they could not actually hold urban areas. Their only real operations in urban areas were the type of spectacular terrorist attacks that Ismaeil had survived at the Ministry of Justice and Zeinab had lived through at AUAF. The cost of this type of warfare on civilian Afghans was extraordinary. In the first six months of 2021, the UN Assistance Mission reported 1,659 civilians killed and another 3,524 injured, representing an increase of 47 percent from 2020.[3] But things were changing.

While Joe Biden had not mentioned Afghanistan much in his election campaign, many policy makers focused on Afghanistan were optimistic that his election might at least bring some stability to the US policy toward Afghanistan and the immigration of those at risk. On February 4, 2021, the Biden administration issued the cumbersomely named and sprawling "Executive Order on Rebuilding and Enhancing Programs to Resettle Refugees and Planning for the Impact of Climate Change on Migration." The order stated that: "The Special Immigrant Visa (SIV) programs for Iraqi and Afghan allies provide humanitarian protection to nationals of Iraq and Afghanistan experiencing an ongoing, serious threat because they provided faithful and valuable service to the United States, including its troops serving in those countries. The Federal Government should ensure that these important programs are administered without undue delay."[4]

In many ways, this was a victory for those who had been working to support the SIV process. The executive order asked for an immediate review of the process, particularly areas of concern such as when "an applicant's employer is unable or unwilling to provide verification of the applicant's 'faithful and valuable service,' and provide for 'alternative forms of verification,'" and it requested a review of methods of digitally streamlining the process. Even more ambitiously, the order requested "The review should also evaluate whether it would be appropriate to seek legislation that would create an SIV program for individuals, regardless of nationality, who faithfully assisted the United States Government in conflict areas for at least 1 year or made exceptional contributions in a shorter period and have experienced or are experiencing an ongoing serious threat as a result of their service."[5]

Such an expansion of the process had not been the goal of most advocates and suggested that the Biden administration was perhaps thinking even more radically about ways of supporting those who had supported the US government in various conflict zones. At the same time, however, intertwined with the recommendations around SIV from Afghanistan were concerns about policy for migrants due to climate change, which was a signal that the administration was looking past Afghanistan to new foreign policy concerns.

Pressure from veterans groups seeking to support translators they had worked with multiplied. Groups like No One Left Behind had pulled together support from a wide array of government officials and military officers. There was even a sense that these groups were making an impact on the national image of Afghan interpreters, something that became apparent with the debut of *United States of Al*, a comedy on CBS about an Afghan translator who moves in with a Marine he worked with from Ohio.

At the same time, however, the veterans community and others were increasingly alarmed by the Biden's administration's commitment to withdraw hastily from Afghanistan. While the Trump administration had agreed to do this by the spring of 2021, there was the widely held belief among both US policy makers and ordinary Afghans that this date would be pushed back. The Doha Agreement even explicitly allowed for this, since the Taliban themselves had not fulfilled their end of the agreement by starting peace talks with the Afghan government.

At that point, the Taliban already had significant momentum, and the announcement that all US troops would leave by the end of the summer came as a shock to many in Kabul. "My first response was, 'What the hell?'" said Arsalan. "This is really dumb. After all this time, they are just going to leave? But honestly, my friends and I, as we discussed, we also weren't really believing it. It was too stupid. Surely there would be pressures from other NATO partners or the Republicans or the generals who had been running the war or something would make them change their minds."

When Biden announced in April that he would completely withdraw American troops by the end of August, concern for those likely to be targeted became more acute. On May 6, representatives from some of the key organizations focused on protecting Afghan refugees, including Human Rights First, IRAP, and NOLB, had a Zoom call with National Security Council members where they raised their fears about the safety of those who had worked with the United States. National Security Consul representatives were "cordial but noncommittal" according to a participant interviewed by the *New York Times*.[6]

But as the withdrawal ramped up, it became clear that something had shifted in the US mentality. It was as if they were abandoning the country entirely, and this was particularly problematic for the Afghan forces, which they had spent $83 billion on building up.[7] Beginning in 2013 and continuing in the years that followed, as US troops withdrew from an area there was careful hand over to Afghan troops, often integrating forces, making sure that the ANA had the ability to control the territory, and then sustained air support once US ground troops had left the area. In the 2021 phase, there were no formal hand overs of any of the major US bases. American troops left Kandahar Airfield after almost twenty years in the middle of the night, not alerting even their Afghan counterparts, for security reasons supposedly. They did the same at Bagram, and the Associated Press quoted the new Afghan commander of the base as saying: "We (heard) some rumor that the Americans had left Bagram . . . and finally by seven o'clock in the morning, we understood that it was confirmed that they had already left Bagram."[8]

Such moves did little to reassure Afghan forces or simply make sure that they were well-positioned to take over the roles their American counterparts had filled. If the United States thought that the Afghan troops could continue to hold the territory that they had, they certainly weren't acting that way. With the abandonment of Bagram, the United States lost access to a large military airport within easy driving distance of Kabul. While there certainly would have been other challenges, having access to Bagram would have at least given the Biden administration many more evacuation options after the August collapse. Instead, the airport in Mazar-e Sharif would become the go-to airport for independent groups trying to extract Afghans who thought the Taliban government in the north was more willing to turn a blind eye to departing flights than the government in Kabul. But Mazar was a full day's drive from Kabul, which was not convenient, and it had few of the resources that Kabul airport or Bagram did.

Several members of Congress, some with personal ties to the war, like Seth Moulton, a veteran and representative from Massachusetts, pushed the Biden administration to do more. He and many of the groups advocating for these Afghans wanted the government to stop the current visa process for SIVs and simply to evacuate those most at risk to a third country and then work on the visa process. Congress did pass a new Afghan Allies Protection Act, which again increased the number of visas available, though did little to mandate that visas get processed any faster.

The State Department managed to process 5,600 between April and July, a rate that was much faster than previous quarters. But at the same time, this was only a small dent in the number of Afghans threatened by the Taliban for their service to the United States.[9] The act also allowed for the medical exam to be postponed and in the case of applicants who were killed while waiting for their visas, allowed their spouses and children to still receive the visa. But none of this was enough.

For Afghans, it became increasingly apparent that the people in the US government running the withdrawal process and the people processing visas were not speaking to each other and had completely different perspectives on the long-term hopes for a peaceful Afghanistan. The SIV process seemed to imply, "don't worry, you will have time to wait several years for your visa," while anyone watching the military withdrawal understood, perhaps they had only a few months.

Further complicating the processing of visas, Ghani and Biden had a tense meeting at the White House on June 25. During the meeting, Ghani asked Biden to be "conservative" about processing SIVs, worried that having thousands of Afghans with connections to the United States fleeing the country would undermine confidence in his government.[10] Not long after this meeting, Ghani had his own passporting process center stop processing passports to similarly slow the exit of Afghans.

***

That spring, Najeeb returned to Kabul for an extended visit, plus to get married to his fiancé who was living in Afghanistan. Like other American citizens, he applied for a visa for his new wife using the I-130 form that gives citizens the ability to get visas for their spouses. In July he filed the case at the US embassy.

This was a busy time for travel to Afghanistan. The spring and early summer was the time that many Afghans who had moved abroad returned to visit family, so it was a good opportunity to spend some time with both friends and family. Many other SIV recipients who had immigrated to the United States and received their green cards also returned regularly to Kabul. The embassy asks US citizens to register through their online tracking system, the Smart Traveler Enrollment Program, or STEP. But in reality, many travelers don't do this, particularly Afghan-Americans who might have concerns about their immigration status still. In general, the registration system was something of a hassle that many avoided. This would have consequences later when US citizens rushed to the airport.

While he was in Afghanistan, Najeeb also spent time with his brother, who had also worked for the US military and had applied for the SIV. He was hopeful that soon, he might have both his wife and brother in Texas with him. But, as he prepared to leave in July, he was still aware that "the situation in Afghanistan was not good." Not long before he was set to leave, Najeeb got a phone call from his friend who worked for Emirates Air. He knew that Najeeb had a ticket booked with them and the company was discussing canceling its Kabul-Dubai route due to the increasing insecurity. "There were talks about the Taliban advancing, but the expectations were still that the big cities would hold up for at least many months. No one expected that it would be possible for Kabul to collapse in a single day." So even with the security concerns, Najeeb kept his original flight booked for July 29.

Najeeb was not the only one concerned about the security situation. With the August 31 withdrawal deadline looming and increasing pressure from veterans groups, the State Department was forced to respond to criticism that they were working too slowly on visas. On July 17, 2021, US Chargé d'Affaires Ambassador Ross Wilson issued a bland statement announcing the embassy's support for Operation Allies Refuge: "These relocation operations will allow the United States to fulfill its commitment to those who have served our country here at great personal risk. They build on the successful acceleration of SIV processing since visa interviews resumed after the COVID suspension ended in 2021." The press release went on to assure that the government would "continue strongly to support the people of Afghanistan and its institutions through security assistance to the Afghan National Defense and Security Forces, development and humanitarian aid, and diplomacy on behalf of peace and stability here and in the region."[11]

Two weeks later the first plane arrived at Dulles International Airport carrying 221 SIV recipients, who were then bused to Fort Lee, Virginia, for processing. It was a drop in the bucket since at that point more than 20,000 SIV applicants remained pending in the processing line.[12]

On August 2, the State Department announced a new potential immigration designation for Afghans who did not qualify for the SIV program but still were particularly at risk. The announcement stated that: "The US objective remains a peaceful, secure Afghanistan. However, in light of increased levels of Taliban violence, the US government is working to provide certain Afghans, including those who worked with the United States, the opportunity for refugee resettlement to the United States."[13] One of the major differences with the P-2 status, however, was that individual Afghans could not apply for it; the organization where the individual had worked itself had to nominate the individual.

The other major difference was that applicants had to be interviewed at a US embassy outside of Afghanistan for their applications to be processed. This generated a great deal of confusion among applicants, but also advocates and the organizations hoping to make referrals for the Afghans who had worked for them. (Two weeks later it would be even more complicated because with the collapse of the government, it would get even more difficult for Afghans to leave the country.) The other complicating factor for many who were contemplating applying was that the State Department said it was targeting 12 to 14 months for processing time, which while far less than the SIV process was currently taking was still far too long for those who were most in danger.

This new program seemed to acknowledge that the SIV program was not working and that Afghans were at risk. But designing a completely separate parallel track hardly seemed like an effective response.

***

In the meantime, we continued talking on the phone regularly as we normally did. We were working together on an assessment of the Ministry of Public Health's response to COVID and had designed a series of interview tools and surveys that they were using to look at where supplies were needed and how they had been used. Frequently, however, we'd discuss the political and security situations more generally.

Arsalan also had family members who were thinking about leaving the country, and we discussed their options. For instance, his brother Yousuf worked for a bank in Kabul, but like many young professional Afghans, he had also bounced around a series of organizations and businesses connected with the international community. For a while, when Arsalan had been studying in Turkey, Yousuf had worked with Noah on a series of projects, mostly conducting interviews. Noah had received funding for these projects from a Kabul-based think tank funded by the US government and a couple of US universities. So, it seemed, perhaps Yousuf could apply for an SIV as a subcontractor. The issue was that Noah had documentation from the funders stating that he was employing Afghan researchers, but they had not asked for documentation with Yousuf's name on it. Furthermore, the government might view this as not really employment, according to lawyers we discussed this with. So we started exploring the Priority 2 option despite the fact that it was confusing and seemed likely to take a while. Already, SIVs were taking three years to process, so if P-2 really did take around a year, that could be faster, we thought. And while everyone was more concerned with the announced US withdrawal, some leaked security reports suggested the government would last at least a year, and most assumed longer.

During this period, Munir also became more active in seeking ways to get his family out of the country. He knew several Afghans who had secured Turkish citizenship. This was possible by purchasing a house there. He had already begun the process of doing this, but several documents had to be approved by the Ministry of Foreign Affairs and this had not yet happened. His real hope after the State Department announcement on August 2 was the Priority 2 visa. Since it relaxed the requirement that you work for the United States for two years, he was convinced that the eight months he had spent interviewing criminals for Pacific Architects and Engineers (PAE), the State Department contractor, would qualify him. PAE, however, would not respond to any of his emails. Additionally, since P-2 required that the contractor submit the application package, Munir needed them to finalize the application for him. He began sending emails, but received no responses.

"I had prepared all the documents. 'Just take my documents,' I kept telling them. Just a click was needed. All they needed to do was send them, but they wouldn't even do this," he said.

He even contacted a US lawyer who had sent some emails on his behalf, but they had no more luck than he did. It was like he had never existed to them. Munir had also become friends with a psychologist named Lyla Schwartz, who had worked in Afghanistan for several years. She had set up an NGO, called Peace of Mind, providing psychological support for some of the same prisoners Munir had worked with when conducting interviews in prisons for PAE. He reached out to her over the summer to see if she had any ideas, and she said that she would begin working on a P-2 application for him as well. Still, it was unclear how long that would take or whether it would be successful or not. The instructions on the website were so vague, what would happen if there were two P-2 applications filed on his behalf? No one seemed to know. Would the government count it against him? Or would it strengthen his case? As the summer went on, it seemed like there were more and more questions, and fewer and fewer answers.

***

One of things, however, that Arsalan, Yousuf's, and Najeeb's brother's cases reflect, is that by early summer of 2021, there were many Afghans who had not yet applied for the SIV, or later the P-2, but who were considering it. In some cases, this was because they were so threatened, they had already fled the country, but for many others, the bureaucratic regulations dissuaded them from applying. So while the State Department was aware of the number of SIV applicants waiting to hear from them, they were unaware of the tens of thousands of other potential applicants. This was true even in the days just before the evacuation. On August 2, when the State Department announced the Priority 2 program, a senior State Department official was asked how many applicants they thought they would receive and responded: "We don't have an estimate yet. We'll have to wait and see how many referrals we get for the program."[14]

This led to one of the most frustrating aspects of the evacuation. Time and time again, we and thousands of others were asked by Afghan friends and colleagues, "Where am I on the list?" And yet, many were shocked to find out there was no list. In fact, there was not even a proper count by the State Department or anyone else of who might be eligible for the various programs they were creating.

The question of numbers became a crucial one in the days of the evacuation, and one that it became increasingly clear few in the government had really wrapped their heads around. Part of the issue here was that for both SIV and P-2, and later Humanitarian Parole, it was not just direct US government employees who were eligible, but also those who had worked as contractors for the government or on US-sponsored programs. And, the war had become increasingly contracted. In fact, since the September 2001 attacks, the Department of Defense had spent fourteen trillion dollars, and contractors had directly received half of that money.[15] In the last quarters that the United States actually reported the number of US troops in Afghanistan (2016—under the Trump administration the government stopped supplying even these basic figures), there were at least three contractors for every US military personnel just working on Department of Defense projects.

Despite this, there was no central database of US government contractors and so answering questions like, how many contractors were there and how long had they worked for the United States, which were essential to determining SIV eligibility, were basically impossible to answer. The Department of Defense did count the number of contractors it had each quarter, but other departments, such as USAID, did not. Even the Department of Defense numbers, however, were not helpful during the evacuation since, if the department counted 100,000 contractors one quarter and 100,000 contractors the next, there is no way of knowing whether these are the same 100,000 contractors, or whether, because of high turnover rates, it was really 150,000 or 200,000 who had worked as contractors over these six months.

Trying to get a sense of the actual numbers was incredibly difficult. Consider the case of one small group: Nepali security contractors in Afghanistan. Nepalis had been recruited into the British Imperial Army since the beginning of the nineteenth century. Because of this, these Gurkhas, as they are often referred to as, are a common fixture as private security contractors across the globe. They guarded compounds in Kabul like the US embassy and the so-called Green Zone, but also smaller NGO compounds.

Noah had spent the academic year in 2015–2016 tracking down many of these Nepalis to write a history of the conflict through the eyes of these private security contractors.[16] One of the issues, however, was that no one knew how many there had been. There was no Nepali embassy in Kabul and the Nepali government made no real effort to track Nepalis in Afghanistan. They asked contractors to register, but after several attacks, the government attempted to stop anyone from going there. As a result, most Nepali contractors would fly through Dubai or elsewhere in the Gulf and never report to the Nepali government that they had been in Afghanistan.

When Noah first attempted to do a survey of the Nepalis who had been in the country, several experts told him that there were around 5,000 Nepalis who worked there. However, as Noah conducted interviews with individual contractors and they reported the numbers working for various contracting companies, it became apparent that the number was much, much higher. Eventually he developed a list of the dozens of companies that employed Nepalis, with approximate estimates for each one. The highest were employing more than 300 at a time. This did not include Nepalis who were unemployed but living in labor camps in Kabul looking for work.

Ultimately, the list showed that at any one point there had been up to 10,000 Nepali contractors in the country and, given turnover rates with most spending three to six years in the country, ultimately at least 50,000 Nepalis participated in the war in Afghanistan. And this was just Nepalis.

On the Afghan side there were hundreds of thousands more. The 20,000 who had SIV applications pending were just the tip of the iceberg, and many, many others had been rejected or not applied either because they were reluctant to or because they thought they did not qualify. When Noah published a report on the problems with the SIV process for the Costs of War Project at Brown University six months before the evacuation, he did follow-up interviews with reporters. Each one wanted to know how many potential SIV applicants there were. Since Noah had struggled over the numbers repeatedly, he was reluctant to give an estimate, but the other estimates floating around in the media—mostly based on the current SIV waiting list—were far too low. So, based on our research, Noah told reporters that there were at least 100,000 Afghans who had a credible case to make for receiving an SIV. Adding in family members, that was probably actually 300,000. Most reporters were incredulous. One researcher from the Congressional Research Service even called to double-check the number. Surely, there can't be that many Afghans who worked for the international presence and potentially want to leave Afghanistan.

But, six months later, as the evacuation began, it was clear, there were that many. And the US government was not prepared for them.

CHAPTER 12

The Collapse

EVEN IN THE EARLY HOURS OF AUGUST 15TH, SOMETHING FELT OFF TO Amena. The city had seen an increase in refugees from around the country over the past weeks. Yet on her way to work things were quiet. There were a larger than normal number of ANA soldiers on the street and at the various checkpoints, but they seemed subdued. There were also several ambulances parked near the checkpoint closest to her home, as if in preparation for someone needing immediate help.

At work, Amena went about her morning, answering emails. Her office was on the second floor of the organization's building, and towards the middle of the morning, she went down to the first-floor meeting hall to meet with a visiting women's group. Not long into the meeting, right around 11:00 a.m., the internal alarm went off. The organization's security team rushed them to the safe room in the basement.

This had happened before in the case of nearby suicide attacks or other threats, so Amena was not immediately alarmed. The organization's security team seemed more serious than usual, and as the time passed, she worried more. They sat there for an hour, checking their cell phones and texting family members for updates. They half expected there to be the sound of gunfire, explosions, or some other cataclysmic event.

But what had happened was far quieter and far more devastating: The Taliban had returned to Kabul, meeting no resistance as they drove into the city.

Not long after this realization, the security team decided that keeping all the employees in the office was probably more dangerous for those in the safe room—there were many professional women in the office and they were well-known as an advocacy group. If the Taliban arrived and demanded to be let in, would the guards resist? Would there be some sort of shoot-out? No options seemed good; the guards hurried them out of the basement and into some of the organization's vehicles. They decided that there was not enough time for them to return to their offices, so Amena climbed into the car, leaving her laptop and other belongings behind.

The roads were busy, particularly the Darulaman road leading past many of the newly built government ministries, the parliament building, and AUAF, heading towards the largely Hazara neighborhood that Amena lived in. Government workers were pouring out of these compounds and joining everyone else in the street. Amena worried that they would not have time to make it through the traffic and actually get everyone who was in the car home. So she got out and walked.

It was a hot day and there is little shade on the Darulaman road. AUAF and other government compounds had cut down most of the trees near the road so that they could more closely monitor the people passing below their walls. So Amena plodded slowly down the same road that Zeinab took on some of her morning runs. Since she was wearing her work clothes, the walk was uncomfortable, and by the time Amena had covered the five miles home she was exhausted.

But more than that, Amena said, it seemed as if the world had entirely shifted. "I was glad to be home, but I felt like a stranger to everything outside of my window. I no longer belonged here; my country was destroyed."

***

Amena and others had little sense of exactly what was happening politically as the Taliban advanced. There were plenty of rumors, mostly focusing on Ghani's increasing reluctance to understand the gravity of the situation the government was in and his increasing isolation.[1] In his final meeting with his cabinet, as provinces were falling around Kabul, Ghani did not consult with his ministers as much as he gave them what several attendees later called a ninety-minute lecture.

In an effort to show that he was taking the Taliban advance seriously, Ghani had put Sami Sadat, a young and charismatic former Afghan army commander in Helmand, in charge of securing Kabul.[2] Sadat had connections to private security contractors as well as working closely with the US military, and perhaps, it was thought, he could use these connections to reinvigorate a demoralized and slowly crumbling Afghan military force. The momentum of the past week, if not twenty years, however, clearly favored the Taliban.

Zaranj, the capital of Nimroz Province, a rural province on the border with Iran, fell to the Taliban on August 6. The next day Jawzjan, the capital of Sherberghan, in the north of the country, followed suit. On August 8, Kunduz, Sar-e-Pul, and Takhar all fell at least partially to the Taliban.

Joining in the attacks were many of the prisoners who had been released by the Ghani government (at the request of the Trump administration) the year before, including Mawlavi Talib, a key commander in the attack on Lashkar Gah in Helmand Province.[3] Video clips posted by various reporters and on social media in Kunduz showed a battleline in the middle of town with Taliban fighters on one side of a street and ANA forces on the other. Afghans in other towns and cities started to worry about the effect of urban warfare if the advance continued.

That week, even while the Ghani government refused to acknowledge the victories, local politicians and militia leaders in provinces across the country were starting to cut deals with the Taliban. While fighting continued the next day in Herat, Kandahar, and Lashkar Gah, the capital of Samagan fell without a shot being fired.[4]

Dostum, the Uzbek commander and former vice president, and Mohommad Atta Noor, the former governor of Balkh, briefly took up arms in the city of Mazar-e Sharif, the last large government stronghold in the north. On August 13, the Taliban took Herat, Kandahar, and Lashkar Gah. And on August 14, Dostum and Atta abandoned Mazar-e Sharif, ceding all of the north to the Taliban. Still, even the day before fleeing, Ghani remained publicly defiant. In a prerecorded message to the nation, he said "Under the current situation, remobilizing of the security and defense forces is our top priority and required measures are underway for this purpose." This, just three months after an often-replayed interview in which Ghani said, "If there is war, I am the commander in chief. I will not abandon my people. I will not abandon my forces. I am willing to die for my country."[5]

***

Meanwhile, over that summer, many Afghans with international connections, like Zeinab, were working through any other channels they could to leave the country. Zeinab had gotten a taste of what it might be like to be a professional athlete finishing her first Ironman triathlon in February 2020, just before COVID shut down travel. She had flown to Dubai with two other Afghan athletes. The race consisted of a 1.2-mile swim out into the Arabian Gulf and back, followed by a 56-mile bike race through the city and into the desert, before a final 13.1-mile run along a shoreline road. The other two Afghan competitors dropped out during the cycling section of the race. They were just not ready to ride that long on a bike, but mile after mile Zeinab kept moving forward, listening to the crowds, watching the skyscrapers of Dubai pass her by. And just more than seven hours after starting the race, she made it to the finish line at 7:01:48, the first Afghan woman ever to finish a triathlon.

It was a triumphant moment because she had proven to herself that she could do it, but it also heightened her understandings of the inequities in the sports world. She met other international athletes in Dubai who had sponsorships and were paid stipends to train by their governments. Afghanistan, unfortunately, had none of this. Their few meager funds might go to help cover travel, but not to train, and Zeinab had been working to cover her expenses for some time now. Furthermore, in 2018, the head of the Afghan Football Federation, the most important sports group in the country, and other coaches and trainers were accused of sexually assaulting female athletes and using their positions to cover up the crimes. While Zeinab was not at all involved, it further convinced many Afghans that having women play sports was scandalous and wasn't what proper young ladies did.

In the meantime, Zeinab had been hired to work for Free to Run to help organize their events. While she was doing this, she dreamed of going abroad, not just as an athlete, but to study. In order to do this, she began preparing to apply for the Fulbright program. She took the GRE (Graduate Record Examination), GMAT (Graduate Management Admission Test), and TOEFL (Test of English as a Foreign Language) exams. She asked Jackie to write her a letter of recommendation. She made it through the first round and was invited to interview. After waiting almost a year, in early 2021, Zeinab heard that she had been selected as a Fulbright Fellow and would be studying in Colorado. She began to prepare.

With the scholarship in hand, it was far easier for her than other Afghans to go to the embassy to apply for a J-1, exchange visa, instead of the Special Immigrant Visa that most others were applying for. This student visa would cover only the time that she was studying, but she knew several Afghans who had applied for asylum while studying or gotten jobs that allowed them to continue living in the United States. She had also just gotten married to a young man named Ali that summer in a simple ceremony, and they were looking forward to starting their lives together. Besides, she was committed to her country and planning on returning once she had her degree. She was fine with the fact that the visa would cover only her course of study. Finally, she learned that her student visa was being processed and she was scheduled to fly out of the country on August 16.

As the days passed and she heard about the Taliban nearing Herat, where her father still lived, she grew more and more nervous. As the Taliban advance continued into the summer of 2021, Free to Run, which had previously been working in five different provinces, was slowly forced to stop operations even in the provinces that were considered safest, like Bamiyan. The entire summer felt more and more surreal. She checked in on her family in Herat daily to keep abreast of conditions in the west of the country. She hoped to visit them before leaving for Colorado, but that seemed less feasible as the days passed. She spent the final days before her flight packing and spending time with her sister. They chatted about what life in the United States might be like and went through her clothes trying to organize what she would need.

COVID restrictions meant that she was required to get a test done the day before boarding the plane. So on August 15, she headed out to a clinic that conducted COVID tests. The streets were busy, and outside the clinic there was a long line of women and children. She submitted her sample, and the nurse at the clinic said that she should come back later that afternoon for her results. So she decided to go home to wait. But on her way home, she said, "Cars were speeding by and shopkeepers were pulling down the grills on their stores and the streets seemed to suddenly empty. I had no idea what was going on, but people looked nervous, so I just joined everyone in hurrying home."

Then, at home, after logging onto Facebook, she saw images of Taliban soldiers driving into Kabul. Her phone buzzed and one of the other students who had been awarded a Fulbright told her he had heard their flights were canceled. "Fear engulfed my entire body," she said.

On Twitter, it said that Ashraf Ghani had fled the country. There were reports of the Taliban in various parts of the city, but news was now coming in so rapidly, she was no longer sure of who to believe. She texted another friend, who said she had heard that there were going to be commercial flights the next day. However, the internet at her home kept going out, and she was struggling to confirm this.

"I was worried about my flight the next day, but I also was asking, what is going to happen to my country, to my people, to my brothers? We are going to have no future. All our dreams are gone."

But she was not ready to give up like that. She decided that if there was a chance for her to get on the plane the next day, she still needed to have a negative COVID test result. So she and Ali prepared to head back to the clinic. But this time, she dressed in conservative Afghan clothes, covering herself entirely, very different from the casual outfit she had worn that morning. Ali also put on the robes that more traditional Afghan men wear, and they headed out.

As she returned to the street, everything had changed. Their neighborhood was usually vibrant with cafes and young people hanging out. Now the streets were almost empty. There were men with guns pulling cars over. They were dressed like Taliban in military fatigues, but they did not have uniforms, or any clear markings. There was no way to tell whether they were Taliban fighters or thieves. Later there were reports of looters who used the chaos to empty police stations of their weapons and computers and steal cars from passersby.[6] Luckily, Zeinab and Ali were in an old taxi and the men with guns seemed focused on those in nicer, newer cars and SUVs.

Elsewhere in Kabul, people were rushing to the banks, hoping to withdraw some money in case this was their last opportunity to do so, but in many cases the banks were simply closing. A friend of Zeinab's who was passing by Kabul University said that students were streaming out of the college dorms with any luggage they could carry, heading back to their villages or to the homes of any relatives they had in Kabul. Another friend said that she had seen a man loading his motorbike when two other men simply walked up to him, shoved him to the ground, hopped onto the bike, and drove off. This friend, who had studied at AUAF, had hurried home and started burning all her books and photos that had the AUAF logo on them, along with any documents that might connect her to the international community. She took her diploma and some of her most important documents, scanned them, put them on a hard drive and buried the drive in her garden. Then she burned her diploma too.

In the meantime, when Zeinab and Ali got to the clinic doing the COVID testing, they could hear the constant drone of airplanes. An airplane was taking off every thirty seconds it seemed. She thought of all those Westerners who worked in embassies and for international organizations, they were the people she had run with, and had worked with, and now they were leaving. She asked herself, "How can this be?" And she resolved that she would do whatever it took not to let them just leave her behind.

***

At around the same time, Jackie had woken up in her condo in Austin, checked her phone, and was shocked by the flood of messages. She scrolled through Twitter, unable to believe that the government had collapsed so quickly and that the international pullout seemed to be accelerating. She called a friend who worked in the office of General Miller, the head of US operations in Afghanistan. Despite the fact that the US embassy was advising both citizens and visa-holders, like Zeinab, to shelter in place, Jackie's friend said, "You should tell her to get to the airport." So, she texted Zeinab.

Zeinab and Ali returned home and, since their internet connection was not reliable, she texted a friend asking him to look up her flight, which was on Turkish Air, scheduled for the next day. Shockingly, the Turkish Air website still said that the flight was on schedule. Jackie told her that she should consider going to the airport immediately. Zeinab's sister agreed. "She said, 'Zeinab, this is your chance, do your best, try and go. If you stay here, no one knows what is going to happen.'"

But they had waited too long. It was now getting late and it seemed too risky to set out at night. Friends had been posting photos of the airport on Facebook. The initial ones just showed long lines, but then airport personnel had started walking off the job and passengers had been pushing and shoving, fighting for the last seats on the final commercial flights. They looked at all these images and kept discussing, but then they heard the Taliban had announced a curfew. No one was to leave their homes after 9:00 p.m.

Zeinab recalled, "In those hours, we went back twenty years. That was the darkest night for me."

***

Earlier that day, it was not just at the airport among civilian passengers that there were physical confrontations to get on aircrafts and out of the country. One eyewitness account of the escape of the four helicopters that took Ashraf Ghani out of the country said that "I saw that the president's bodyguards punch and kicked each other, each trying to push the other out of his way and board into the helicopters. As the helicopters peaked, several [security team] members, despite many efforts, were unable to board and remained [left behind at the presidential palace]." Apparently, half of the thirty bodyguards with Ghani were able to get on the helicopter, while the rest changed into civilian clothes and attempted to blend in as they walked out of the palace.[7]

Accounts of the decision to evacuate the presidential palace remain disputed, but almost all reports highlight the disorganization of the process and the lack of planning. By most accounts, Abdul Salam Rahimi, head of the government negotiations team in Doha that morning, had worked to arrange a transitional government plan in which Ghani would hand over power to a *loya jirga*, or group of elders. That morning, however, the plan began to unravel as Taliban fighters gathered at the gate. Ghani held several meetings to discuss the situation but remained undecided about his next steps.[8]

Phone calls were made back and forth with the peace negotiation team in Doha, but it wasn't clear whether the Taliban leaders they were talking with were in full communication with the Taliban currently at the gates of Kabul. According to a BBC source inside the palace, Ghani's security team was in favor of remaining there, but Mohib was pushing for an evacuation. (Four months later, when Mohib spoke publicly for the first time, he claimed that they had intel suggesting that the Taliban were planning on executing Ghani.[9]) At 3:30 p.m. three helicopters arrived, and after the brief shuffle over who would get a seat, they were loaded and departed.[10]

In the days that followed, other accounts, particularly from Russian-friendly news sources, as well as the Afghan embassy in Tajikistan, accused Ghani, Mohib, and others of escaping with millions in cash from the treasury as well. While there has been little subsequent evidence to support this at all, the details circulated rapidly on Facebook and probably helped reinforce the idea among many that Ghani had taken what he could during his flight and would not be active in whatever negotiations might follow.[11] A later US government report said that it was unlikely that the group had taken more than $500,000 in cash with them.[12]

When Ghani himself surfaced for the first time three days later on a Facebook live post (and his only public statements during the next months), he referred to the fate of Najibullah, the Afghan president during the Soviet occupation who was mutilated and tortured before being dragged through the street and strung up on a telephone pole outside the presidential palace by the Taliban the first time they took Kabul. The possibility of history repeating itself appeared to be too much for Ghani: "I would have been hanged in front of the eyes of the people of

Afghanistan and this would have been a dreadful disaster in our history," Ghani said in subdued tones, to explain his "hasty" departure.[13]

Few agreed with his assessment of his choices in those final moments. His own defense minister, General Bismillah Mohammadi, tweeted in reply: "They (Ghani and his associates) tied our hands behind our backs and sold the homeland, damn the rich man and his gang."

Arsalan agreed. "How could those that we entrusted, those that we elected, just leave like that? The entire government vanished, as if it had never been there."

When the four helicopters took off, they carried fifty-two people, including Ghani, Mohib, and Fazly, and, after twenty years, that was the end of the Afghan Republic.

PART V

AFTER AUGUST 15

ARSALAN—DECEMBER 2, 2021:

In the first days of the evacuation, everyone's focus was really on the airport. Some of my friends, even my aunts and uncles, had rushed there in those first couple of hours to see if they could get on a flight. Some were beaten by the Taliban with pipes and whips. Some were tear gassed by US and ANA soldiers.

For a moment or two on August 16, I considered it as well, but it just seemed so shameful to run off like that. We watched some of the images on TV of people trying to get into the airport and it was all so depressing. What was happening to our country? Watching this drove my mother crazy. "Why are they abandoning their homes?" she asked.

On August 17, the second day of the evacuation, I heard that a friend of mine had been shot dead at the airport. He had a Turkish visa and was trying to get on a flight. Still we don't know where the bullet came from, whether it was the Taliban or the Americans, or whether it was an accident or on purpose.

It was around this time that I went from sitting at home, mostly watching TV idly, to working around the clock. It was like I had been shocked into motion after a two-day stupor. In those first two days, some of my friends sent me messages asking if I could help them. Many assumed that since I had worked for the foreigners for so long that I was already out of the country. Others were asking if our office had any evacuation plans, since we had been funded by various foreign governments and organizations. Many were angry when I had no good answers for them. Former international colleagues, like

Noah, who were outside of the country also reached out to check in on us and ask if they could help, but, honestly, I did not know what to tell them either.

So I got our HR team to start working on writing letters for everyone who worked with us. I had them help our employees who might be illiterate or did not speak English well fill out forms requesting assistance. I filled out dozens of these for my friends and colleagues as well. Other organizations, particularly those run by internationals, seemed to have shut down completely, so I had dozens of other former colleagues sending messages asking for letters from us, since they could not get anything from their current employers.

Then there were the family members, first and second cousins, other relatives I had not heard from in a long time, all asking for help with their documents. While we only have 300 employees, when I asked the HR head how many people we were helping, he said, when you included the former staff members, temporary workers, and others, it was more than 1,000.

Family members were often trickiest to help. My uncle had been a driver for a security company that left Afghanistan more than ten years ago. At first, he did not really think that there would be a way for him to leave the country, but he heard more and more reports about those who had done work like he had making it out. He started sending emails to some of his former colleagues, but his English is not so good. I read one of the emails he had sent to an international colleague and in an attempt, I guess, to show him that he remembered him fondly, he signed it, "I love you."

So, he asked me to pretend to be him and send some emails on his behalf. I did this and after several emails back and forth, they finally sent us an employment verification letter. Now we had to get something from his direct supervisor. Once we found him on Facebook, it took some time before he responded to our messages. He finally agreed to write a letter. When he sent it, however, the dates were slightly different from the dates in the employment verification letter and we had seen cases delayed for discrepancies like this. So, I tried to ask politely for another letter. This time he sent a Word document and said:

"Here, you can edit it as you like, but please don't bother me anymore with this!"

At least my uncle then had a pending SIV case.

The problem was that my aunt told some other relatives that I had done this, and now everyone was sending me texts or calling me, asking me to help

174

them. Many were people I didn't know, distant relatives of distant relatives, or, as we say in Dari "relatives of my sheep."

I finally had to tell all my family members, "Listen, stop telling people I am doing this work, and if anyone asks, tell them I am too busy."

Part of the concern that people have is that there is not just one way out; there are many. And people are constantly discussing and debating, spreading rumors about the best way to leave. For instance, the United Kingdom and then Canada announced that they would take more refugees and everyone rushed to see if they could find contacts at those embassies. People were circulating Google forms that said they were organizing evacuations. It was hard to tell if these were real and who to believe, but people started asking me to help with these forms as well. But then, the websites were so overwhelmed by the thousands of applicants filling out these forms that the sites stopped working and some of these embassies then announced they would not be taking any new applications.

For the next week, I had no real life. I was on one call and then another. I sent voice messages requesting documents from internationals who were in other time zones. I didn't sleep. My parents and my wife were getting increasingly anxious, especially since I was annoyed all the time. "Stop worrying about these other people. What are we going to do?"

To be honest, I was also angry with myself. Why hadn't I submitted my SIV application before? Why did I assume it would all be alright? Now I barely had time to work on my own applications and my brother kept asking for help with his.

As one of my friends said: "We don't have just one plan. We have a plan A, a plan B, a plan C, and maybe even other plans after that."

I realized that I had so many potential plans, it had paralyzed me and I had been unable to really begin working on any one of them. I reached out to the organization I had originally taught English at. I contacted the head, who I had been good friends with, and she forwarded my email to their HR office. But then, I didn't get more of a response. It was discouraging, so I remained busy contacting friends and trying to get updates from the airport, but not really doing anything to move my own case forward.

In the meantime, one of my good friends assumed that I had already submitted my SIV application and so he kept calling, asking for help with his.

I had worked with him at a think tank, but he worked on one of their small local projects, and I don't think he had a formal contract, so I didn't think he had a chance of getting an SIV. I kept putting him off, telling him, "No, I am too busy. Perhaps later in the week."

But he was persistent, and finally he came to my house one evening around 5:00 p.m. with all his documents. At first, I tried to tell him I was busy, but he replied, "Don't worry, I have brought my blanket. I can sleep here by your door until you have time." I wanted to be angry at him for being pushy, but he was so funny about it that I just sighed and agreed to help him. So we sat there, working on my computer, scanning documents on his phone, editing his threat statement for the next six hours. Finally, a little before midnight, we hit the submit button. He smiled. And I realized that I needed to complete my own application soon. I couldn't put it off any longer.

Noah had already written me a letter of recommendation a long time before, and I had made some progress writing a threat statement, but the real issue was the employment letter. Most of my work during the past eight years had been on a series of projects for the USAID, UNICEF, and many other international organizations. In each of these cases, however, the organization basically hired my company to conduct a research project or some other project for them. So, while I was constantly working for these various organizations, I had never been a permanent employee. None of them would give me an employment verification letter.

We had to consider other options. Starting in 2011, I worked with Noah on a series of projects for a think tank in Washington. I had conducted interviews and done some research in the areas around my father's home village. Noah was happy to write a letter saying that he was my direct supervisor, as the application required, but we had both technically been subcontractors for the think tank, and when I had asked them previously, the think tank had said they would not give me a letter confirming this employment.

On August 17, I sent another email to the think tank asking for an employment verification letter. A program manager there followed up and said that I should just apply for P-2. I asked again, since I did not think the P-2 would be processed for at least a year. Again, they said no.

Noah sent another email, attaching my contract and requesting the employment letter again. They forwarded the email to another office. Around and around the email thread went. At one point, Noah wrote a stronger email and cc-ed the country director and the head of the Afghanistan office. He pointed out that we still had a contract for my work, and one of the officers wrote an angry email back saying they were overloaded with requests and doing their best. At that point, I was worried they might not give me any additional documentation.

Finally, a week later, they sent a single-line letter: "Through this letter, I would like to confirm that Arsalan worked as a contractor in multiple capacities since January 2011." It was certainly annoying that they did not reply to my emails and that they did respond to Noah's, but that is the way these things go with many organizations. I'm sure it was difficult for the HR people who were getting all these requests, but surely they must have understood that it was even harder for us on the ground. In the end, it seemed, they paid attention to the expats, but not the Afghans. At least with this I could finish my SIV application and, the next day, after organizing the documents, at last, I was done.

Of course, during all this time, like everyone, it was not just the SIV we were talking about. The SIV would only get me and my wife to the United States. If we wanted to get the rest of my family out, we would need to do something else.

As those first two weeks passed, my mother became more and more annoyed and would pace around the house. She would watch the television and then comment to no one in particular, "Look at all these fake promises. Things have just been getting worse and worse and no one from the foreigners acknowledges this. They just run."

A little later she returned to the room, looked at the television. "All there is on the news is evacuation: look at the crowds, all the people being left between. Look at the children, how alone they are. And even those who are getting out, they are not going to a better future. They will just be poor in some other country." And then she walked out again.

My mother's anger, like many of my friends and family, flows in many directions. The United States and Biden, in particular, because of some of the terrible things he said during the evacuation, but also Khalilzad, who everyone still thinks had some secret hand in the collapse. Of course, the various Afghan leaders, who are all gone now, Atta, Dostum, Ishmael Khan, the ministers and businessmen who had made so much money. Still, the most anger is undoubtedly at Ghani. He knew that all this was happening. He could have stayed and negotiated, or even fought, but instead he left us behind.

In the news they keep showing pictures of the men running towards the US military plane and, in the cases of some of the men who had managed to grab onto the landing gear, the bodies falling from the sky to their deaths. They were the most horrific scenes. We learned that one of the bodies that fell from the plane was a seventeen-year-old boy who had been trying to make the national soccer team. They showed pictures of him on the news again and again. He looked so young.

My mother said, "The world needed to see that. If it hadn't happened like this, no one outside of Afghanistan would have noticed what was happening here. Shame on the United States. I am glad the world has seen how terribly they acted."

I sighed. It was more complicated than this, but now, trapped inside our home, with nothing to do but watch these images on the television, it's difficult to disagree.

Maybe this all was inevitable—the collapse of the government, the rise of the Taliban, the end of the international presence here—and it was a terrible way for it all to end. But perhaps the one good thing is that at least the world was forced to watch, as we watched.

CHAPTER 13

Chaos

ON THE NIGHT OF AUGUST 15, ZEINAB DIDN'T SLEEP AT ALL. IT WAS warm that evening and she, her sister, and Ali sat out in the yard where the cell phone reception was best. Zeinab had hoped her father would come and join them from their home in the west of the country, but he canceled his trip the week before as the Taliban advanced on Herat. So the young people were left in Kabul on their own.

Finally, they decided that Zeinab should leave for the airport first thing in the morning. The problem was how to get there.

She texted with Jackie, who tried to get the driver from She Can Tri to take her, but given the new Taliban checkpoints, he refused. Zeinab then called four or five different taxi companies. Each one either didn't answer or said they wouldn't come to pick her up. Finally, Zar, the other woman who she had run the triathlon with in Dubai and who had also been selected for a Fulbright, said that her uncle had a taxi and could pick her up at 5:00 a.m.

The next morning, as they got into the car, Ali handed his phone to her and told her to hide her own phone and laptop deep in her bag. If they were stopped by the Taliban, she would give them his phone and still have hers hidden. She worried what pictures and messages they would see on it if they were searched. What would they think of the photos of her crossing the finish line of the triathlon in Dubai? She told the taxi driver, "If anyone asks, you are my uncle and this is my husband and we are just a family, going to the airport." They set off.

At first, on the quiet side streets, things seemed normal. She even saw a group of school girls in their uniforms, skipping down the road. For a moment, she thought perhaps it had all been a dream. But as soon as they made it to the main road, it was clear how things had changed. There were checkpoints with young armed Taliban soldiers going through trunks and looking in bags. They seemed a little less aggressive than the fighters they had seen the day before. In retrospect she thought, "They were trying to play nice, since it was their first day, and they realized the internationals were watching them." Luckily, they were waved quickly through most of the checkpoints.

The scene at the airport when they arrived, however, was surreal. The car could not get anywhere near the main gate. There were long lines of cars on the road leading up to the airport and people on foot around them, all pushing ahead. Others sat by the side of the road with bags, looking as if they had been there all night. A month later, describing the situation, one scene still haunted her in particular: For some reason there was a large pile of shoes, sandals, and slippers by the airport gate. What had happened there the day before? Whose shoes were they? What happened to their owners?

"I am still thinking about that," she said and sighed.

When she saw the crowds already there, she and Ali made the difficult decision to leave her beloved bicycle and one of her bags in the car and launched into the crowd with just one bag.

Meanwhile, Zeinab kept messaging her friend Jackie. Cell reception was not good. The military had set up cell phone jammers around many of the entrances. Since calls weren't connecting, Zeinab kept sending texts and voice messages to Jackie, who was in Texas and frantically trying to get a hold of some of her contacts within the airport compound. Suddenly there were gunshots from inside the airport. Some of the Taliban fighters outside responded by firing their guns in the air. Zeinab started to panic as the crowd rushed in all directions. No one seemed to know where it was safe.

She sent Jackie a desperate voice memo, with gunshots in the background: "Jackie, Jackie, there is no possible way to go there, there is only one plane and the American soldier . . . I don't know, I don't know . . ." she trailed off in a sob.

Jackie recalled sitting in her condo in Austin, crying at this point. She had gotten a hold of an Italian Special Forces officer inside the airport, but with jammers and poor cell coverage, they kept getting disconnected and she couldn't be sure her messages were getting through. She remained convinced that there was a spot for Zeinab on a Turkish flight, if she could just get inside. "Stay with me, you sweet girl," she responded, "you have to get to the gate."

But to reach the plane, Zeinab had to get through the crowds and the checkpoints. She hesitated for a moment, and then she pushed into the fray.

Inside the airport there were US troops from two Marine battalions, the Minnesota Army National Guard, the 82nd Airborne Division, and the 10th Mountain Division, as well as British, French, and Turkish soldiers, not to mention security personnel from a variety of other embassies and missions. For the Afghans outside, however, these were faceless soldiers, almost all of whom seemed to be wearing sunglasses and masks. Their stares felt cold. It was hard to imagine they were real people with families and kids. It was impossible to tell who was in charge or who might be able to help them.

There were no airport officials to be seen anywhere. The US soldiers on the civilian side of the airport where Zeinab had entered had set up barbed-wire rolls around the crowd, trying to keep back the passengers. She tried to shout to them across the barbed wire and show the Marines her visa, but the crowd was too loud and everyone around her was also trying to show documents of one kind or another. The crowd pushed her from behind and she fell, cracking her phone and cutting her leg on the barbed wire. Her clothes ripped. Ali told her, "This is it, Zeinab, we should return home."

But she replied, "No, let's push it. Let's be here and see what happens. I can do it."

Finally, she managed to get the attention of one of the guards, but he just told her if she didn't have a US passport, they wouldn't let her through. She showed him her visa for the United States, but he said it was not up to him. Then she watched some wealthy, well-connected Afghans with second passports from America or some Western European countries get waved through. "I wanted to shout, 'it is not just Americans whose lives have value, our lives have value too!'"

Zeinab asked, "Why do you get to choose whose life has value?"

The Marine looked at her and said, "It doesn't work that way." And then more menacingly, "You need to step back."

***

In the meantime, she was sending regular text messages to her sister and brother, who were watching many of the scenes from the airport get posted on Facebook and Twitter. They were horrified. The crowds were overwhelming, and it seemed possible that soldiers from either side could open fire or maybe a suicide bomber would choose that moment to try to kill some departing American troops. It felt that the uneasy truce between the US soldiers and the Taliban fighters, separated by just a roll of barbed wire, could break in an instant. Civilians would certainly be killed by the dozens in any sort of firefight.

Zeinab kept texting with Jackie, and Jackie had again connected with the Italian officer. Jackie asked Zeinab to send a full-length selfie of herself, so he could recognize her and the clothes she was wearing. The officer texted Jackie, "I can't get to her." He was on the military side of the airport and on duty. He told Jackie to tell Zeinab to go to the gate on the far side of the airport. She began to despair. The military airport was directly across the runway from the civilian airport, but to get to the other side, you had to walk all the way around the airport; the gate was at least a mile away. She would have to go back through the crowds she had come through and who knows how long it might take. She started walking back and thought to herself, "That's it, I will stay in Afghanistan forever, there is no hope."

Just then, her cell phone buzzed with an incoming number that she didn't recognize. This in and of itself was a small miracle because of how spotty the cell coverage was. It was the Italian officer. He had come to the civilian side of the airport. That meant that he was somewhere close by. She went back towards the checkpoint where she had been previously and saw the officer with sunglasses and a mask waving at her. She ran towards him. He had a quick conversation with the US soldier guarding the checkpoint. She couldn't hear what they were saying, but the mood was tense. The US soldier appeared stiff and unhappy with what the Italian was saying. Finally, the American gestured that she should come through.

She turned to Ali and realized this was her last moment with him. She hadn't thought that it would happen so quickly, and young Afghans are not used to any sorts of displays of public affection. All she could do was reach out and shake his hand. It felt awkward, but then she was walking towards the Italian officer, not knowing what to say.

Luckily, the officer took over and said that they needed to get into his car and drive around to the military side of the airport. She got in. "All I was thinking this whole time was that 'I was going for a Fulbright scholarship, I was going to study for my Master's degree, this was a big achievement, but then all this happened.' I imagined that this day would come and I would have my family at the airport. They would say goodbye and we would take some photos that I would keep with me in America to remember them. And we would embrace each other . . . but none of that occurred."

Instead, it was just an awkward handshake with Ali in a mass of desperate travelers. What made it almost worse was that she could see just how happy Ali was that she was going to make it into the airport. She could see the real joy on his face even while it felt like her heart was breaking.

***

Fifteen minutes later when they made it to the military side, things were calmer, but still confusing. Soldiers, pilots, and officials were nervously milling around, and it was unclear what might happen next. They all had a clear view of the civilian side of the airport, which was across the runway, and the crowd there seemed even louder than it had been when Zeinab had left. The air was hot.

A Turkish Airlines plane had arrived, and Zeinab joined the line on the tarmac in front of the plane with its distinctive red tail with the silhouette of a bird. One of the officials came through the line, asking whether her name was on the list. She gave them her ticket and said, "Yes, here is my ticket."

But the official responded: "No, what is your name? Is it on the list? How did you get over to this side of the airport?"

Zeinab protested. She had a ticket for Turkish Airlines on August 16. Here it was August 16 and here was a Turkish Airlines plane. She said, "Look, I have all my documentation, here is my passport, my visa, my COVID test, and my school documents. I have everything."

But the official said, "No, you cannot be on this flight, this is not a normal flight. It is a charter flight only for Turkish diplomats and Afghan VIPs."

She pushed back. "Listen, here is my ticket. I did not know that all these things were going to happen."

The man just walked away shaking his head and went to talk to another group from the Turkish embassy who were closer to the plane. Zeinab began to cry. She could not accept that she could have made it this far, all the way to the plane itself, just to be turned back, so she stayed in line.

Finally, a Turkish diplomat, who had overheard the conversation, walked over and said, "Don't listen to them. I am the one who gets to decide and I will tell them you can get on the flight."

The Turkish Airlines official looked somewhat disgruntled when the diplomat walked over to him, but he wrote Zeinab's name on his list at the bottom. Another official then announced that the weight on the plane was too much and that she would need to leave her final bag behind while pointing to a pile of discarded bags off to the side. It was as if she had to leave absolutely everything behind if she wanted to make it out. The diplomat, however, quietly stopped her again, pointed at another pile, and said, "Go to the backside of the plane and act like you are putting your bag in the discard pile, but put it in the other pile. Those are the bags getting loaded."

She felt so grateful for his kindness at that moment.

Not long after this, the passengers were finally allowed onto the plane, climbing up the steep steps. It was 8:00 a.m. and it had been only three hours since Zeinab left her home, even though it felt like a week had passed. As she sat down, it should have been a moment of relief, but just moments later on the civilian side of the airport, some of the soldiers lost control and the crowds overran one of the checkpoints across the tarmac. Zeinab watched with horror from inside the plane as young men started running out onto the runway where several planes had been preparing to depart.

Zeinab knew how much Afghans had suffered over the past forty years of war, but looking at the scene, she couldn't believe such misery was possible. Dozens of young men sprinted across the runway towards a US military cargo plane that was about to take off. They flung themselves at it.

"Some Turkish diplomats started taking out their phones to film it all, but I couldn't watch those poor people," she recounted, her voice breaking. "They were all so terrified, and irrational, it was a terrible feeling to see our countrymen in this situation, everyone was just trying to save their lives. It was like a movie." She paused in her retelling, grasping for words. "I couldn't believe all this," she finally finished.

She could see that the crowd had also swarmed a Kam Air commercial plane. The flight wasn't preparing to talk off, but people were instead literally climbing up the side of the plane. They were clinging to the side of the boarding bridge and bodies were trying to crush their way into the open door.

The images of bodies trying to push their way on, overwhelming a tilting walkway, shook her. Some older people were trying to get off the plane, but the crowd just pushed them back in. They seemed to be struggling for air, drowning in the sea of people. Nicola Careem, BBC South Asia's bureau chief, tweeted of the scene: "This is, perhaps, one of the saddest images I've seen from Afghanistan. A people who are desperate and abandoned. No aid agencies, no UN, no government. Nothing."[1] Footage from inside showed the plane vastly overloaded, with bodies pushed up against each other and men occasionally exchanging blows as they tried to remove enough passengers to take off.

Meanwhile, the crowd on the tarmac grew. It was now not just men, but she could see women and children too, and she could see other people trying to climb the wall and join them. The US soldiers fired tear gas at the crowd and tried to clear the runway. The passengers sat on the plane unsure of what would happen next. She was sure at any moment they might be asked to get off the plane.

Time passed slowly and she could hear the occasional sound of gunfire, but there was nothing to do but wait, as the soldiers slowly tried to clear the runway.

An hour passed. And then another.

The air grew stale. Zeinab fell into something of a stupor.

Finally, five hours later, the plane started to move with a jolt. The pilot came on the loudspeaker and told everyone to take their seats. Zeinab held her breath.

And then, they were taking off.

She watched as Kabul disappeared into the haze below, unsure of when she would ever be able to return.

***

She felt some relief once they landed in Istanbul. The passengers were quiet, yet she again felt nervous as Turkish officials met the plane and asked the passengers to hand over their passports. They were put on buses to the terminal, and Zeinab got a better look at some of the other passengers. She quickly recognized Vice President Sarwar Danish. Also on the plane were officials including Afghan Foreign Minister Haneef Atmar, the former National Security Advisor Rangin Spanta, and family members of other high-ranking officials like former Vice President Abdul Rashid Dostum's daughter.[2] She was even more amazed that she had gotten on the plane now knowing that almost everyone was someone powerful. She felt their gaze on her, as they wondered why this young woman had been on the plane with them. Zeinab stared back, refusing to show them the deference that they seemed to be demanding, thinking, "'You all are the ones who are fleeing and running away, how can you look at me in such a condescending way?' Still, it made me feel terrible since I kept thinking, I too am fleeing and leaving my family behind. Who knows when I will be able to see them again or what might happen to them with the Taliban there. I felt so guilty knowing that I am safe, but they may never be safe again."

The bus stopped at the VIP lounge and almost everyone got off. "I wanted to shout at them: 'You have sold our country,' but I controlled myself and decided not to make any trouble."

Zeinab was only one of four passengers on her bus that was not considered a VIP and instead she was told to head toward the "Inadmissible" sign for passengers who did not have visas or some sort of connection. She was still nervous that they might not let her pass, or even worse, perhaps try to send her back to Kabul. She tried to make small talk with the couple of other passengers, but they had no documentation at all and seemed terrified, refusing to say anything at all to her.

Once in the airport office, however, things seemed to move more smoothly. Or perhaps, the Turkish officials just wanted to make sure that she was no longer their problem. The woman behind the desk confirmed her seat and handed her a boarding pass for the Turkish Air Flight bound for Chicago in twelve hours. Finally, Zeinab allowed herself to believe that she might be on her way to America.

Still, she was now completely alone. Every other Afghan woman she had run, studied, or worked with remained behind to face unknown futures with the Taliban. At that moment she said, "Every Afghan felt as if they had been betrayed by their leaders and by the world."

CHAPTER 14

In Afghanistan, It's Still Who You Know

THE FOLLOWING DAY, MANY AFGHANS TUNED IN AS PRESIDENT BIDEN made his remarks on the situation in Afghanistan.

"American troops cannot and should not be fighting in a war and dying in a war that Afghan forces are not willing to fight for themselves. We spent over a trillion dollars. We trained and equipped an Afghan military force of some 300,000 strong—incredibly well equipped—a force larger in size than the militaries of many of our NATO allies. We gave them every tool they could need. We paid their salaries, provided for the maintenance of their air force—something the Taliban doesn't have. The Taliban does not have an air force. We provided close air support. We gave them every chance to determine their own future. What we could not provide them was the will to fight for that future."[1]

Most Afghans listened in stunned silence. For those in Kabul, watching Taliban vehicles drive down the street filled with soldiers, it was galling: How could Biden say they were unwilling to fight? What did he mean they determined their own future? These were not the futures that they had asked for or the futures that American officials had promised them again and again over two decades.

While there were some truths embedded in the remarks, they certainly mischaracterized the situation massively. Afghan troops had fought in many areas. They had been dying by the thousands for the past decade. Most felt it was not the soldiers who had run, it was the Afghan political elite, who the United States had given money and visas to. Furthermore, in those hurried days before the Taliban took Kabul, the Biden administration repeatedly referred to the fact that they were hamstrung by the agreement that the Trump administration had signed. Certainly, the Trump deal with the Taliban was not a good one and seriously delegitimized the Afghan government, but since the Taliban had not made good faith efforts to negotiate with the Afghan government, as they promised in the deal, it would have been possible for the United States to say that the Taliban had not lived up to their end of the bargain. They could have kept troops in the country or at least slowed the withdrawal. Even a few thousand soldiers at Bagram Air Base could have helped ensure the Taliban would not commit the most egregious of atrocities. Until the very last minute, Arsalan and many, many Afghans still felt that the United States would change course and at least ensure that not all the work of the past twenty years was lost.

But Biden's course was set and, in the eyes of most, the betrayal was complete. More Afghans ran toward the airport.

While the administration at a senior level had turned its back on Afghanistan, on the ground, a herculean feat was unfolding. Diplomats and soldiers, Afghans, Americans, and others, all working together as best they could to get out as many as possible: When the airport was initially overrun on August 16 there were thousands of Afghans inside the terminal, in the VIP parking area, on the runway, and just wandering around the airport grounds, hoping to find a way onto a plane. Some of them were high government officials. US soldiers attempted to clear the airport of everyone who was not supposed to be there, which, of course, was difficult because those who had made it in were unwilling to leave, and how did the soldiers know who was "supposed" to be there?

There were no airport officials and there was no Afghan government anymore, so they weren't deciding. By 4:00 p.m. on August 16, the Taliban Special Forces had secured the area around the airport, along with the presidential palace and other key sites. After this, to get into the airport, you had to pass through both Taliban checkpoints and US ones, which were oftentimes being guarded by Afghan soldiers of an army that no longer existed.

On the military side, there were diplomats, aid workers, and others who had been allowed into the airport on August 15, who on any normal day would not have been authorized to be at the airport unless boarding a flight. More civilians were at embassies waiting to get bused to the airport. In addition, there were Afghan security forces who had retreated to the airport, including the Khost Protection Force, the CIA-run militia group accused of executions and other abuses of power. (The next day, on August 17, the Pentagon would announce there were six hundred Afghan security forces at the airport assisting US troops.[2]) Now the US soldiers overseeing the evacuation had to start making sense of who was there and what to do with everyone.

The plan to withdraw the final US troops out of Afghanistan had been drawn up in a Pentagon meeting four months before, on April 24. By July 4, the last troops from Bagram Air Base were to be removed, which would have left 650 Marines and soldiers at the US embassy to protect the 1,400 Americans at the embassy. The estimate presented at the meeting in April was that the Afghan forces could hold off the Taliban for one to two more years. The group briefly discussed an emergency evacuation plan involving carrying Americans from the embassy to the airport by helicopter, but no one considered the possibility that the Taliban might actually gain complete control of Kabul.[3] They assumed that the Americans, Afghan-Americans, and others, including aid workers, journalists, and contractors, who might want to leave the country would just buy tickets on commercial flights. There was no plan for what to do if the government collapsed, commercial flights stopped flying, and there was no way out.

Having given up most of their military assets in the country, the United States was now working with a dangerous and unreliable partner in the Taliban in trying to move tens of thousands of American citizens and Afghan allies out of the country. In some ways, simply the fact that the operation continued for as long as it did is a testament to the military's ability to respond in emergency situations. The 618th Air Operations Center at Scott Air Force Base in Illinois, which oversaw the bulk of US flights, organized 2,600 flights on 85 aircrafts, evacuating 124,000 people in just fifteen days.[4] Most of the evacuations were done on C-17 or C-130s. A C-17 is generally configured to transport 100 passengers. In the evacuation they were modified to accommodate 400, and in one case, there were actually 823 on one flight, which was the outer limit of the weight the plane could hold based just on the passengers with no luggage.[5] The United States eventually ended up relying not just on the airport, but also the CIA base located close to the airport where they could collect US citizens, as well as certain at-risk Afghans, apparently primarily members of the ANA commando units and their families, before ferrying them to the airport.[6]

At the same time, however, the evacuation was still messy and poorly organized. Tensions everywhere were high. As one State Department official complained, the Taliban changed the criteria for passing through their checkpoints "on a day-to-day, sometimes hour-by-hour basis."[7]

The scene at the airport remained chaotic. It seemed as if some were randomly making it through, while others were being turned back for similarly unpredictable reasons. One person Arsalan knew had tried to travel to the United Kingdom a couple years before using a not-very-convincing fake visa he had purchased from a smuggler. At the airport in Turkey, the forgery was discovered and he was deported back to Afghanistan. He still had the fake visa in his passport, however, and in the days just after the collapse of the government, he used it at the gate of the airport. The soldiers at the gate waved him through, and he eventually got on a plane to the United Kingdom. The fake visa was later discovered in the United Kingdom, but the British government was not about to send someone who had just gotten out back to Afghanistan, so he was processed as a refugee.

Zeinab's husband, Ali, had returned to the airport and tried to get onto one of the evacuation flights, but he was turned back, told that he didn't have the right paperwork. But what was the correct paperwork?

Some of the procedures put into place by the US government seemed woefully unthought out. For instance, at one point, diplomats sent electronic codes to those Afghans they were attempting to evacuate, but there was nothing to stop these Afghans from forwarding the codes onto their family members and friends. Soon these were shared so widely, it was not clear who was supposed to actually be allowed in.[8]

Other nongovernment groups and networks also sprang into action in the days following August 15. A group of prominent journalists, veterans, and other internationals who had worked in Afghanistan organized charter flights with support from the Rockefeller Foundation.[9] They used personal connections with the US military to get buses of Afghan activists, journalists, lesser officials, and their families onto the airport and into private planes. Communication between these groups was poor and other attempts were not successful, turned back either by the Taliban or the Americans manning the gates.

The group that probably received the most media attention called itself Taskforce Pineapple. They attempted to ferry Afghan interpreters, in particular, into the airport to be evacuated and veterans associated with the group appeared on Fox News, CNN, and elsewhere, drawing attention to the plight of some of those who had not made it out, while quickly raising millions of dollars. In the first eleven days of the evacuation before the bombing at Abbey Gate, which made extractions even more difficult, Taskforce Pineapple claimed to have helped extract more than five hundred Afghans.[10] Other groups were less benevolent: Erik Prince, former Blackwater head, told the *Wall Street Journal* that his company would evacuate individuals from Kabul for $6,500 each, with an additional charge for escorting them to the airport.[11]

For ordinary Afghans, of course, none of this was visible from the outside. All they could see were the soldiers and the walls that appeared to be denying them an escape from the unknown reality of life under the Taliban.

***

Arsalan's friends Jalil and Sahar both worked with him at his research firm and were friends with Zeinab. They had recently married and had both worked with various international organizations. They also had some relatives living in the United States, and Zeinab's husband, Ali, had been the president of the student union at AUAF. They were some of the people who had been frantically texting with Arsalan in the hours and days following the collapse of the government.

Unlike Zeinab, they did not have visas already, but they did have relatives in the United States and previously had been there on scholarship programs. Sahar also had a pending SIV application. In the days before the collapse, they began discussing just what they should do, while looking for alternative ways out of the country. Sahar in particular did not want to leave the country without her father's blessing and was worried about his health. So, at first, she did not even tell him that she was applying for visas to the West. When he found out, he said, "Why are you wasting your time on these things?"

In the meantime, her mother and other relatives had begun packing up some household supplies and their best carpets, so they could flee to either Iran or Pakistan. But her father refused. "I have built us a house here. I am not going to leave it. I'm not going to be a refugee again. If you want to go on your own, go."

Through the first weeks of August, Sahar continued to file applications, but she did not talk about it because it upset her father, who thought that if the neighbors heard about her desires, they would tell some of the people with connections to the Taliban and the family would be in even more danger. It was already known in the neighborhood that they were a family that worked closely with the Americans.

When the government collapsed, Sahar and Jalil started looking more frantically for a way out. Two of Sahar's aunts already had US visa applications that were being processed and the embassy had sent a message, telling them to come to the airport on August 18. When they got there, the American guards at the gate were struggling with the crowds, trying to explain to them who could come in and who could not. One of Sahar's aunts helped defuse a tense situation between the crowd and the guards.

The soldiers asked her to remain with them after checking on when she was to be evacuated and promised her a spot on a later flight. She ended up spending the entire next day translating for them, and when finally, the time drew near for her flight, the guards told her aunt that if she had some family members who could continue to help them with translation, they would evacuate them as well. So, Sahar's aunt called Jalil and Sahar.

At that point, some of the American soldiers at the gate were telling those inside the airport that if one person in the family had a visa, the entire family would be allowed in. This made Sahar and Jalil hopeful. If they could get into the airport and find Sahar's aunt, perhaps that would mean they could escape.

They packed quickly, said goodbye to family members, and at 4:00 a.m. on August 19, three days after Zeinab had left, they set out to the airport, along with a friend of Sahar. They were nervous about Taliban checkpoints, but the streets were quiet. The airport, however, was a different scene. They first went to the gate under Taliban control. There were several hundred people pushing up against the barriers there. Taliban soldiers were walking through the crowds beating any man who appeared to be standing near a woman who he was not related to.

"What are you doing here?" one of the Taliban soldiers yelled at Jalil.

"I'm sorry, my wife is sick, we are just trying to leave to get her care," he replied.

A few minutes later, one of the soldiers fired shots in the air. Others joined him. This caused a quick scattering of the crowd and people started pushing against each other, unsure of where to run. Sahar's friend stumbled and was on the verge of being trampled, but Jalil picked her up and they ran from the crowd, leaving behind the friend's one bag of luggage.

As they were considering what to do, they received a text from Sahar's aunt: They were at the wrong gate. So they started the long walk along the airport wall to the Abbey Gate, which was controlled by American and British troops. Along the way, they stepped around bodies of people laying in the street, asleep, who had been there, waiting for a gate to open, all night.

The gate with the international soldiers was just as disorganized. The situation was made worse by the fact that the road here was narrower, and running alongside the wall, there was a drainage ditch that separated most of the people from the gate. Barbed wire had been set up along the wall and spilled down into the dirt street. Concrete barriers had also been placed haphazardly, trying to reinforce the military's position and slow anyone who might attack it. The ditch was filled with muddy water and trash. Some of those waiting outside had climbed into the ditch, hoping to be noticed by the soldiers as they held their documents up. The crowd surged towards the gate.

Sahar and Jalil pushed their way through the crowds. Jalil saw an opening in the wall, just beyond the gate that had previously been used just by those exiting the airport. The guards were focused on the main gate and did not seem to be watching this area. He took Sahar and they pushed their way in. Others quickly followed them. They were now in an area inside the outer wall, but still surrounded by barbed wire. They were away from the main crowds, inside the first wall, but had not made it all the way into the airport yet. In a matter of minutes, there were approximately two hundred of them in this space, Jalil estimated. Several of the British soldiers shouted at them and tried to push them back. The soldiers were shouting and swearing at the crowd. All Jalil could hear at some points was, "Get the fuck back."

Some soldiers had laser sights on their weapons, and Jalil and Sahar could see the red dots moving around on people in the crowd. Then a soldier fired tear gas into the crowd. Sahar fell, cutting her foot. But there were too many of them and eventually the soldiers gave up, allowing them to remain in the area between the walls.

"Sahar's aunt had told us the name of the soldier who was working with the translators, I think his name was Smith," Jalil recounted. "I was told to call him loudly and I did so by the barbed wire when I saw some American troops come near. I called him, and one of them came over. He told me to note down our names on a paper, and I did. Then, he asked me to wait."

When he returned, they were then taken through another gate, farther into the airport into a holding area that gradually grew into a camp for those waiting to be processed. It was the first of three days they would spend at the airport.

***

Looking around, Sahar saw that they were now in a slightly more open fenced-in area, where Sahar's aunts were also being held. They were a ways away from either of the terminals, but now they were within the airport walls. The area had no place to sit and most of the ground was large chunks of gravel, which made sitting uncomfortable. So, a few hours later, when some of the soldiers brought food into the area in a series of large plastic tubs, those who had been waiting started fighting to get the tubs, so they could turn them over and sit on them. Sahar and Jalil were lucky to get one each, and once the tubs had all been snatched up, the food, ready-to-eat packets that the military used in the field, was passed around in a more orderly manner.

If the process for supporting the Afghans who had made it into the airport seemed unorganized and confusing to Sahar and Jalil, it is, in part, because it was. The 110 Marines from Ghost Company, which had been assigned to Abbey Gate, had been in Jordan just two days before. They had arrived at Hamid Karzai International Airport (HKIA) on August 18 with no vehicles. As a result, according to a series of *New York Times* interviews, they had hot-wired a blue bus that had been abandoned at the terminal and also used a motorized baggage cart to get around.[12] The instructions they received on processing the Afghans inside the airport were also unclear and seemed to change rapidly. They were being told contradictory things about who could and could not be evacuated and when it would all happen. Luckily, they at least could rely on Sahar and Jalil to translate for them and to begin organizing the Afghans in the holding area.

The area they were fenced in also had no shade, and the day was hot. People used headscarves and other clothes if they had them to try to make some shade. A few women were trying to nurse their infants. Later, some soldiers brought sunscreen, as well as diapers and formula for any- one with small children. The soldiers there said little but were generally reassuring. Surely someone would come and process them soon.

The first night inside the airport, there was no place for them to sleep. Sahar and her two aunts were able to find some space off the gravel with some other women, but there was no space for Jalil, and he spent the night pacing. As he walked, however, it got colder and colder. Finally, he saw some soldiers distributing some sheets of plastic. He rushed over but had to wait for thirty minutes before he could get one. When he finally did, he brought it to Sahar and her aunts and covered them with it.

Still, he couldn't sleep. Planes were taking off every few minutes it seemed, and some of the small children there wailed all night long. At one point, after a particularly loud plane took off, a woman cried out, "The sky has been torn apart."

***

The next morning soldiers came and distributed food, but there was less than there was the day before. They each got one meal ration, but that was all they would get for the day. People were growing despondent and refused to wait in line, pushing each other to get their meal packets. Occasionally, they could hear gunfire just outside the gates of the airport. There was only one bathroom for men and one for women, and the line was so long that at one point, it took five hours to get a turn. A woman sitting next to Sahar fainted, and in a couple of cases, some of those who had been there the longest and were growing hungry asked to be let back out of the airport. But the soldiers wouldn't even let them leave.

At one point, several men started shouting and throwing things towards the soldiers by the checkpoint leading further into the airport. The soldiers then handcuffed the men to the fence. At least, the crowd was told, they would be given large tents to sleep in that night for those who were still not evacuated.

Jalil and Sahar, and a couple of other younger Afghans there who spoke English, continued to help translate and organize the group. Medical workers came to check on the sick and they translated for them as well. One of the soldiers they were working with reassured them. He told them that by helping them translate, they would be helping their own cases and promised that they would get them all out. At one point, when there was a rumor that they would be leaving soon, one of the soldiers asked them for a photo, so they could remember the moment of working together. They took a photo on his camera and on theirs. In the photo, the soldier looks grim, while Sahar and Jalil have hopeful smiles.

They spent another night in the holding area, this time in the tents.

***

On the third day, there was even less food and water. The soldiers distributed two large water bottles for every ten people. The only thing that made it bearable was that they were told by the soldiers that they would be evacuated that day. At one point the soldiers asked Jalil and Sahar to help organize those who remained in the area into groups based upon the documents they had. One group was those with foreign passports, another was those with Afghan passports and some sort of visa or other travel document from a Western country, a third was those with Afghan passports and no visas, and finally there were those with no documentation of any kind. Those with no documentation were then divided further into two groups: single individuals and families.

Sahar and Jalil were in the second group with those that had some sort of documentation since they had their SIV applications, which was reassuring.

Meanwhile, the numbers had swelled. What had been just an open area surrounded by barbed wire was now a makeshift camp. At that point, there were about four thousand people in the holding area, Jalil estimated. The translators were told to select a leader from each group who was responsible for gathering the paperwork for the group, listing down their names and details. They also helped distribute the food and water. The groups were each given a letter, A, B, C, and so on, and Sahar and Jalil were in group B. At several points, Jalil asked the soldiers where they were being taken and when they thought they would leave, but the soldiers told him that for security reasons, they had been instructed not to say anything. Then, the group that Sahar's aunts were in was taken out of the camp.

Sahar's aunts sent them a message shortly after saying they were in the military terminal and were told they would be leaving soon. Sahar and Jalil started to gain hope. Finally, at around 7:00 p.m. on the third day, a bus came and took twenty more people from group A towards the military terminal.

Shortly after another bus came to take their group towards the terminal and they excitedly boarded. It felt so good to be leaving the holding area they spent the last days in. The bus drove through the gates and towards the terminal, but before it reached the fence separating the terminal from the rest of the airport, the driver stopped. He spoke to someone on the radio. Jalil tried to see what was happening, but he was towards the back of the bus. Then, the bus started up again, but instead of continuing straight, it slowly made a wide turn and started heading back towards the exit gate. The passengers began to murmur to each other. They were so close to the terminal, they couldn't be going back to the holding area, could they, Jalil thought. Maybe they were picking up some more people or maybe they would be brought back to the terminal later. No one wanted to complain since they had heard that anyone who caused problems would not be evacuated, but people shifted restlessly.

As they reached the exit gate, one of the first things Jalil noticed was that the American troops, who had mostly been cordial if distant, had been replaced by soldiers with Turkish military insignias on them. A soldier got on the bus and told them gruffly to get out. They did so, reluctantly. The bus was parked in such a way that there was really only one path forward. Turkish soldiers lined the roadway towards the gate. They pushed them towards the gate. Maybe, they thought desperately, they were being taken a different way to the planes. Jalil tried to ask what was going on, but the soldiers just told him repeatedly to "shut up." They tried to protest, but the entire group was pushed towards the exit. And just like that, in a matter of a few seconds, they were no longer in the airport.

Sahar said, "I was crying and laughing all at the same time. It all happened so quickly. I didn't know what was happening to me. Jalil brought me some water and hugged me. I felt light-headed for a while but really couldn't understand what was happening."

They had been so sure that they were going to make it out. The US soldiers had promised them. Now they stood there, just outside the wall to the airport, in stunned disbelief.

After a few minutes, Jalil tried calling Sahar's aunt who was still inside the airport being processed. The aunt called one of the American officers they had been translating for who had given her his cell number. He told her to tell them to go back to the entrance gate and try again, but she didn't have much of a charge for her phone, so they could not keep talking. Sahar and Jalil did return to the Abbey Gate, but the guards weren't letting anyone in and just shouted at them. "Back the fuck up," one yelled.

Jalil tried to explain that they had been inside and told them the names of the soldiers they had been working with. He even tried showing them the picture on the phone they had taken with the American soldier inside the airport the day before. They just swore at him and told him to get back. Later, some of the people who had been on their bus speculated that the US military had received intel of a suicide bomber at the airport and had hurried to get anyone who did not have clear documentation out. But Jalil and Sahar are still not sure. Some of the others waiting at the gate had said that the Taliban had come by and taken some of those who had been inside the airport and beaten them up.

Some men squatting by the canal across from the gate were smoking hashish. It made the air heavy. Sahar kept coughing. It was getting late and the fear of being beaten by the soldiers hung over them. Finally, dejected, they went to try to find a taxi home.

CHAPTER 15

Unaccompanied Minors

WHILE SAHAR AND JALIL WERE CAUGHT IN THE HOLDING CAMP, between the main airport wall and the military terminal area where evacuees were actually being put onto the planes, Munir had made it, somewhat unintentionally, to the area where evacuees were being processed.

After the chaos of August 15 and 16, when civilians had pushed their way into the airport and onto the tarmac, the State Department started trying to determine who everyone was that had made it inside the airport, and they found diplomats, translators, aid workers, and ANA fighters. They also discovered dozens of children inside the airport who were unaccompanied by any adult. In some cases, they had been separated from their parents who had sometimes already left on earlier flights. In other cases, Munir said, "These were just the children who you would see begging on the streets around the airport. Some would clean your shoes for money."

On August 16, they joined the crowds rushing through the airport gates and ran around the tarmac like everyone else. Some had stayed on the airport grounds and were now hungry and tired. While the military had pushed out many of the adults, it was harder to decide what to do with the children.

"Some of them were there crying and the soldiers didn't know what to do," Munir said.

As a UNICEF employee, Munir had been asked to come to the airport and oversee the processing of the cases of twenty-eight of the children who were at the airport being cared for by the Norwegian military contingent, which was running a clinic at the airport. Munir was asked to interview the children and send the details to the UNICEF office so that it could start working to reunite those families when possible. For those street children, who had no families abroad, Munir was not sure what UNICEF would do with them. But looking around at the crowds outside the airport, surely any place was better than this for them, Munir thought.

There were also rumors that even though there was still a week left before the August 31 deadline that Joe Biden had imposed on the withdrawal, civilians would be allowed to leave only for the next day or two, since the final days would be reserved for evacuating the military. Munir was asked to process the cases quickly. His boss said that once the children were in Qatar, they would have time to search for families, but for now, Munir should just prepare the children to depart as quickly as possible.

***

This was a strange process to be a part of, Munir said. "One child was maybe seven years old, and he may have had family in Kabul, but when I asked him about them, he refused to give any details. He just kept saying that he wanted to go to the United States. We are told that we need to act on the best interests of the child, and we couldn't just send him back into the streets. So, I told him we were transferring him to Qatar, and he was so happy, he was jumping and clapping. I didn't know what to think.

"Who knows, maybe he will have a future in the United States. Here he just knows abuse from the streets."

In the days leading up to the collapse of the Afghan government, Munir was, perhaps, more concerned with security than many others in Kabul. In part, this was because the international UN officials he worked with were clearly worried, but also the US embassy, which he lived close to, started testing its warning siren in the middle of the nights. It would wake his children and he would try to comfort them.

The UN officials who ran Munir's office had numerous meetings about security and how they might continue their work there, but the Afghan employees were excluded from meetings, which previously would have had international and Afghan staff in them. "They didn't want to think about the Afghan staff. They just wanted to get out of the country and make sure they could take all their things with them," Munir said. "They didn't consult us, even though we were the ones doing the real work. At that point, I was actually happy to keep working in Afghanistan, I just wanted them to get my children out to India or Turkey or someplace like that."

The lack of trust between the international staff and the vast number of Afghans working for them bothered Munir. In those final days, it seemed, all the work was focused on protecting international staff and UN property. They reassured them continually that everything was under control, even when the Afghan staff could clearly see that it wasn't. This would continue until the very last minute.

In fact, on the morning of August 15, at nine o'clock, Munir got a call from a couple of his staff requesting permission to leave and go home to their families since they were concerned about the security situation. Munir had just received a UN security update saying that they did not have any new information or any reason to be more worried than normal, so he told his employees that they should stay on the job.

"I felt very bad after that," Munir said later, because just thirty minutes after, he received a call that insurgents entered different parts of Kabul and that the government had started collapsing. The soldiers in the Juvenile Rehabilitation Centre where they worked had apparently put down their guns and just left. Some of his employees worked in the detention center and inmates had apparently started to leave as well, so Munir's top priority became making sure that those members of his staff were safe.

He had teams in the provinces of Parwan and Wardak, both several hours from Kabul, and he told them to return quickly. He was particularly worried about the women on his staff traveling, but he was also worried about his own family. One of his cousins worked on the political programming for TOLO, Afghanistan's most Western TV channel, and he was worried that the Taliban would target him. His cousin had been sitting with Munir's father-in-law, who was in the hospital, so Munir called his nephew to go sit with him instead, and his cousin went to a safe house.

All of this meant that it was midafternoon before Munir was able to head home. There was gridlock on the main road heading east, so he sat in traffic for several hours and watched as, at first, one or two, and then groups of five or six, and finally a steady stream of men walked between the cars toward the center of the city. It was all the prisoners who had just been released by the Taliban.

***

In the days that followed, Munir's work did not stop, though he did do most of it from home. They had been working on a program providing support for some of the young children who were displaced from other provinces and had come to Kabul during the recent fighting, living in makeshift camps around the city. He wanted to make sure that the support would continue.

UNICEF also had taken on the issue of the unaccompanied children at the airport and, a few days later, Munir was asked to go and help with their cases. One of the problems was that the Taliban had taken over the guard duties for the UN compound where Munir worked, and he was afraid of returning, wondering whether the Taliban were really there to protect the compound or figure out who worked there so they could later punish them. However, if he was to get into the airport, he would need a UN vehicle, so, he went to the UN compound to get a car and driver. When he arrived at the office, he saw Taliban soldiers milling around outside where previously there had been Afghan police. Several of the Taliban's senior fighters had organized a convoy to get him to the airport. There was one UN vehicle, but then a Taliban armored escort car ahead of them and behind them. When they got closer to the airport, they had to slow down since there were so many people in the streets. The Taliban blared their horns and pushed their way through.

At the first Taliban airport checkpoint, there were Taliban fighters from the 313 Brigade who had been in charge of the Taliban suicide bombing campaign. Named after the Battle of Badr, when the Prophet Mohommad took Mecca with 313 men, the group was closely aligned with the work of the Haqqani network and was said to have ties still with al Qaeda.[1] These were some of the most hardened of the Taliban fighters.

Looking at them, Munir said, "Their equipment, their uniforms, everything was almost identical to what the United States was wearing. The night-vision goggles, everything, even the way they were looking and acting." They were standing there, just feet away from the last remaining US forces in Afghanistan. Munir wondered, was this to be the future of Afghanistan? Munir and the others in the car were studied intently by the Taliban fighter manning the gate and then waved through.

"I was so scared," Munir said, "and then, they treated us just like VIPs. In all my trips to the airport, I had never gotten through so quickly and easily."

A similar thing happened with the US soldiers. And just like that, they were in the airport.

***

Inside the airport things were quieter, but tense. Munir said, "There was so much pressure in the airport, you could feel it at the gate, but even inside, the officials and soldiers seemed to be working without a break. The rush had been constant and there was stress in everyone's eyes."

UNICEF had been given a makeshift room where Munir went to work processing the children. They were lucky to have that room, since every other part of the airport seemed to be taken up by people trying to sleep or waiting in line. Some were on chairs, but others were on the ground. Most flights were not allowing passengers to take any baggage beyond a small backpack, so there were also discarded bags everywhere. The bags weren't just castaway materials, but the things that people treasured most: the mementos they'd hoped to bring with them, the clothes and necessities to start a new life, all left behind because they were told there was no room on the flight.

After working for that first day, Munir was able to sleep in the UNICEF office on some cushions that someone had left there. It was better than what most of the evacuees were enduring outside.

The next day, he finished his assessment and sent the paperwork to the UNICEF office. He was told to wait with the children and that they would be assigned one of the next planes. Later in the day, an official told him to bring the children to one of the main rooms in the terminal where they were issuing the final tickets to board the planes. This was when the US Marine, to Munir's surprise, handed him a ticket as well.

Later he said, "It was really chaotic and it was like, once you were in the airport, you were basically in the United States. No one was asking anything, and they assumed that we all were leaving. They were just trying to evacuate as many people as they could and finish the airport as soon as possible. They were not questioning who you were or what you were doing, they just kept saying, 'Go, go.'

"Some people didn't have any documents at all, and they said, 'just go, get on the plane.' At least I had a scanned copy of my passport on my phone, so they wrote down that information and told me to get on the plane."

He hadn't intended to leave. He had almost nothing with him: no passport, no national identity card, no phone charger, laptop, or clothes. He didn't even have time to go back to the UNICEF office just across the terminal. Up until the final moments he was torn as to whether he should get on the plane or not. Calling his family had not helped. His mother was upset, but his brother pushed him to go. Then, he was getting on the plane with the children he had processed, and they were closing the door.

And almost without realizing it, Munir joined the tens of thousands fleeing the country, heading towards unknown destinations.

***

By the time Munir left, the officials and soldiers inside the airport knew there were only a few days left for them to get as many people out as they could, but they were also rushing because of how tenuous the entire situation was. Outside the airport, Taliban soldiers continued to patrol the perimeter of the airport, operating just feet away from the American and British soldiers they had fought against for the past twenty years— the entire lives of the younger fighters. After ten days, the atmosphere remained tense, but there had been no significant incidents between the two groups. In many ways, it became clear that it was also in the Taliban's best interest to help the Americans leave as quickly as they could, and they seemed to think that if they wanted to take the corrupt government officials and loud voices of civil society leaders with them, that would only help the transition. Not everyone who had been fighting against the United States agreed with the Taliban stance, however.

The uneasy peace was broken on August 26, not by the Taliban, but by a suicide bomber from IS-K, the Afghan iteration of the Islamic State, who detonated his vest in the crowd right outside of Abbey Gate, where Sahar and Jalil had walked away the day before. IS-K saw the evacuation as their last opportunity to target US soldiers in Afghanistan, and also to destabilize the takeover by the Taliban, who they viewed as not adhering to an extreme-enough vision of Afghanistan as an Islamic state. After the initial explosion, gunfire erupted, with several eyewitnesses claiming US soldiers fired into the crowd in a panic. In total, 169 Afghan civilians and 13 US service members were killed. Reports afterward suggested that while most had been killed by the bombing, others had been trampled or shot in the aftermath.[2] Bodies lay in the sewage ditch that Sahar and Jalil had climbed through.

In the days that followed, Arsalan and others read news articles and listened to international media reports that all seemed to start with, "US service members killed at Kabul airport," either relegating to the second paragraph or farther down the fact that ten times as many civilians were also killed trying to get processed into the airport.

After the attack, President Biden said, speaking to those organizing the bombing, "We will not forgive. We will not forget. We will hunt you down and make you pay."[3] Three days later, a drone fired a Hellfire missile into a car that the military claimed was being driven by the man responsible for organizing the attack. Tragically, it became clear that he had nothing to do with the incident. The Pentagon later acknowledged that the bottles they had seen going into the car before it exploded were probably water bottles, not explosives as they had assumed, and that the ten civilians, including seven children, killed by the drone strike had no connection with the bombing.[4]

As Arsalan remembered, "The speech Biden gave after the attack was nonsense. He blamed IS-K and maybe the attacker was IS-K, but he had created this entire situation. It feels bad to say, but people were thinking, 'this is the situation you made, you deserve this.' How is it possible that they are still firing missiles at civilian cars just because they happen to be a certain color or match a certain description, without confirming that it is what they think it is? The United States always makes these mistakes—mistakes that seem to end up killing many Afghans."

It was as if in its final days in Afghanistan, the US military had to again make all the mistakes it had been making for the past twenty years: killing civilians with drones, lashing out over situations of their own making, and responding with inappropriate force.

***

The attack changed the calculus for some of those who were still hoping to leave. The crowds around the airport were more tense than ever. Many of those who had come in the initial days had given up hope entirely, but word had spread that many of the former ANA soldiers were making it out, so military families increasingly flooded the area.

For someone like Amena, who had been waiting to hear from her international colleagues on whether there would be any evacuation of the Afghan staff, the window for escape seemed to be closing. Her own home felt increasingly unsafe since all the neighbors knew that her husband's family was in America.

Amena's organization's low profile had been helpful in their work with endangered women. Their website had very little information, and it was difficult to find their address if no one had passed it on to you. This allowed them to avoid some harassment and get more done. The benefit of being low profile was quickly lost, however, during the evacuation when some of the more public, well-known organizations were able to both quickly raise funds and get government officials to prioritize their cases. Amena's organization was not able to do either, she said.

In the meantime, Amena had been alerted by her organization that the German authorities were working to evacuate them, along with other Afghans who worked for German organizations. The largest of these was GIZ, the German equivalent of USAID. The German authorities had granted them papers that would get them on an evacuation flight out of HKIA and they had been told that a bus would take them to the airport. The family packed hastily. Amena had an excited nervousness in her stomach. If everything went well, they could all be out of the country in a couple of hours. She didn't want to think about what the alternative outcomes might be.

When they arrived at the office they had been told to gather at, however, the man organizing the group said that the situation had changed. It was no longer safe and the bus was not going to go. They were too concerned about getting the bus through Taliban checkpoints and didn't just want to hand over an entire bus full of Afghans who had worked for German organizations to the Taliban. Amena and her family left, dejected. Later, she said, she realized that she should have stayed and waited. After they left, apparently, some others had come to take a second bus, and then for some reason they allowed the second bus to go and not the first one. Amena later heard that the second bus had been reserved for the actual employees of GIZ and that they had been prioritized, but she was not able to confirm this and, in those days, it was difficult to know what to believe.

According to a GIZ release, 1,000 Afghan employees registered to request evacuation, but only "a small number of these" were able to leave the country before Germany ceased its airlifts on August 26.[5] Other reports, however, claimed there were as many as 2,500 employees seeking evacuation who had worked for GIZ, as well as 3,000 who worked for the UN, another 6,500 who worked for the Swedish Committee for Afghanistan, and thousands of others working for numerous NGOs across the country.[6] GIZ said that they were offering cash payments to those Afghans who remained in the country but insisted that this was "no way intended to encourage staff to stay in the country, but is designed as bridging assistance in a difficult situation."

Amena heard this and felt even more frustrated. She did not need cash. She needed help getting out of the country, and her international bosses seemed to have no plan. The small NGO that Amena had worked for also released a statement blasting the German government, saying that they had received assurances that their staff would be evacuated by the Germans, but then, they were ultimately not allowed onto the buses, and others who made it to the airport were not allowed inside. Still, after this initial statement there was no public follow-up and the message that Amena got from her international colleagues remained vague.

Germany and the United States were not the only NATO countries that were ineffective in their attempts to evacuate Afghans who had supported them. The British government evacuated 15,000 people during those two weeks in August, but in many cases, a later whistleblower report alleged, those who were most deserving did not make it out. At any given moment during the evacuation, the Foreign Office had 5,000 unread emails in their inbox, and only 5 percent of those requesting assistance actually got out of the country. More controversially, the Foreign Office allegedly "received an instruction from the prime minister to use considerable capacity" to transport animals from a dog shelter set up by a former Royal Marine called Nowzad.[7] (The day after the report, the Marine denied the allegations in a tweet: "Let's make this bloody crystal clear & on the record. NOT 1 single British soldier was used to get me or the @Nowzad #dogs & #cats into #Kabul airport.") Boris Johnson, the prime minister, later echoed this denial.

Even if there was no favoritism being shown to certain shelter animals, it was clear, as the days went on, that the process was not getting any more transparent or efficient. Instead, it was rumored that a family who lived next to the airport could smuggle people into the terminal through a hole in the wall. For $4,000 each, they would get you inside. For those trying to get in through legitimate means, the coordination between those evacuating Afghans and those providing security at the gates remained challenging. As more private efforts ramped up, there were reports of individuals with seats on flights not able to make it through the checkpoints into the airport. On August 22, the *Wall Street Journal* reported, two different private flights ended up taking off mostly empty. Activists chartered a plane for vulnerable women, but many of the women were denied entrance to the airport, leaving 70 of the 240 seats empty, and in a more extreme case, a Washington development firm hoping to get 1,000 Afghans out of the country chartered a plane with 345 seats, but could get only 50 passengers on board.[8]

Accusations of corruption around the evacuation process were not confined to the ground in Afghanistan. The extensive media focus on the situation led to a series of questionable fundraising efforts by individuals and groups, some with little to no experience in Afghanistan. For instance, Tommy Marcus, an Instagram influencer, used a GoFundMe campaign to fund evacuation flights, raising $7.2 million in less than two weeks. Yet a month later, a *Washington Post* investigation found that no flights had been chartered by the campaign and $3.3 million dollars in flights had been reserved but had then been canceled.[9] There was no word on what had happened to the money that had been donated.

Other operations showed just how far corruption had seeped into the security system in Afghanistan. For example, Erik Prince's offer to fly individuals out for thousands of dollars each. Prince, of course, was the former head of Blackwater and the brother of Trump's secretary of education, Betsy Devos. He had also previously pitched a proposal to the Trump White House to remove all US troops and replace them with private security contractors. Prince and other mercenaries who had profited so much from the last two decades of war clearly were trying to make a few more dollars in the war's final days.

Some operations, however, were more successful. A group from the Silicon Valley, including LinkedIn co-founder Reid Hoffman and some executives from Facebook, sponsored a charter flight aimed at evacuating primarily journalists, as well as some high-profile members of civil society. One of Zeinab's friends, Farkhunda, had managed to get on the flight after one of the journalists had listed her and her husband as family members. The flight was thrown into further turmoil, however, when at the last minute, the airlines allowed on another 155 passengers who were primarily employees of the airlines.

According to a Bloomberg report, the State Department internal communication said that "The 155, not on the FB [Facebook] manifest, were placed on the FB airplane by KAM airlines. . . . FB (and everyone else) learned about these individuals when they landed in Abu Dhabi."[10] The 188 others on the flight were then flown on to Mexico. A month later, the State Department said it was still "awaiting guidance" on those others who had managed to board planes out of the country but did not fit into one of the categories of Afghans that the US government considered at risk. There, Farkhunda was told that she would be able to resettle in Canada, perhaps.

The process of sorting through who had made it out, who had what papers, and where these Afghans would resettle was just beginning.

The next day, on August 30, just before midnight, Major General Chris Donahue boarded the last of five C-17s at Hamid Karzai International Airport. With lights dimmed to prevent any final attacks, the five planes took off in rapid succession.

Around the city, Taliban soldiers fired celebratory shots into the air.

CHAPTER 16

The Women Who Remained Behind

THE NEXT MORNING, FOR THE FIRST TIME IN ALMOST TWENTY YEARS, there was no US military presence in Afghanistan, and for those who remained behind, the reality of living with the Taliban set further in.

The owner of the compound that Amena worked in called her to let her know that some Taliban fighters had ransacked the building and taken her laptop among other official papers. They wanted to know what work they were doing in their offices and asked him to tell Amena that someone from their office should meet with the Taliban to discuss their work.

Amena was the highest-ranking Afghan employee, and she received several calls from the Taliban asking about the work her organization's mission was. Around the same time, some Taliban fighters came to her neighborhood and dragged one of her neighbors out of his house. He worked for the Afghanistan Human Rights Independent Commission. No one was sure what happened to him, but Amena watched and realized that she could be next. So, she and Murtaza decided their family needed to leave home. They packed their things and told their neighbors that they had been able to find a way to leave the country, hoping that anyone who came looking for them might believe this. First, they went to a relative's house, but they were not sure that was safe, so a few days later they moved again.

In Afghan society, where family is so important, moving away from family is considered strange at best and, more commonly, scandalous. But by this point, Murtaza's family was mostly outside of the country already and Amena did not want to put members of her own family who were in the country at further risk, so, they set off on their own. There was a human rights group that had set up a series of shelters across Afghanistan for people exactly like Amena and so they moved into one of these, joining other families and women, in particular, who had worked for groups advocating for women's rights and were now forced into hiding.

Shelter spaces were in high demand and, as Amena put it, "it was more of a prison than a safe house." The compound rented by the organization was in the center of the city. For their own safety, they were told, once they were inside, they were not allowed to come and go. The organization did not want to attract the attention of the Taliban or their neighbors. The high-walled compound was composed of two buildings with four rooms each. The men were separated from the women and slept in the basement, and in each room, the women and children from three or four families were crammed in. There were eleven people in her room. The other older kids were unruly and constantly fighting with each other. Their mothers appeared shell-shocked and said nothing to them as they screamed. No one cleaned the bathrooms and the entire place smelled like waste.

Amena tried to get her infant to sleep, but it was difficult with all the noise. They only were given two meals a day, and dinner was served around 9:00 p.m., when her older daughter was already asleep. The baby cried constantly, and her older daughter complained that she was hungry. They would give Amena boiled water only once a day to sterilize her baby's bottle. The lack of hygiene rankled her as a mother and a doctor. From behind the curtains of their room they could look out onto the busy street outside. Taliban vehicles passed by regularly. One morning, they watched a group of ten or so soldiers knock loudly on the door across the street. The men went inside and there was yelling. A few minutes later they dragged a man out, kicking him. He stumbled, and they picked him up and put him in the back of a pickup truck and drove off.

Amena and her family lasted there only four days.

"We decided to go to my friend's house instead. It may have been riskier, but it was better than that place," Amena said.

But, after that, where could they go? Her sister worked for the UN and she had been evacuated to Macedonia. She had helped to arrange for Pakistani visas for Amena's mother, sisters, and brothers. They were hoping to either join her sister in a European Union country or apply for refugee status through UNHCR.

Amena spoke on the phone with them most nights. It was good to know they were out of the country, but it made her feel even lonelier. Also, even though she was in a place where few knew her, it was clear that someone was looking for her. Shortly after arriving at her friend's house, her phone rang and when she answered it, there was a man's voice that she did not recognize. He said that his name was Jamshid and that he was a mujahideen, a fighter for Allah and a term often used by the Taliban, but also the US-backed anti-Communist groups of the 1980s. The term now, however, was used by the Taliban for those who had fought the longest and most loyally. He asked her for the password to her computer. She immediately hung up the phone and blocked the number. She then went online and deleted everything she could from her organization's network.

***

Amena was not the only one to have this type of experience with the Taliban intelligence units as they started sifting through the records of various organizations and government offices from the past twenty years. And it quickly became clear that while the original version of the Taliban had shunned technology, this new version knew their way around a computer. They knew what passwords to look for and how to find the files that mattered the most to an organization.

While the Taliban had yet to impose some of the same censorship measures they had used previously, in many instances they did not need to, since women were so fearful, they imposed the measures on themselves. It became increasingly rare to see women out and about. While many offices did not fire their female staff, in many cases they simply stopped showing up for work. "I myself haven't even gone out to the market in two months," Amena pointed out in late October.

Amena said the message was clear, "everyone who worked for women and to advance Afghanistan for the past twenty years is of no value to the

Taliban. I went through a lot of hardships, sleepless nights, and sometimes suffered hunger to get to where I am now, but it seems the achievements have no use under the Taliban. Under the Taliban rule, women are considered just things to be incarcerated at home and be used by men."

As Taliban "justice" returned to the country, it was difficult for Amena and others to determine exactly what that would mean for them. The Taliban claimed that they were ruling by Sharia law, but it soon became clear Sharia law was being applied inconsistently and somewhat randomly. Kidnappers were publicly hanged in Herat "to deliver a message."[1]

Amena worried in particular about the violence that would not be seen publicly. She suspected that the return of the Taliban would lead to an increase of violence against women inside the home. Having worked with so many women who suffered during the more liberal Ghani government, she saw clearly how physical abuse and the psychological torture of being confined to the home also led to self-harm, suicides, and even cases of self-immolation.

One of her relatives, a young woman who had just scored well on the TOEFL exam and was preparing for the Kankor, had already killed herself after hearing the Taliban would no longer let girls older than age twelve attend school. "She was so disappointed that she could not continue her education and fulfill her dreams, that she preferred to die," she said sadly.

A few days later, her Facetime app rang with a number she did not recognize, and she answered it since she thought it might be a relative. Instead, it was a man in a turban who stared at her and slowly drew his finger across his throat, not saying a word. "It haunted me," she said.

By mid-September, Amena realized that her family had only two choices: flee to Pakistan or flee to Iran. Even though both Amena and her husband had lived previously in Iran, it was not an appealing option. Iran was going through a COVID spike and a related economic slump, which often seemed to trigger increased harassment of Afghan refugees. Plus, there was no US embassy in Iran, so if their visa applications were processed, they would have to go to yet another country to pick them up. So, the one remaining option was Pakistan.

Amena's husband's passport had expired and her infant daughter had never had one. The family had applied for passports earlier in the year, which meant the Passport Directorate had their applications, but they had not yet been processed. The Taliban, however, while opening some government offices, had not opened the passport office, so if they wanted to cross to Pakistan, they would have to do it illegally.

During more ordinary times, it was possible to cross the borders with Pakistan and Iran informally. Bypassing checkpoints was one option, but an even easier one was a well-timed bribe to one of the officials there. The problem with both Pakistan and Iran was that crossing illegally might get you out of the country and away from the Taliban, but unless you had family there, you were likely to struggle to make ends meet. Crossing illegally would also make it much more difficult to get any sort of visa from a Western embassy. Still, it seemed worth the risk to Amena and her family.

With all the turmoil happening in Afghanistan following the evacuation, both the Iranian and Pakistani borders had gotten more difficult to pass. The nearest crossing to Kabul was to the east, past Jalalabad and through the famed Khyber Pass; however, rumors in Kabul were that the crossing to the south, close to Kandahar through the Spin Boldak crossing, was easier at that point. So, even though Kandahar was the original homeland of the Taliban movement, the family decided that it was their best option and headed south.

***

Amena had been given the contact information of a smuggler in Kandahar by a friend in Kabul, and when they arrived in Kandahar the smuggler instructed them to meet him at a hotel later that evening. "The smuggler was extremely paranoid," Amena recalled. He seemed on edge and was always glancing around. He instructed them to say nothing about his identity if they were stopped at any of the numerous Taliban checkpoints. "Just tell them you are going to a wedding in Quetta," which was just across the border, he said. He then told them to quickly get into his old taxi, which was waiting outside.

The border crossing at Spin Boldak is about two hours from Kandahar and has long been one of the two central transit points between Afghanistan and Pakistan. Spin Boldak had also been one of the first major victories of the summer, with the Taliban taking the border crossing on July 13. While Taliban fighters had showed some restraint against civilians elsewhere, in Spin Boldak they reportedly killed at least 100 civilians, with some reports as high as 380, including the relatives of government officials.[2]

The next two hours were terrifying for Amena and her family. They drove eighty miles an hour, down a road that had been torn apart by bombs. At times it was more like a dirt track than a road. They jostled against each other in the backseat. The smuggler, who had stopped talking, told them to be quiet as they approached each Taliban checkpoint. The fighters looked in the car, but seeing a family, they just waved them through. Over the next two hours they would pass through another four checkpoints, each of which unsettled Amena, but the smuggler said not to worry about the Taliban, it was the gangs of thieves that sometimes take over the road after nightfall that they should really worry about. Amena looked out the window. No one out there had electricity and the barren landscape was pitch back.

Finally, they arrived in Spin Boldak and the smuggler dropped them off at a building he called a "hotel," but Amena said it looked more like a prison. On the first floor, there were two large rooms that were shared by a group of men. Three families had the upper floor, which was quieter, but filthy, crawling with bugs. The floors of most of the rooms were just dirt. There were no bathrooms, just a pit toilet. The smuggler brought them some dinner, but it was served on dirty plates and looked like it had rotten meat in it, so they pushed it to the side. He then demanded that they pay 16,000 Pakistani rupees or around $100 for the ride they had just taken from Kandahar to Spin Boldak. Although they had not agreed on that price before leaving, they didn't feel like there was anything they could do but hand over the money.

He then laid out the plan for the next day: At 7:00 a.m. he would take Amena and her two children from the hotel to the border checkpoint, which was just five minutes away. Usually, women and children could go straight through the post. Since they attracted less attention, it was likely that a bribe to the border officials could be enough to get them through. If anyone asked them anything, he would say they were going to a nearby family wedding and would be gone only for a couple of days. Often, Pakistani officials would allow Afghan women and children like that on family visits without passports, he explained. It was harder for the men. Another smuggler would then pick up Amena's husband at 10:00 p.m. and take him and another group of men around the checkpoint through some of the nearby rocky hills. There were fences, but they could be crawled under if you knew the route. He would charge them 40,000 Pakistani rupees or around $250 each. He said, "I won't charge you for the infant." It seemed like hollow generosity to Amena.

The smuggler was clear, however, it was possible that they could be shot and killed along the way. Perhaps even your children, he added darkly. Now with the Taliban here, things had been less predictable and there had been other shootings recently. "Whatever happens, I am not responsible," he concluded.

Reluctantly they agreed.

Amena was nervous, and in the dirty room mosquitos buzzed constantly around her children, who were exhausted from the travel. They remained quiet, aware of just how tense their parents were. Amena did not sleep at all.

The next morning, however, the smuggler did not return as they had agreed. At one point they heard some gunfire in the distance, but no one seemed to know what was happening. They waited for an hour in their room and then called him. He said that there was "a problem" at the border and they should wait. He would come later in the day. But he didn't. Instead, he called again and told them to spend another night at the hotel.

The day passed slowly. There was nothing to do in the small room. Her children wanted to go out, but the men downstairs were noisy, speaking loudly in Pashto, a language they understood little of, and a group of single men hanging out at a smuggler's preferred hotel might be dangerous, they concluded.

She did talk with one of the women from one of the other families staying on the second floor. The conversation had not been reassuring. The woman told her how they had tried to cross the border several nights before. They had been forced to climb under some barbed-wire fences that the smugglers pulled up for them. The wires, however, had snapped down on her baby's head, causing blood to run down his face, and he started to cry loudly. This had attracted the attention of a Pakistani patrol, who had started firing their guns. It seemed that these were just warning shots and no one was hit, but the entire party had been forced to retreat back under the fence and into Afghanistan. Now they were sitting in the hotel, trying to figure out whether it was worth the risk to try the crossing again.

The next morning the smuggler did come back and said a dispute had erupted between the Pakistani guards and the Taliban guards, and shots had been fired. The border had been closed, but his contacts assured him it would open again soon. He said that the plan was now for him to take Amena's husband that night at 10:00 p.m., and then he would return the next morning for Amena and her children. They rejected the offer. The idea of a night alone with those men downstairs was too much for Amena to imagine. And what if the border was not open the next morning? They had been there two days already. Amena could not stand waiting for another night, particularly alone with her children.

So, her husband remained with them and they debated what to do. Perhaps they could wait there until the situation at the border was resolved, but later that night, Amena was checking her Facebook account, and she finally saw a piece of good news: the passport office had reopened. The Taliban government announced that they would begin allowing Afghans to apply for passports again. There were few specifics about who was getting passports and how long it would take and, in fact, they had start handing out passports with the former government's seal on them.[3]

They worried that being Hazaras, the new Taliban officials might not allow them to get their passports, assuming they would try to flee the country. There were also rumors the Taliban were using the passports to lure those who were opposed to the new government to their offices and, in fact, one analyst suggested, "it is likely that the Taliban view the process of issuing identification as an intelligence collection operation as much as anything else."[4]

Still, the possibility of having legitimate passports in hand seemed better than staying at the border, so the next day they took a taxi to Kandahar and flew back to Kabul.

Once back in Kabul, Amena's husband quickly went to the government offices to check on their applications. He was not the only one. He arrived at 5:00 a.m. in the hopes of being one of the first in line, but the crowds at the office seemed to almost rival the ones at the airport the month before. The disorganized line wound its way down the street. It was 2:00 p.m. before he was able to make it to a counter to speak to someone. Amazingly, since they had submitted their applications before the Taliban had taken over, their passports were almost ready. They were told to return in two days.

When he went back, the passports were ready. It was a small miracle.

The passports were just the first step and the family was reluctant to return to the border. There were reports that it had closed again, and they still didn't have Pakistani visas, so any crossing would still be technically illegal.

Additionally, they were far from the only ones trying to leave the country, and travel agents and brokers had started raising prices to take advantage of those looking to flee. Airline tickets to Pakistan used to be $200, and now they were more than $1,000. And that was only if you could find someone to sell you one. There was also a danger of buying counterfeit tickets, and Amena had heard of families spending thousands of dollars on bogus tickets.

Agents sprung up on the internet making all sorts of promises about visas and tickets if you were willing to pay. And many, it seemed, were. There were Facebook pages for those applying for the SIV, some with helpful information, but others were clearly scams. One, for instance, listed the required biographical information needed for the application process, but then said to text the poster if they needed recommendation letters. "HR and Recamandation are 100% of the reputable companies in

America and the Superweiser gives 100% positive answers to this VC," the post read.

Amena, Arsalan, and other Afghans who had not been evacuated continued to call former colleagues and seek other ways out of the country. There were still occasional rumors of others who had plans to leave through Pakistan or elsewhere, but day by day, it felt like the door shut a little further.

PART VI

TEA WITH THE TALIBAN

ARSALAN—DECEMBER 21, 2021:

As the winter sets in, you can see poverty grip Kabul. There are more beggars on the streets than I have ever seen before. Many of those who came from rural areas into the city to avoid fighting between the Taliban and the government have stayed, since their homes were destroyed in the war or just because they didn't plant any crops this year and had nothing to return to.

Some of the teachers from my sister's school have started pushing carts of bananas around the city, buying from wholesalers in the morning, hoping to sell enough to make a profit by the end of the day.

People are selling their household goods on the streets for next to nothing, and prices, particularly of anything imported, have skyrocketed. Last year, before I got married, we installed a fancy new LPG gas heating system in my house, but fuel prices have tripled and now we can't even afford to use it. So, my brother and I had to go out and buy burkharis, the old-fashion stoves that burn wood or sawdust and cause rooms to fill with smoke. Since our new house had gas heat, we didn't have the smoke holes that older homes do, and we had to drill holes in our new walls. We're lucky that we can at least have that. Other families I've seen are burning tires to stay warm and some people don't have anything at all.

Some of the things that the Taliban did in their first days in power were hard to understand. For example, they opened up the prisons and let all the prisoners out. Not just the Taliban fighters, but the murderers and thieves, and even some members of IS-K who were fighting against the Taliban. At first it

225

just appeared foolish, but the Taliban leaders seemed worried that perhaps the Americans would not just leave and perhaps power would somehow slip out of their hands. So better to get all the Taliban fighters out that they could, particularly since the release of prisoners was something that the Ghani government had opposed. Getting those fighters out was symbolic as well as replacing members from their ranks who had been killed in the summer offensive.

Other things we hear and struggle to believe. For instance, my father's home district where I had lived as a young boy had been taken by only ten Taliban fighters. There had been no resistance. The new Taliban governor was a man who used to work as a day laborer in some of the orchards my family owned.

These things, however, are now just parts of our new reality.

One of the problems is that our office is in a part of the city where lots of officials had their homes and offices. Hamid Karzai's cousin lived next door to our office and on the other side, the minister of defense. Now all these compounds have been seized by the Taliban. They walk past our gates constantly, and our guards are always asking, what should we do when they ask us who we are and what we are doing in our office?

So, we discussed it with Kabir, "the consultant," and he again suggested we invite some Taliban members to lunch.

At first I thought, this is impossible. Why would we invite the Taliban here? The government had been fighting against this group for twenty years, and we had spent the last decade trying to avoid Taliban bombings and making sure our researchers weren't kidnapped by them. During the first weeks of the Taliban government, while others fled, every instinct told me to hide behind our walls and not let them know who we were or what we were doing. But slowly I realized he was right. Better that we have some relationship with them than for them to just come in here and shut us down.

Reluctantly, I agreed and, far too quickly for my comfort, Kabir reached out to some Taliban leaders who were in charge of some local security units and invited them to lunch.

Now, the game was to make it seem like we were an Afghan organization with only limited ties to the international community. The research we had been doing, we told them, was working to make sure aid was being distributed effectively. In fact, we were monitoring the Ghani government. We agreed that they had been weak, wasteful, and too beholden to the Americans. Or at least that was the story.

Because of both COVID and the insecurity of those early days under the Taliban, I still had most of my team working remotely, so at least there would be no women in the office. The day before the Taliban were set to come, I went through the office carefully, looking for anything that might make it look like we were anything other than what our story said. We went through the desks of the female workers in particular: We put perfume, makeup, key-chains with fuzzy animals on them, anything else that might be considered feminine-looking in boxes, and I had the guards drive them to the women's homes.

The Taliban arrived in trucks. There were about fifteen of them.

Three of them were, for lack of a better term, liaisons. They looked like they had worked for the previous government and quickly shifted sides. They had beards, but they were neatly trimmed. They spoke clearly, with urban accents, and took the lead with the introductions.

The other twelve looked more like the Taliban fighters we had seen racing around town in pickup trucks. Their hair was long, and they spoke with strong accents that sounded almost Pakistani.

Since my Pashto is not as fluid as some of my colleagues, the idea was that I would hang back and try to stay in the background, acting as the quiet host who oversees everything. When they arrived, they were all wearing the traditional robes that Taliban fighters always seem to prefer, black or dark brown. For my part, I didn't even own many robes, and that morning I had worn a cream-colored one. I realized too late that it made me stand out clearly as a "Kabuli," urban, educated, and, in their eyes, too Westernized.

The fighters themselves seemed particularly unsure about what the protocol was. But for that matter, I realized, I didn't know what it was either, so we all walked into the building. We have a large meeting room with a table and chairs where the staff usually eats lunch, but this, we decided, could be perceived as too Western. We had taken the room that our staff used as a call center for our surveys and taken out the desks, bringing in cushions, so we could all sit on the floor as traditional Afghans would.

Before eating, everyone went to wash in the bathrooms before the noonday prayers. As they went off, I worried. Was there anything in the bathrooms that *might make it seem that until a month ago, dozens of women worked here? I had taken down the "Women" sign from one of the bathrooms, but I worried that there might be flip-flops or something like that left behind that appeared to belong to a woman. They were slow in coming back, and I waited in the hall nervously.*

After we prayed, two of the boys we had hired from a local restaurant came out to serve the food. There was a bit of everything: different kinds of kebab, rice, some stews, bread.

As the meal began, I tried to act like a good Afghan host:

"How is the meat? Would you like some more? Please, you have not taken enough."

Often in Afghanistan, it is considered polite to decline initially when the host offers you something, but these men seemed eager to eat. They quickly dove into the kebab.

I had told the restaurant catering the meal to prepare enough food for fifty since we were unsure how many people might come, and I was glad we had ordered for so many since the fighters tore through the dishes quickly.

We joke in Afghanistan that you don't want to invite over to your house a mullah who lives in a madrassa, or religious school, where life is hard and there is not much food. They will eat and eat to make up for everything they have been missing. And in some ways, it felt like that's what those fighters were doing.

For the most part, the groups just talked among themselves. The Taliban fighters were telling stories about Taliban leaders they had fought with and places they had been. They compared the reputations and exploits of different leaders and reminisced about their days living in Pakistan.

I kept waiting for them to ask us about our work or to deal with our situation in some way, but they seemed uninterested.

Then, dessert was served. Since I lived in Turkey, I have always been a fan of baklava. It's not too hard to find in Kabul if you know the right pastry shops, but it is still considered a treat and Afghans don't often eat sweets like that after meals. The soldiers each took several and commented on how delicious they were.

"Oh, this is so sweet," one sitting across from me exclaimed. "Did you make it yourself?"

"No," I said, "it's from Turkey."

"How did you find out about it?" he asked.

"I used to study there," I replied cautiously.

"They are Muslim, right?"

I nodded.

"I hear that they are corrupt though and too secular," he continued.

I thought about Turkey, the classrooms I had studied in with both men and women, and the dinners I'd had with classmates along the Bosphorus.

"Perhaps," I said, "but the food is delicious."

The Talib chuckled. "Well, now at least we have these in Kabul," he said. "I'd like to get more."

And then, rather suddenly, the head liaison got up and said that they had another pressing meeting to attend. They started to say their goodbyes, and the Talib I had been speaking to picked up the plate with the remaining baklava and asked, "Can I take it with me?"

"Sure," I said, and he patted my shoulder, in the first friendly gesture of the meal.

I realized that this was one of probably dozens of meetings that these soldiers were having with the various businesses and families living in the neighborhood. They couldn't just shut every business and organization down. The country would grind to a halt. Instead, they were trying to figure out how to manage all these new relations just as much as we were trying to manage them.

At the door, the head liaison stopped and turned to us. "We are in your service. If anything comes up, just tell this guy to contact us," he said, pointing at Kabir, our consultant. And like that, they climbed up in their trucks and were gone.

***

For the first month that the Taliban were here, while everyone was afraid of the Taliban soldiers, things felt safer since there was suddenly less crime and no more suicide attacks. A couple of my friends just took a bus from Kabul to Herat, passing through Kandahar. That used to be a dangerous road, but since the Taliban arrived, there are not the same attacks and kidnappers on the road. Another friend just went to the mountains along the Pakistani border that had long been off limits, and I was considering traveling out to check on some of our field sites.

They said that all the criminals feared the Taliban and what they do to punish thieves. But after a few weeks, many of the thieves and gangs seemed to realize that while the Taliban are brutal if they catch you, they did not have all the sophisticated technology that the Afghan government had for monitoring phones and tracking down criminals, and they didn't seem to be concerned about whether the public felt safe or not. In fact, they clearly benefited from all of us being afraid.

Then, the crime restarted: One man was robbed by two men with knives right at the gate of my house. We have some trees there and apparently the thieves hid there waiting. Now my mother makes me call whenever I'm on my way home, and my father and brother go out with big sticks to open our gate as I pull in. I'm not sure what they would do if someone with a gun did appear, but they stand there and try to look threatening.

In a more serious case, the father-in-law of one of my colleagues was a well-known doctor in the north of the country. He had a successful clinic that many people went to and then, one day, he was kidnapped on his way home. The band of kidnappers demanded a million dollars for his return, but while his family had some money, there was no way they could get that much. So they offered to pay $300,000. At first the kidnappers refused, but a few days later the kidnappers finally agreed and told the family where to drop the money. The family handed over the money, but instead of returning the man alive, they just returned his dead body.

The Taliban government in Mazar said that they had later caught the men who did this and were going to punish them, but no one actually believes they caught the right people. It was probably some enemy of the Taliban leader up there who would now suffer for a crime he didn't commit.

Because of this, people remain desperate for any way out. One of my friends received a phone call in the middle of the night from a friend who worked at the French embassy. He had not been planning on leaving the country since he had a good job at the Central Bank, managing some of the bank's various branches. That night his friend from the embassy said, if you come to the airport now, we can get you on a flight to France. So, my friend left, still wearing his *pajamas with nothing but his documents. Two days later, he posted a photo on Facebook with the caption, "Sending you love, from the city of love, Paris."*

This man had a wife and children, but I suppose it makes sense. If he makes it to France, he could potentially send for the rest of his family later. But if he is stuck here, there might be no way to leave.

A month after submitting my SIV application, I received an email giving me a case number for my visa, but, honestly, I have begun to lose hope in the SIV process. Now they are saying that you must go to a third country to get an interview and I have heard that it will take more than a year after the interview possibly. Who knows if they are really processing these visas at all? In the past months, I have heard of friends and distant relatives who have left, and none of them left on the SIV. Instead, they all had some connections in the United States or, we heard of other cases where they paid some company like Blackwater to get them out.

More recently, we have heard of some families that left for the United States through the Humanitarian Parole process. When I first heard about it, I thought that it would just be more of a waste of time, but then a family I knew had their parole applications approved and suddenly, all twelve of them left. So Noah and I decided to submit a Humanitarian Parole application for all the members of my family. The other issue, however, is that you need a sponsor to file the application, and it's better if a lawyer does it. Luckily, Noah has a friend who is a lawyer who used to work in Uzbekistan and came to visit him in Afghanistan, who agreed to do the work for free. There is also a $575 fee for each application, which will be difficult to pay, especially since there are six of us. I also saw a report that said 28,000 Afghans had already applied for Humanitarian Parole, and so far 100 visas had been processed.

But it seems worth it. I think.

Just yesterday, we were all watching these reports on television and looking at our phones as we had for weeks, and finally I said, "Enough. We can't just sit and watch this, we need to discuss what we will do."

In previous weeks my brother and I had talked about going abroad to find work. Once we establish ourselves, we could send for the rest of the family, but with the Taliban announcing they would not allow girls to be educated and that they were going to reimpose amputations as a punishment for stealing, it feels more and more unbearable for all of us.

My mother is the one who is probably most opposed to leaving. She said, "Anyone who leaves is abandoning their family, their country, and their home. I hate thinking about it." And yet, I think now that she has seen how keen the rest of us are to leave that even she has agreed that we should be ready.

My father has been feeling anxious and stressed by the constant news, and he really wants to go. That's interesting, since he is probably the one whose life has changed the least. He is retired and is no longer going to his veterinary clinic. Before the Taliban came, he was mostly at home, working in his garden, watching football on television, occasionally visiting friends.

Now he says, "I don't see a future for us or Afghanistan."

This is even though he has worked so hard to build and renovate our home. It will be difficult for him to leave his gardens behind, but he also doesn't want to have us go and leave him here. He says it would worry him too much. But, it also makes him worry every time my brother or I go out with the Taliban here.

So far, my family has managed to stay together and that seems like a small miracle. Other families have been torn apart. Afghans are always proud of their strong family connections, the ways in which cousins, grandparents, aunts and uncles, all support one another, look out for one another. Right now, however, everyone is looking for a way out. People are looking out only for themselves. Everyone is worried about families splitting apart, spouses leaving each other, parents leaving their children, but they also know that this could be the only way out for them.

***

Sometimes people start to feel that perhaps we can survive this and stay here, but then something happens and we realize all over again just how dangerous things are now.

Just yesterday, I was on a call with the World Bank. We had colleagues from the United States and France on the call. I was the only one on the call still in Kabul. I had my headphones on, so if the Taliban fighters knocked on the door, I didn't hear them.

Luckily my computer was turned away from the door, so I had time to minimize the call, though I didn't hang up. I was grateful the Taliban did not think to unplug my headphones or look closely at the windows on my computer.

When the Taliban had arrived, the guards had simply let them in. I was angry at the guards, but I also understood why they were reluctant to protest.

There were six of these Taliban soldiers looking around the office, though only one asked questions rudely. The others poked randomly around piles of paper, maybe expecting to see pictures of naked women, or some documents that might reveal that we are spies, or something like that. That is what they seem to think all these offices working with the internationals are hiding. It's very strange.

I explained to them that we were helping hold the old government account-able for not delivering humanitarian aid and being corrupt. I showed them some spreadsheets and made it look like I was being transparent with them.

In the meantime, I had sent a text to Kabir to say that our office was being searched. He must have called some of his contacts in the Taliban government, because about twenty minutes later, one of the Taliban commanders from our neighborhood arrived with a few of his men. He was really pissed. Not at us, but at these other Taliban who were searching our office. That made me feel better about the connections that Kabir had, but it made me wonder even more just about how this new government will run when it is made up all of these different groups that don't talk to each other.

While all this was happening at my office, the meeting with these guys from the World Bank working remotely in France, the United Kingdom, Paki-stan, and the United States just kept going. I don't think they were aware of what was happening at all. With some of them, I think they are just trying to make sure they keep collecting their paychecks, so they keep having these remote meetings where they talk and the Afghans listen and nothing much happens.

I returned home and told my wife about it, but I tried not to make a big deal about the incident.

In the meantime, I have told my own family, mostly jokingly, that we need to be ready to leave at any moment and we should have a backpack ready to go. My mother, particularly, does not like this. "How can you just leave everything behind?" she asks. "Our friends? Our family? It's too much. I'll go, but it must be prepared, orderly."

When I told my wife about the man leaving in his pajamas, she just said, "You can kill me, but don't make me leave like that."

So, still, we wait.

CHAPTER 17

Airplane Hangars

THE C-130 CARRYING MUNIR ARRIVED IN QATAR IN THE EARLY EVEning of the same day he had stepped onto the plane, despite having no plan to evacuate. The temperature in Doha climbed to 115 degrees Fahrenheit that week, and inside the plane it was sweltering. Unfortunately, on the plane they did not fully realize the fact that the processing center they had just arrived at was far beyond capacity. For an hour they sat and waited, and nothing happened. Inside the overcrowded plane the situation was becoming unbearable. Finally, some of the passengers convinced the crew, who were also clearly hot and impatient, to open the back ramp of the plane. The passengers spilled out onto the runway and milled around the plane. It was even hotter outside, but at least they were free from the press of bodies.

Some people on the flight had been in the Kabul airport for over a week since the government collapse. They were exhausted, Munir said, from having slept on plastic chairs or not at all for the past seven days. Some of them curled up on the runway beside the plane to try to get some sleep. Looking at those exhausted bodies by the plane, more doubt started creeping into Munir's mind.

Finally, after three hours, buses arrived to take Munir and the other passengers to a large airport hangar. They taxied across the tarmac toward what Munir would later be told was Al Udeid Air Base. They pulled up alongside a massive hangar. There were more than 1,500 people in the room, and there seemed to be no order whatsoever. Some of those evacuees who were already there were on cots, but they seemed to be reserved mostly for the women and children, and most people were sitting on the ground or leaning against the walls. The line for the bathrooms was twenty people long, and you could smell that the toilets were overflowing.

"What is this place?" Munir wondered.

Munir was not the only one repulsed by the conditions. An email to State Department officials that Axios later published contained notes from the embassy staff about the conditions at the base in Doha where many of the evacuees were processed. It contained comments including: "A humid day today. Where the Afghans are housed is a living hell. Trash, urine, fecal matter, spilled liquids, and vomit cover the floors. . . . I spent an hour in there picking up trash . . . almost suffocated . . . Another flight arrived and there's no resources to solve the sanitation problem. . . . These human beings are in a living nightmare."[1]

Flights to Qatar had been paused just three days before Munir's arrival but had resumed after the United States opened up a processing center in Bahrain as well.

In the hangar, Munir finally found a trash bag and spread it out on the ground. It was difficult to sleep because the only space he could find was near some overflowing trash bins. After trying to sleep for about an hour and listening to some of the children around him crying, Munir couldn't take it anymore. He stood up. Nearby a couple men were discussing that they had heard they would be kept in the hangar for days.

There was a desk at the front of the hall. Munir approached it and told the soldier at the desk, "I want to go back to Afghanistan. This is horrible, I cannot survive this situation. Just put me back on one of those flights that are returning empty to Kabul." The soldier there just shrugged. He said there was nothing that they could do. "You have to stay here."

The rest of the night passed painfully slowly, in a sort of haze. Neither asleep nor awake, Munir paced. The next day was no better, particularly since the temperatures climbed rapidly as soon as the sun came up. There was nothing to do but wander around and try not to be overwhelmed by the misery that surrounded him. Despite the heat, going outside was more pleasant than being inside with all the crying children and the awful smell. Munir walked around the outside of the hangar.

Then, around 4:00 p.m., there were suddenly some people running towards one of the gates in the fence surrounding the hangar. Munir jogged along with them just to see what was happening. One of the gates that had previously been shut tightly was now opened and they were allowing evacuees to pass through one at a time. Munir wasn't sure where they were going. Someone said they were to be transferred to Germany, but at that point, the destination didn't matter to Munir. He just needed to escape this place. The soldiers at the gate tried to make lines, but the crowd grew and threatened to overrun the narrow opening. The soldiers just started handing out paper tickets to those who passed through. It appeared that the officials there had decided it simply couldn't process everyone, and Munir, being one of the first ones at the gate, got a ticket. Before the day ended, he was on a flight—this time, a typical commercial plane run by Qatar Airways—happy to leave Qatar behind him.

***

They were not headed to the United States, however. Few of those evacuated from Kabul were. Instead, they were transferred to Ramstein Air Base, a massive US base in southwestern Germany. This was better than some of the other options that Munir had heard evacuees discussing in Qatar. Some of those who had been evacuated had been taken to Uganda, others to Kosovo and Albania, and another friend he knew had been transported to Mexico. Among those discussing options in the hangar in Qatar, there appeared to be no logic as to who was being shifted where.

In Germany, however, they started processing the evacuees more systematically. The officers running the center took their biometric data, checked their documents, gave them a health screening, and conducted initial interviews. While the conditions here were somewhat improved, it still felt they were being treated more like livestock than as human beings, as they were corralled from one holding area to another, each surrounded by fencing. Officials at the base had not been alerted that they would be processing evacuees until August 19 and by the time Munir arrived, a week later, there were ten thousand Afghans living temporarily on the base in 350 tents.[2]

The weather was cool compared to Afghanistan, and they were put into military tents, twenty to thirty people in each. Since Munir was an unaccompanied man, he was put in with other men, primarily from the CIA-funded Khost Protection Force (KPF). While most of those evacuated were from Kabul or other Afghan urban areas, some of the exceptions were the soldiers from the KPF.[3] These were rough men, Munir said, who had been fighting the Taliban for years. Few spoke English and instead spoke a dialogue of Pashto that was difficult even for a native speaker like Munir to understand. They tended to swear as they spoke, Munir noted. Members of the KPF had been accused of killing journalists and activists. They were the worst elements of the US-funded support for the Afghan military, and if the Taliban were to harbor a grudge against anyone, it would probably be these men who had tortured their comrades. It made Munir uncomfortable sitting with them. At that point, however, he had little choice—they were the ones who made it out.

Those with families were given separate tents—in fact at least three women gave birth on the base—but their tents were no better, and in those moments, Munir said, "I was so happy for one thing—that I hadn't taken my family with me."[4]

The time between stages of the processing allowed Munir to take stock of his situation. After four days in the same traditional robes he arrived at the airport in, he was finally able to take a shower, but washing his clothes was impossible since he had only one set. Two days later, the military went room by room with donated clothes, and he received a pair of pants and a shirt. The pants were too big for him and fell off when he walked, but at least he could put them on while he washed his other clothes. He also had an Afghan bank card that was useless in Germany and, most importantly, his cell phone.

This presented a new issue: He had no charger. He started spending a good deal of his free time trying to figure out how to get his phone recharged. This meant finding other people with his same model phone and asking if he could borrow their chargers—something many were hesitant to do—and then getting time at one of the few outlets that was available. Once he did have a charge in the phone, he tried to connect with his family, but here he was faced with a new issue—no one in the camp had a German SIM card, since no one knew they were going to Germany. There was WIFI available, but nothing on the base was designed to accommodate ten thousand refugees, and the WIFI allowed only a few people on at a time and kept kicking them off. This of course further drained the charge on his cell phone, and Munir had to start all over again.

A few days later, he got lucky chatting with one of the former interpreters in his tent. The interpreter had a background in IT and Munir wasn't sure exactly what he did, but he somehow changed his VPN number so the WIFI system wouldn't kick him off. This meant that for the first time in seven days, he was able to talk to his wife and mother. They had been worried, having not heard from him in a week, and were surprised to hear that he was in Germany.

He also sent an email to his boss. He struggled to write it.

"They must have been wondering, 'What happened to that guy?'" he said. The last they had heard from him, he had been processing unaccompanied minors at the airport and then he disappeared. Munir decided the only thing he could do was be honest.

"I told my boss, 'I'm so sorry. I didn't plan on this happening, but suddenly I had this opportunity. And I didn't do this for myself, I only did it for my children. I don't think that I will have much opportunity in the United States to get a good job and advance, but if I take my children there, maybe they will have such opportunities. This was a hasty decision, I know, and maybe I made a mistake, but now, it is done, and I have to inform you.' And then, I asked him for a two-month leave."

At this point, in Germany, he was still hoping that if he received a green card quickly, perhaps he could actually return to Afghanistan and work to get his children out. He knew some SIV recipients who had done something similar. He was, however, going to be disappointed again.

***

By that point, Zeinab had been in Colorado for a week and was trying to settle into her new life while also talking regularly with her family back at home, trying to figure out what to do since Ali had failed to get anywhere in his attempts to be evacuated. Zeinab was also in regular contact with her two younger brothers and one older brother. She was particularly worried about the older brother because he had served in the Afghan military. Already, several members of his unit had been killed by the Taliban, and the family was worried that reprisals might come soon, so he had left their family home and gone into hiding. There was nothing they could do for the youngest brother because he did not have a passport.

Zeinab contacted one of the groups that had sprung up to help evacuate Afghans. They said they would work to get Ali, her older brother, and one of her younger brothers onto an evacuation flight. Then, in mid-September at around 3:00 p.m. in Colorado, she received a message that there was space for them on a flight leaving from Mazar-e Sharif first thing the next morning. The problem was that it was 2:00 a.m. in the morning in Kabul, and Ali would have to be in Mazar by noon to get on the flight. There were no domestic flights flying, so he would have to leave immediately, but Ali had turned the ringer on his phone off. She desperately started messaging friends to see if there was anyone who was awake who could go to his house and rouse him. When she finally did get him on the phone, she told him, "Listen, this is your opportunity, you can't let it pass."

And so, he set off. It was early, so there were no buses at the bus station yet. However, there were some shared taxis that generally waited for four passengers to arrive and then had them all split the fare. Since there was no one else around, Ali told one of the drivers he would pay for all four seats if they could leave immediately, and so they did. He kept texting with Zeinab all along the way, and she kept telling him to tell the driver to keep driving faster. And they barely made it. He joined Zeinab's younger brother, who she had also messaged. Once they boarded the private evacuation flight, they were on their way to Abu Dhabi, where they would join the long processing chain that Munir was in, but their stay would be much longer.

At the last minute, Zeinab's oldest brother decided not to go because there was no space on his flight for his wife. "I feel helpless, but it feels like there is nothing that I can do," he said.

He was not the only one in despair. During the month after the evacuation, Jackie Faye had grown more and more frustrated. She had flown to Colorado to meet Zeinab and help her settle into her new college life. And while she was happy Zeinab had made it out, she thought more and more about the others who had not. Was there more that she could have done for them?

She had submitted piles and piles of paperwork, sponsoring various Afghans she had worked with. One of the first applications she had sent in was a P-2 visa for the driver of her NGO. They had sent it in five days after the program had been announced, received an email confirming its receipt, and then nothing. No one she called could give her an update. It was frustrating how the evacuation did not have any logic to it at all. Those who were at the most risk, those who had done the most for the United States, those who were the most likely to create productive lives in the United States—none of them seemed to be prioritized over those who could simply get through the right gate at the right time.

At one point, Jackie had worked teaching English to sixty Afghan Air Force pilots. They all now spoke serviceable English, they were pilots, so they had real skills that were in demand in many parts of the world, and they were certainly a likely group to be targeted by the new Taliban government. And yet, almost none of them had made it out in August.

In one case, Jackie had been on the phone with a friend in Virginia who had a contact in the Special Forces working at one of the checkpoints. She knew that one of the pilots she had worked closely with was at that gate and ready to go, he just needed to get in. He even had printed out a picture of himself with some of his American trainers. Jackie pleaded with the contact to give her the number of the Special Forces guy at the airport. "The problem," she said, recalling it later, "is that these Special Forces guys think that they are so special. I was like, 'Give me his damn number! He's right there!'"

The pilot didn't make it through.

In the days and weeks that followed the withdrawal of US troops, the formal evacuation ended, but the more informal network of NGOs, veterans groups, and Afghans continued to organize ongoing operations to keep flights of those wishing to leave the country continuing. More and more of these started leaving from Mazar, since it was said that it was easier to get evacuation flights out of the north than out of the

Kabul airport, which the Taliban was watching more closely. By the second week of September, NPR estimated that there were seven thousand Afghans in Mazar waiting for flights out.[5]

In the meantime, the US government had also started pushing on some of the groups attempting to run independent evacuation operations. During the evacuation process in August, there had been a good deal of informal cooperation between the State Department, the military, and various donors and groups looking to help Afghans. A sense of urgency helped push away at least some of the red tape and get 125,000 individuals out of the country. Now, with the formal US presence gone, some of those hoping to help Afghan friends found themselves receiving more scrutiny, and not just from the Taliban.

The FBI contacted several of the veterans groups that had evacuated Afghans and were attempting to continue keeping flights coming out of the country. The FBI stated that this was due to increased activity in 503ce accounts coming from outpouring of donations as groups quickly raised funds to charter planes. But several of those we interviewed suggested that the motive for the investigation appeared to be aimed more at sending a message: Independent operations that could be seen by the Taliban as having a military component were to be halted.[6] There seemed to be a concern that if one of these informal evacuation flights ran into issues, it could cause a diplomatic incident or, worse, pressure the United States to engage formally with the Taliban. As of August 31, the administration wanted it clear: The United States was no longer in Afghanistan and had no ties to the new government there.

While some Afghans were still managing to get out of the country, after August 31, flights were largely curtailed, meaning for those who remained in the country, like Arsalan and Amena, it became a waiting game to see whether the new Taliban government would begin allowing planes out or whether the dangerous land routes were the only option.

As Arsalan was waiting, it was also becoming increasingly clear to him and others in the country that making it out was not the end of one's struggles.

**

After six days at Ramstein, Munir's initial paperwork was processed. He was boarded onto yet another flight, this time to New Jersey. Munir arrived at Fort Pickett, where there were 8,500 Afghans living in massive tents with some others in makeshift housing. The base had previously housed 4,000 refugees from Kosovo, and it sprang into action with surprising speed. A report commissioned by the base in August estimated that they could house up to 9,500 and looked at the impact of the arrivals on everything from housing availability to noise pollution.[7]

Munir was lucky to get put into a small room with just one roommate, a soldier from Khost. In the first few days, a few people managed to get SIM cards and contact their relatives back in Kabul, but there were few of these cards and there quickly sprang up a market for the buying, selling, and borrowing of them. Conditions were much better than on the bases in Germany or Qatar, but the treatment was in some ways worse, Munir said. All the military personnel there were helpful, he recalled, the problem was the other workers and civilian contractors who were supposed to give them food and care. They spoke to them rudely. One referred to them as "shit" and others told them they were not welcome in America.

At Fort Pickett there were more donated goods like clothes, which was helpful, but also seemed to bring out the worst in people. People fought over the clothes that were being handed out, and certain families seemed to be hoarding them, Munir said. The Red Cross also provided soap, toothbrushes, and other toiletries. This was helpful, but they had to stand in line for two hours just to receive these things, and it pained him to feel that he was receiving charity like this. The recent arrivals all sat consumed by a mixture of boredom, uncertainty, and anxiety. There were doctors' visits and interviews that were conducted, but mostly they waited. This gave them plenty of time to discuss and speculate all about the potential legal questions of their cases. They gave each other advice and debated the best approaches to take.

In the detention center Munir was told confusing, sometimes contradictory things. At one point they said that once they were released, they would all get to choose where they were resettled. Munir's brother was in Sacramento, so he would definitely go there, he told himself. The next day they told them, no, the resettlement agencies would be making that decision. Munir was distraught. How would he start over if he didn't know anyone? Two days later they were again told they would be able to choose where they resettled. Munir spoke English well, and he worried particularly about those Afghans there who didn't speak English at all. How were they going to navigate the process?

"Some of the other Afghans I was with were sent to Alaska. They were crying because they heard that the nights were so long there."

The most confusing, however, were the different categories that they were being assigned. "Before we arrived at the camp in the United States, none of us understood that there were different categories and that perhaps we would be treated differently depending on what category they put us in," Munir said. "We just thought, 'We are escaping Afghanistan and coming to the United States.'"

For those who had applied for the SIV and had already passed through the initial of the thirteen steps, it was said that the government was working to move them through the final steps as quickly as possible. For those like Munir, who had not applied for SIV, the only initial option was to receive Humanitarian Parole. Generally Humanitarian Parole is reserved for those who cannot receive a US visa through normal means, and there are relatively few processed each year. With tens of thousands of Afghans evacuated from Afghanistan without US visas, however, the program was expanded to allow them to live temporarily in the United States, but it did not put them on the path to a green card, as an SIV would.

This process was confusing since the details of the program were in flux, even as they were being processed. As Munir learned more about his potential status as a parolee, he felt worse and worse about his decision. He had assumed that, as with the SIV program, he would receive a green card pretty quickly, then he would be free to travel and return to Afghanistan and bring his family back with him. Now that was clearly impossible.

His situation was made more complicated when he finally received an email from PAE, the contracting firm he had worked for in the prisons, months after his initial message to them. They were apologetic and said that they had been buried under requests for employment verification.

They asked Munir to send his documents, even though he had already done this several times, and they submitted them. Now he had an active P-2 application.

Coincidentally, he also received confirmation that his friend Lyla Schwartz, an NGO worker he had worked with in the prisons, had also finalized paperwork on his behalf. Now he had two active P-2 applications, though he had still not received case numbers for either application. In some ways this gave Munir hope, but it also increased his uncertainty about his situation. If he received Humanitarian Parole and then applied for asylum, it would most likely be years before he could leave the country and it would not be easy to sponsor his family to get US visas. If he waited, however, and received the P-2, this would make travel possible and make it easier to get visas for his family, but it seemed like the backlog of applications would take months, if not years, to clear. Maybe they would prioritize cases for people in Munir's situation, who were already out of Afghanistan, but that would require decision making and logic that the process seemed to lack.

Sitting in the camp, he began to despair. "I had no information about any of these processes. If there had been someone to explain these things, I would never have made such a decision."

There was a State Department office at the camp and Munir booked a time there. He asked about the difference between P-2 and being a parolee. The official said that they were also confused since the process was so new. They went through some of the parole language together. The more he heard, the further he felt from his family.

At the end of the meeting, for a second time he asked, "Please, can you just put me on a plane back to Afghanistan?"

Again, the answer was no.

CHAPTER 18

Making Compromises

LIVING WITH THE TALIBAN CHANGED THINGS IN SMALL WAYS AND large. Arsalan said, "I am not very religious, but I used to go to the mosque at least weekly. But now with the Taliban here, I can't even go anymore. It doesn't feel right to be in the mosque. The Taliban say we should be religious, but they have made me want to be less religious. When they force you to pray or fast or wear certain conservative clothes, it just makes me feel so unnatural—it makes me feel far away from my own values."

In the first days of the Taliban in Kabul, most residents were unsure what to expect. During the early days in mid-August, before a formal government was established, most women were left to guess what the Taliban restrictions would be and were terrified that even if the Taliban had an official policy, what would the random young Taliban fighter manning a checkpoint do if they saw a woman out trying to go to work or school or simply do some shopping. As for lower-level government officials, teachers, and others, should they return to work? If so would they be paid? If not, how were they expected to feed their families? Arsalan's older sister for instance was principal of a school. Afraid of what some Taliban fighters might do if they found her in the principal's office, she had handed over most of her materials to a male colleague and was having him represent the school whenever anyone inquired.

During their first months in control of Kabul, the Taliban seemed at first to be allowing more rights for women than they had in their previous regime, but many felt that this was simply a show for the international community. On August 28, before the withdrawal was complete, the Taliban announced that all female government health care workers should return to work.[1] Another official announced on September 13 that women could work, but not in offices alongside men, which would essentially bar them from most government ministries but could potentially mean some women working in offices that had segregated spaces dividing the women and men.[2]

But then a week later on September 19, the mayor of Kabul announced that only essential female workers, in particular "those working in the city's design and engineering departments and women's public toilet attendants" should be working.[3] The new government also seemed to flip-flop on girls in schools, initially saying that they could continue studying, but then, in September instituting a ban on girls in school past the sixth grade.[4] Officials said repeatedly that they would reopen schools once it was possible to do this in an Islamic way, but this was said to include strictly segregated school spaces, only female teachers, and male family escorts to the school buildings. Finally, it was announced that secondary schools would not reopen for girls and while universities remained open to them, it was difficult to imagine that there would be any women in the universities in a year or two if the high schools remained closed to them. (A little more than a year later, in December 2022, the Taliban would formally ban women from universities as well.) Still, other messages were less subtle, and the Taliban shut down the Ministry of Women's Affairs, putting in its place the reestablished Ministry for the Propagation of Virtue and Prevention of Vice, which was notorious for enforcing the Taliban's strict dress code for women, as well as enforcing other "moral" issues.

Minorities, particularly Hazaras, who had been treated brutally by the initial Taliban regime, were also very weary of the new government and rightly so. During their rapid rise in June, July, and August, there were several incidents reported by Amnesty International, among others, where Hazara men had been executed, particularly in rural areas of the country. Two young Hazara men had been executed at a checkpoint heading to Jaghori, Ismaeil's home district.[5] As with everything else with the Taliban, it was difficult to determine exactly how high up the order to carry out these killings had come from, but the result regardless of who ordered the killings was a deep fear of the new rulers.

When the Taliban announced their cabinet, the fact that there were only men and no non-Pashtuns included in the initial list of ministers and only one Hazara later announced as a deputy minister suggested an additional message to women and minority groups: This is no longer your country.

Even under Taliban rule, some brave women did come out to protest. These initial protests were covered in the international press and followed by many Afghan women over social media. Zeinab, watching from afar, was impressed with them, but also realized how much had changed: "They were protesting for women to have the right to work and the right to education, but I didn't see anyone protesting for the right to participate in sports or just live a normal life."

***

While some brave women were protesting, for others the risk was too great. Amena at this point said that her life was "suspended." They had already sold their car and were thinking about selling their furniture and other household items to raise funds to perhaps buy a Pakistani visa, but it was difficult in those fall days to know what to do.

Then, out of nowhere, around midnight on November 3, Amena's cell phone rang with a call from an unknown number. She was reluctant to pick it up, since she had already received threats by phone, but it was late and she had been somewhat caught off guard by the call. When she did answer, the caller was speaking English.

"Are you Amena?" the man asked.

"Yes," she replied hesitantly.

Then he asked her to confirm the names of her children. Somewhat startled, she answered. He then asked if she was pregnant.

"No," she said, now completely confused.

The man then said that he had been instructed by the International Organization for Migration (IOM) to prepare her for evacuation. He went on to ask about her health and whether anyone in her family had been harmed by the Taliban. Then he said he would contact them again soon, but he gave no information about when or how they would be evacuated or even where they might be going. Amena and Murtaza were left in a state of nervous confusion.

Five days later, she was called again at night by a different man who was calling from Dubai on behalf of the German Foreign Ministry. Be prepared to leave the next day for Qatar, he said. And don't tell anyone, he added, since the flight was secret.

They were to be at the airport at 9:00 a.m., but before that, he gave them an address and said to meet a man there in a white Toyota Corolla at 7:00 a.m. to collect their visas. The household flew into action, packing and preparing to leave, but still Amena worried, it did not seem realistic they could get a visa and get to the airport and on a plane in just two hours. It didn't seem real. But if it was a trap, finally, she thought, they might as well step forward boldly. Having lived under the Taliban for two and a half months, she had seen enough. They had no other options and she was exhausted from living in fear.

Murtaza went to the address the man had given Amena at 7:00 a.m. the next morning. There was a white Corolla just as they had been told with two Afghan men inside it. Nervously he got in. The men too seemed anxious, but they took the passports and began to inspect them and went through a folder of papers. Not long after, they handed the passports all back, now with official Qatari stamps on the inside. Murtaza got out, paused to marvel at the transaction that had just taken place in the back of the car in a few minutes, and rushed to get his family to the airport.

But, Amena wondered, would the Taliban even allow them on the plane with these stamps?

***

The Taliban's silence and inconsistent declarations meant it was difficult to try to decide what to do and left Afghans still in Afghanistan guessing what the Taliban policies might be. At the same time, life had to go on, so people were left proceeding cautiously.

Arsalan and several of his friends, for instance, had been supporting a local orphanage for the past three years. Before the Taliban arrived, Arsalan's wife would go over every other week and give the children art lessons. It was a fairly informal place, as many Afghan charities are. There were approximately fifty orphans there when the Taliban arrived and it was run by a man who had worked for the Afghan Ministry of Justice and his wife. They had, on a few occasions, received funds from international donors, but they were not directly affiliated with any groups and when they needed more funds or specific items, they would appeal mostly to upper middle-class Afghans, like Arsalan, who would attempt to give what they could.

A lot of the children there were the children of drug addicts who had been abandoned on the streets. One girl's mother had died after her father had beaten her—angry that she had only given birth to girls. The family left the mother's body at the hospital and the baby girl alongside her, saying that anyone who would bury the mother was welcome to take the baby, since they had enough girls already, they said. The hospital had called the head of the orphanage and he had come instead.

While the orphanage had no direct international ties, the Taliban associated places like this with the West and the American presence. Arsalan worried that the older girls could be forced into marriages with Taliban fighters. The youngest ones might be sent to the Taliban madrassas, where they would receive nothing but rote religious education. Finally, the head of the orphanage decided that their building was in too central a location and that it would receive less attention in a quiet, more residential area. So, they rented a new house and began moving the orphans, a few at a time, not to draw attention to themselves, to the more secluded, residential neighborhood. Arsalan helped with some of the move. Just as they were finishing, however, there was a commotion on the street. In a neighboring compound, there had been a former Afghan army officer living. The Taliban had heard about the compound and a couple of the higher-ranking members of the Taliban decided to claim the home as their own. As Arsalan and his friends watched, the Taliban threw the Afghan army officer and his family out, along with their belongings.

Now the orphanage is right next door to the Taliban, and the orphanage workers still don't know the best way to keep the children safe, move them again or attempt to meet the Taliban and gain their sympathy. Arsalan's family still tries to visit every other week or so, but the children don't receive many other visitors, in part because many of those Afghans who supported the orphanage have fled the country and in part because the orphanage was still trying to keep a low profile. Some of the kids still went to school, but not the older girls since the Taliban had closed their schools, and not the youngest kids, since the director was concerned about them being out on their own. Arsalan had gotten a Ping-Pong table for the orphanage and especially for those who were not able to go to school, as this was one of their few escapes and, Arsalan joked, they practiced so much, some were on the verge of becoming professionals.

It would have been funnier, these tiny boys and girls who were so skilled at Ping-Pong, he said, if it didn't show just how dire their situation had become.

***

When Amena, Murtaza, and their children arrived at the airport, a line with three hundred people in it stretched out, trying to get onto the Qatar flight. Amena heard from some of the others in line that they would not actually take off until 4:00 p.m., but that was good, because it took three hours for everyone to be processed. The only people there in an official capacity all worked for Qatar Airlines. Everyone in line had worked for an organization receiving German funding, but there was no formal acknowledgment of this as they were slowly processed. There still seemed to be no logic to it, only one of the other passengers had worked with Amena, and she reflected later, "I still do not know what made the German government include my name on the list or how we were contacted."

The Qataris gave the family their tickets and checked them in. They walked through the immigration checkpoint, but no members of the new Taliban government seemed to be interested in even acknowledging that the plane full of Afghans was leaving. It felt strange to simply walk towards the plane when they had for so long feared not being allowed to make it past the airport authorities. Amena kept waiting for someone to call them back or try to prevent them from leaving.

Upon landing in Qatar, Amena felt all the energy just drain from her body: "It was not physical exhaustion, but the mental exhaustion of fear and stress which had held me for weeks." The German embassy took them to some pleasant and clean rooms, and when they woke the next morning, Amena said she could feel the freedom in her body.

They were told they would be processed in Qatar for around ten days before continuing on to Germany. The relief was immense, but many questions lingered. Neither Amena nor her husband spoke much German. What would they do there for work? Where would they live? Their oldest daughter was sad when she heard that they would not be returning, which meant not seeing her friend who lived in the apartment above them. But, Amena reasoned, these were the choices they had to make. Better to wake up with this feeling of freedom and possibility in a strange land, than live in fear at home.

CHAPTER 19

Parole

WHILE THE GERMAN GOVERNMENT FOLLOWED THROUGH ON THEIR promise of processing Amena's family over the next ten days and putting them on a plane to Hanover, the US government continued to struggle to process or even make sense of the evacuation they had triggered.

By mid-October Najeeb's wife and his brother, Haseeb, had also made it out to a processing camp in Abu Dhabi called Humanitarian City. They joined Zeinab's husband and brother, along with several thousand other Afghans getting their cases processed in the camp. Najeeb had contacts with the Department of Defense who promised that his family's cases would be processed quickly, but the department was vague on the details and unwilling to commit to any sort of timeline. His brother's case was just one of Najeeb's worries. His partners and other siblings were still back in Kabul. Najeeb had submitted Humanitarian Parole applications on their behalf using some lawyers who had been working with No One Left Behind.

Najeeb had also been doing some of his own informal advocacy. A friend of his working at an immigrant support center had heard that Texas senator Cornyn was interested in meeting with some SIV recipients and organized a roundtable on October 15. Several SIV recipients and their families were there, but it was Najeeb who was selected to lead the discussion. Najeeb was pleasantly surprised that Cornyn did seem to have some knowledge of the SIV process, but he didn't seem to understand just how slow and ineffective it was. He also seemed surprised when all of the recipients talked about family they still had in Afghanistan who were in danger. "It's not just us who are in danger," Najeeb explained, "it's our parents and siblings too, but none of them have received visas."

After the roundtable, Cornyn, who had a legislative track record of opposing immigration in almost all other contexts, said, "I think this is a special case where we do have a moral obligation to help those who have helped us keep America safe from future attacks."[1] Like other hawkish and anti-immigration Republicans, he tried to walk a fine line between supporting Afghan allies but not making it sound like he was supporting a new wave of immigration. As with many US politicians during and after the evacuation, Cornyn appeared to be saying the right things, but it was not clear that his words were translating into any concrete action at all.

Discussing the challenges that his brother had leaving the country and the fact that he was still in legal limbo in Abu Dhabi, Najeeb concluded of politicians like Cornyn, "The problem is not just that they are not willing to help. The problem is that they are actually hindering some of the efforts by service members. I get it, they do not want to be involved in Afghanistan, like 0 percent, but there is still stuff they should be doing privately. There are things that they can do."

***

For those who did make it out, however, the US government was struggling to keep up with high numbers of arrivals, creating awful backlogs with thousands of Afghans stuck in various states of limbo. Some politicians with connections to Afghanistan, like representative and veteran Seth Moulton, continued to push for action. However, there was not enough political will in the divided Congress to address that from the beginning, and the bureaucracy was not equipped to handle this type of immigrant influx—or the broader consequences of the withdrawal.

The most effective of the series of reforms attempted to move some aspects of the process from the government's hands into those of Americans themselves. In late October, the State Department announced that individuals and organizations such as churches could now sponsor Afghans in the country, expanding beyond the nine designated resettlement agencies that had typically done this work. The program, the

State Department announcement said, "will enable groups of individuals to form sponsor circles to provide initial resettlement assistance to Afghans as they arrive and build new lives in local communities across the country."[2]

Run by the Rockefeller Foundation, the Community Sponsorship Hub would vet these groups and then permit them to support Afghans who had arrived in the United States. Similar processes, which US advocates wanted to imitate, had long been running in Canada and some European countries.[3] But throughout the fall, the flurry of new programs did not seem to be resulting in faster processing of applications or changing much on the ground for applicants like Arsalan. By the middle of November, US Citizenship and Immigration Services had reported that 28,000 applications for Humanitarian Parole had been received, but only 100 cases had been approved. Part of this was due to staffing, and the agency had trained 44 additional staff to help process applications, but by mid-October, Al Jazeera reported, the agency had only 6 staffers working on the program.[4] Other offices had similar backlogs. The National Visa Center, by the first week of December, had not responded to any emails sent after August 21 and said that it was taking two to three weeks just to respond to a day's worth of emails from earlier that summer, not to mention any emails that had come in since.

Even when applications were being processed, however, it appeared that the process was still hampered by vague standards that, to applicants and their advocates, seemed arbitrarily enforced. In the first wave of Humanitarian Parole denials, Axios obtained a letter to an applicant that stated that their case was missing "documentation from a third-party source specifically naming the beneficiary, and outlining the serious harm they face." This was even though the program manual stated that parolee status could be granted for those "facing fear of harm due to generalized violence."[5]

The haphazard, rushed nature of the evacuation meant many of the evacuees were of uncertain status. In fact, one estimate suggested only 40 percent of those evacuated were eligible for the visa.[6] Still, much of the advocacy work being done focused on those who were SIV eligible. IRAP, for instance, had filed another lawsuit against the State Department, this time emphasizing the need to provide protection for SIV applicants and their families. In this case, the SIV applicant was already in the United States but filed a petition asking that his two minor sons be evacuated. The Afghan Allies Protection Act demands the US government make "reasonable effort[s]'to protect or evacuate SIV applicants and their families who are in 'imminent danger' while their SIV applications remain pending," and yet, six months after filing the petition, the applicant who IRAP had filed the case on behalf of still had not even received a response on the case.[7] The lawsuit IRAP filed on his behalf "challenges the US government's unconscionable delay" in the processing of his case.

The IRAP lawyer Noah spoke with was confident that they would win this particular case as well, but it was likely to be slow, and if the State Department continued to ignore the decisions that IRAP was winning, it seemed unlikely that much would change for other applicants themselves. "It's not like anyone is going to go to jail," the lawyer concluded. In the meantime, it seemed that no one in the government was actually interested in solving the problems created by evacuating 125,000 Afghans, but rather in delaying court rulings in the hopes that the Afghans would simply go elsewhere.

Many of the veterans groups had continued attempting to evacuate their allies, working around the Taliban and, at times, US government efforts to get their colleagues out on charter planes or over land routes and through third countries. Inside Afghanistan, rumors of flights out and safe houses continued to circulate. Yet, it became clear that while there were individual successes, these organizations were getting out only a few hundred Afghans per month, not the tens of thousands who had made it out in August. For many, the frustration built.

A group called #AfghanEvac, made up of more than one hundred of these groups, some long established, like No One Left Behind, and many others that had sprung up just in response to the events of August, attempted to coordinate lobbying efforts. In an open letter to President Biden and leaders in Congress, they argued that while they were continuing to work, "The sheer volume and complexity of this crisis, however, renders our work untenable without increasing the formal support of the US Government." The group had several demands that would expedite both the evacuation and resettlement of Afghans in the United States. The first one of these was that "The Executive branch should, no later than February 2022, appoint an interagency leader with tasking authority, oversight responsibility, and a dedicated staff to develop and implement a multi-year, actionable plan for evacuating our Afghan allies."[8] This reflected the problems of the SIV problem from the very start; fifteen years later, there was still no one person overseeing the SIV process. But even the timeline of this request—that the interagency leader be appointed by February 2022, reflected how the glacial response time of the US government would have little impact on any of the Afghans who were most in danger and who had already fled.

***

In the meantime, in Emirates Humanitarian City in Abu Dhabi, Najeeb's brother, Haseeb, and Najeeb's wife waited. Haseeb had worked as a translator at Camp Morehead starting in 2016, when it was a base for training Afghan commandos. He worked for five years but was told initially that he was not eligible for the SIV since he had not been working directly for the military but was translating for an officer who was mentoring the Afghan Army commandos. He had applied again, a little more than a year and a half before the collapse of the government, but his application was still pending when the Taliban returned.

When the evacuation had started in the middle of August, he had been in contact with some of the veterans groups that were aware of his application but had not heard anything. On the night of the bombing at Abbey Gate, on August 19, he got a call to go to Mazar-e Sharif immediately. He had to pack and leave Kabul within the hour to get to the airport in the north where there was a charter flight waiting. He rushed north, but when he got to the airport in Mazar, the Taliban guards there said the flight could not leave since not everyone had their passports with them. His contact told him to get a room nearby and that they would try again the next day. Again they were told to wait. This continued for more than a month. He phoned Najeeb daily, but there did not seem to be much Najeeb could do from the States. At some point he thought about giving up and returning home, but he worried that this would draw more attention to his family.

Then, suddenly, after weeks of waiting, they were told they could depart.

In the United Arab Emirates, they were put in a camp run by the UAE government called Humanitarian City. The camp held between 5,000 and 10,000 Afghans depending on the day and who was counting. By Haseeb's estimate, about half of those there had active SIV applications. Most of the rest either had pending P-2 cases, except for around 1,000, who seemed to have no case whatsoever. Those were the most difficult cases.

In comparison with some of the other camps that Munir had passed through, the living conditions in Abu Dhabi were not bad. "The food is good and there is even a playground for the kids," Haseeb said. The major issue was the lack of transparency for anyone in the camp about their fate. They were given almost no information. How long would they be there? Who would decide when they could leave? Where would they be sent?

Many of the Afghans there had boarded US-sponsored planes under the impression that their cases would be processed and they would be sent to the United States. Now, however, some of the Afghans were being sent to third countries. There were even reports that US embassy staff were threatening to deport some of the evacuees back to Afghanistan.[9] Also, as the days ground by, the place began to feel more and more like a prison. They couldn't leave, which at first was not a huge burden. But there was no school and only basic medical facilities. Babies were being born at the camp and children were missing schooling.

On November 12, dozens of those detained held a protest carrying signs on bedsheets that read "85 Days of Prison Life" and "We Are Suffering from Mental Stress." One young boy held a piece of paper that said "I AM SAD. TAKE US OUT." One of the pieces that frustrated many of those protesters the most was that cases were being processed at very different rates. Some of those who, apparently, had strong applications were processed quickly, while there were others who had arrived in the camp on August 16, just after the collapse of the Ghani government, who had not heard anything about their applications. Six months after his arrival, Haseeb was still in the camp, and the messages he sent out were increasingly dejected.

Haseeb complained that the US embassy staff working in the camp was also rotating on a monthly basis. They were constantly faced with new officials who were unfamiliar with all of the processes. At times, he said, it was as if the Afghans, who had been there for months, had to explain to the new staff members how the process worked, instead of the other way around.

Initially Haseeb thought he was lucky compared with some of the others in the camp. After twenty days, he received his Chief of Mission approval or, as it was more commonly known, COM approval, which was one of the key steps in the process and indicated that the embassy approved the pending case. This was the fifth of the fourteen steps in the SIV application process and had become something of a demarcation line in the camp, Haseeb said. If you had COM approval, they usually allowed you to continue to the United States. The State Department seemed to be working under the assumption that if you got your COM approval, you would receive the SIV eventually. If you did not have COM approval, you were essentially treated like all the other applicants in limbo and the threat of deportation hung over you.

Even with COM approval, the process remained confusing and disorganized. When he was told that he had approval, they said that he would be on a flight as soon as one was available. A couple days later, however, he discovered that he needed to receive his COVID vaccine before they would let him leave—both shots of it. Why hadn't they told him before? Or given him the vaccine earlier? He had been there for months. Everyone in the compound had received the Measles, Mumps, and Rubella vaccine. Why didn't they do it then? No one had a good answer. All they said was, "You have to wait." And so he did.

***

Najeeb was not the only one with relatives in the Abu Dhabi Humanitarian City. Zeinab's husband and younger brother had also managed to get evacuated there in October. Since she and Ali had filed paperwork for the marriage at the court in Afghanistan, he was qualified to apply for a spouse visa. In general, unlike those from other parts of the world, Fulbrighters from Afghanistan were not allowed to bring dependents to the United States, but with the collapse of the government, they had relaxed that policy. The problem was, Zeinab and Ali did not have a marriage certificate, because they had just gotten married and the courts in Afghanistan were under Taliban control. Her brother, in the meantime, was hoping to get in with a P-2 application.

Speaking to them from Colorado, her brother complained that the dormitories were crowded and there was no privacy. On one occasion, a new group of Afghans had arrived and had to quarantine, but instead of just quarantining the group, they made everyone in that dorm quarantine and for ten days they couldn't even leave the building. Decisions like this made them feel like they were less than human.

While Zeinab waited to hear more about Ali and her brother's cases, the rest of the family still in Afghanistan were also struggling. Her older sister's husband had managed to get to Uzbekistan using a business visa and, initially, Zeinab's sister hoped to join him there, but then the Uzbek embassy stopped handing out visas. They had paid an agent to try to get them a visa through other means, but the agent had given her passport back (and only half of her deposit) and said there was no way to get a visa anymore. Instead of fleeing, her sister's husband had returned to Afghanistan. Her older brother had taken his wife and fled to Iran. Things were difficult there economically, but since he had been an Afghan Army commando, it felt like the only way to stay safe. In the meantime, her father was still in Herat, but with the winter setting in and the economic collapse, things were getting bad. Her father had told her that he had spent the day in his shop and earned only ten Afghanis—about ten cents. That was not enough to even buy bread. How could they continue living like that?

Finally, Zeinab managed to have a relative go to the court in Kabul and pick up a copy of the marriage certificate, but then there was no way to send it to Ali in the camp, and even if they could, the US embassy was apparently not granting visa interviews for that type of visa in the camp. Since Ali and the other Afghans were not allowed to leave the camp, there was no way to get to the embassy in Abu Dhabi. So, the months passed.

Soon the two young men had been in the camp for six months. Most of the other Afghans there had found a way to get to the United States, or, more frequently, to one of the other countries accepting Afghan refugees. Some, however, had just gone back to Afghanistan to see what their fates might be. But several thousand remained, just waiting.

The trauma of the AUAF attack also stayed with Zeinab. One afternoon, someone in her neighborhood had set off a firework and she was convinced that another suicide attack had begun. It took her several minutes to calm herself and remember that these things were not common in the United States. It was hard to balance her schoolwork with the emotions of everything that she was still going through. She knew that many of the other international students were far from home, and during COVID, everyone was facing some form of trauma, but she still felt that other students and faculty did not understand what she was going through. And that was lonely.

Zeinab threw herself into her training. She qualified for the Ironman 70.3 World Championships, which were scheduled to be held in Utah in October 2022. Now that she was living in Colorado she had access to a pool, and her cycling had improved. She was feeling much more confident than she had during that first triathlon in Dubai when swimming had felt so strange. The training gave her something to focus on that was different from the stress of worrying about friends and family both inside and outside Afghanistan.

"I sometimes regret my departure from Afghanistan and feel guilty because . . ." she trailed off, before starting again. "Whenever I think about the danger to my family in Afghanistan, I feel pain. When I hear about the Taliban's reprisals against Hazaras, attacks on Panjshir, and the attacks by IS-K, it pains me. I don't discuss these issues with anybody here in the United States because nobody feels the pains people in Afghanistan are suffering.

"I have always had big plans, but now, I don't know what will come to my family and country. . . . Now, there is nothing we can do other than pray for change in our country."

CHAPTER 20

California

THE EVACUATION WAS SUPPOSED TO BE A WAY OUT—A WAY TO SOME-place else, someplace safe, but instead, in many cases, it was a way to nowhere. It was constant uncertainty.

Murtaza and Amena called Ismaeil before getting on the German flight to Doha. They had wanted it to be a surprise, and they were, frankly, worried until the very last minute that the flight might not depart. But they had also heard that sometimes internet was unreliable in the centers where refugees were being taken, and if they were unable to contact their family for several days, they would certainly worry. So Ismaeil was not entirely surprised when he received a text that they had landed in Doha. Still, there was part of him that did not believe that two months after they had started trying, his son, daughter-in-law, and granddaughters were finally out and on their way to Germany.

Still, this instantly opened a whole other set of questions. "What is your advice?" he asked Noah. "Should I apply for Humanitarian Parole for them?"

Now that they were in Germany, he was worried they would be automatically rejected. Besides, it would cost two thousand dollars to apply for all of them, and he had already applied for Humanitarian Parole for his sister and his wife's brother. It would take eight years, he had heard, for them to secure German citizenship. In the meantime, they would have to look for other ways to reunite the family if that is what they wanted to do. "Maybe if my son were to enroll in some graduate program someplace in the United States as a student," he thought.

Despite the uncertainty, some things were better. He had been at his job at the University of Utah for three years now, and so his son and two daughters got a large discount when they enrolled. They had bought a house with a reasonable mortgage and a yard. "I was so thankful that we weren't in a rented apartment during the pandemic," he said. "This way we at least had our own home."

Still, as he pointed out, his family had been literally flung across the globe: "I have four brothers on four continents—Asia, Europe, North America, and Australia. If we were to have another brother, he would have to move to Africa," he joked. His younger brother in Australia had managed to get his family out of Afghanistan, but his older brother who was in Austria had not been able to, and his wife was still back in Kabul. His fourth brother was in Iran, with another sister in Pakistan and two others in Afghanistan. "I hope we will all be able to come together sometime, but I'm not sure it is likely," he concluded softly.

***

Finally, after six weeks in Fort Pickett, Munir was released. On the way out he was handed an *Information Sheet for Afghan Parolees Departing Military Installations*, as well as a stack of other papers that were supposed to tell him how to get a Social Security number and other instructions based upon his uncertain status. They were all somewhat confusing. Among the various instructions, he was required to alert the US Citizenship and Immigration Services within ten days whenever he changed address. He arrived in Sacramento on October 20, almost two months after he had walked out of his house in Kabul.

His brother had arrived about six months before on an SIV. They lived in Section 8 government housing and had struggled in their initial months. With COVID, it had been hard to find a good job, and they had six children. In his first days in California, Munir felt immense relief seeing his brother again. It appeared to Munir that his brother had aged since he had last seen him and he seemed more than ever like his father, and Munir enjoyed the feeling of paternal care. During his two months in detention centers, he hadn't seen anyone he had known before the evacuation. It was good to be with people he was familiar with again.

Still, he was growing anxious about his family in Kabul. How would they make it through the winter? The increase in crime also worried him. He had talked with his wife about potentially moving back to their family village in Wardak. He and his wife had both been reluctant, however, since they wanted their children to keep studying, and the schools in the village were nowhere near as good as those in Kabul.

Still, the village was safe and quiet these days, he said. Everyone there who had supported the Ghani government was mostly staying home and trying not to draw attention to themselves. Everyone from the neighboring villages who supported the Taliban, or at least all the men, had moved to Kabul or Kandahar now that the Taliban had taken over. They were hoping for jobs or other spoils of war. Of course, many were likely to be disappointed, Munir concluded. The only Taliban who were getting rich and living comfortably were the top leaders. It seemed likely that the peace that had settled over the country in the months following the rise of the Taliban government was likely to break at some point. Taliban soldiers were not getting paid, and their families were facing some of the same hardships that everyone else was with the impending winter.

Somewhat surprisingly, the one thing Munir was able to do was continue his work for UNICEF in Kabul. Since many of the work staff had already gone remote during the COVID pandemic, they were able to accommodate Munir living twelve time zones away. He continued to manage forty-six social workers in provinces around the country who were supporting the Taliban government's attempts to protect children, all working on projects valued at $1.5 million. He was grateful for the continued income though there was barely enough to cover his family in Kabul, let alone to contribute to his brother's household.

The Taliban government seemed desperate for international aid to continue flowing. While they had demanded that UNICEF and other organizations shut down any programs that were associated with gender, many programs quietly continued. Munir explained, "Sometimes we are playing with them. We just explain what we do in a different way."

It also helped that much of the work was being done in provinces, working closely with local authorities, and each of the provinces had a very different set of Taliban running it. Some were far more open to international programming than others, particularly when it brought funds to remote districts.

"It's not like there is a law," Munir said. "All the Taliban are different. Some let us continue our work, in other provinces they stop it. My interpretation of Islam is different than anyone else's. And each Taliban is just doing what they think Islam is, it's not centralized at all. In one village, I heard the Taliban came and put an attendance sheet up at the mosque and said each man must come to the mosque five times a day and pray, otherwise they will be beaten. This is not from the Koran, it's just something they have made up, but no one will challenge them.

"In Kabul they are not demanding that men grow beards, but they are in other provinces," he continued. "There is no system to it."

Initially, the Taliban was only sporadically enforcing the rule that women could only travel accompanied by a male relative, a mahram—a rule they had imposed during their previous government, but there were concerns that they might reimplement this practice more aggressively.[1] Since Munir and his brothers were no longer in Kabul, and his wife's father was in their village in Wardak, that would mean the only male relative would be Munir's young son. If the Taliban did not accept him as an escort, his wife might not even be allowed to go out to the market anymore. It was difficult for the public to determine just how conservative and rigorous in their enforcement the Taliban was planning on being.

The Haqqani faction of the Taliban that was closely associated with the Pakistanis was considered more extreme. Other factions, particularly the one led by Mullah Baradar, one of the chief Taliban negotiators in Doha, were more moderate. With all these divides, however, it was hard to imagine that there would not be some sort of civil war, or at least a splintering of the government, Munir concluded. Either that, or just a breakdown of government services, or what was left of them. As the Taliban continued to fill positions at various ministries, it was clear the only priority was that all the appointees had an Islamic education from a madrassa.

"Perhaps at the minister level, it makes sense," said Munir, "since those are political positions. But now they are appointing these mullahs to fill positions as deputy ministers, directors, and other technical positions. What is a mullah going to do at the Ministry of Energy of Water? They need engineers."

With little hope of a functioning government in the near future, it made sense that the government would continue to rely on UNICEF and other international groups to keep delivering programs. The problem with his job was that he was now working from 8:00 p.m. to 2:00 a.m. most nights, attending Zoom meetings and responding to emails. Once work was over, it was difficult for him to get to sleep. He also wasn't good at sleeping during the day. The schedule left him constantly exhausted and even more depressed.

In California, the reality of his parolee status set in further. Two months after his arrival he still did not have a Social Security card, so he couldn't work. The application process had been delayed because he didn't have a passport or any other documents. As long as his status was temporary, he could not travel back to Afghanistan or anywhere else to see his family even if they could make it out. He couldn't even get a driver's license.

He had been advised by the resettlement agency he was working with that he should now apply for asylum. The government had expedited the asylum review process for recent Afghan parolees, and it was said that they were processing cases within forty-five days now. But still, he needed a lawyer to help him with the process, and he could not afford one of the private lawyers who worked on immigration cases. Even though the resettlement agency had contacts with legal groups that were supposed to help with the process pro bono, everyone Munir called said that they were booked solid with other Afghans seeking asylum. They hosted some information sessions that he attended, but the information sessions were not the same as actually getting his case moving.

One said that perhaps they could see him in January, but not before. "It feels like they are just playing with us," he concluded. "If everything goes perfectly, at the fastest, I could see my wife and children in eight months or a year." But of course, that many things could go wrong weighed on him: His asylum case could be rejected, or his wife might not be able to make it out of Kabul. Look at what had happened in the past six months. Who knows what the world would look like in a year?

Another human rights NGO agreed to review his case, and the man who took down his details said that it would likely be a long time before he could get his case resolved enough so that he could apply for his wife and children to join him. Perhaps it would be better to start looking for other countries that Munir could travel to and seek asylum and then try to have his family meet him there. The conversation was not encouraging.

During the day he mostly stayed in their apartment. He was tired and didn't know anyone in Sacramento. This left him halfway between Kabul and California, living in neither place. His brother's oldest children were fifteen and seventeen years old. They seemed to be adapting the best. They had studied English in Kabul and were working to catch up in the local high school. His youngest nephew didn't know as much English, "but kids learn fast," Munir concluded.

"I don't feel like myself here. I am depressed, anxious, stressed all at the same time." An Afghan friend came to visit from Kentucky and they drove to San Francisco. The city was impressive and the bay with its bridge was beautiful, but it was difficult for him to enjoy things like this. He had never been away from his family for more than four days. And while he spoke to them on the phone every day, it pained him when they asked, again and again, when he was coming back to Afghanistan.

"I don't know whether I've made the right choice or not, but I made this decision for my children's sake. It was urgent, I had no time to really think about it, and sometimes now, I regret it."

***

The word that came up repeatedly in the interviews we conducted in English during the last weeks of August was "chaos," from the Greek word for abyss or void. The airport was chaotic; the parolee hangars were chaotic; the US policy towards Afghan immigration was pure chaos. When we conducted interviews in Dari the word that was more common was *gadwadee* or disorder, messiness.

Over the course of our conversations and interviews, we came to believe that *gadwadee* and "disorder" are more accurate in describing those weeks. There was no order, no logic, no reasoning that could explain who made it out and who did not. In the crush of bodies at the airport, in the rushed lines at the passport offices, there was not a void, but a social and political world that no longer made sense. The political hierarchy was completely upended. The politicians, warlords, and gangsters who had run the Afghan government were gone, with no clear sense of who the new rulers were or what type of rule they would enforce.

Of course, that is not at all to say that the events that led up to the collapse of the government were disordered. In fact, they were logical and foreseeable: The Taliban was relentless in its belief that the Americans could be defeated, and the US government methodically sidelined Afghan leaders and misunderstood Afghan political culture, while enriching American and international defense contractors. These contactors, in turn, passed their riches on to Afghan politicians and warlords. These Afghan leaders consistently made logical decisions to reinforce their own positions politically, by negotiating deals that preserved a short-term status quo, with little interest in the long-term prosperity of the Afghan people.

What followed the initial two weeks of the evacuation was more in line with the English understanding of chaos: An abyss opened up for those who were in Afghanistan, waiting for visas that would likely never be processed, waiting for responses to emails that would never come, waiting in airport hangars to be transferred to the next detention center, those who were in detention centers waiting to be assigned new homes for resettlement, those who were in small American towns and big cities, in dingy apartments, with no job prospects and little chance of seeing their family members again in the coming years. They could file petitions with the State Department, their supporters could write letters to their congressional representatives, and advocates could send out scathing tweets, but ultimately, these too all seemed to end up in the abyss.

Later, among those who had been the key decision-makers on the Afghan and US government sides, there was a spirited and inconsequential debate over who was at fault. Khalilzad stepped down from his role as special representative on October 18 and was attacked by many both within the US government and Afghanistan for negotiating a weak deal that led to the collapse. Khalilzad, for his part, went on a media tour trying to rehabilitate his image and put the blame on the Ghani government. "President Ghani made the choice that he did, that caused the forces to disintegrate in Kabul," he said.[2]

Ghani's vice president, Amrullah Saleh, shot back, saying that Khalilzad "was the architect of the grand deception scheme," echoing the sentiments of many in Kabul who still felt there had been some sort of plot by Khalilzad to undermine the government.[3] Mohib reappeared in December and gave an interview on Voice of America in Dari where he claimed, "Unfortunately, Zalmai Khalilzad was bringing the Taliban to Kabul, and he even was telling us, do not put up a defense."[4] His demeanor in the interview was defiant as he criticized Khalilzad's role and the United States more generally. A day later, in a far more subdued appearance on CBS in an interview conducted in English, he concluded, almost with a shrug, "I felt that our partners, and the United States included, believed in a democratic Afghanistan, a place where we were going to preserve the gains of the last twenty years. I thought those gains meant something."[5] In the days that followed, there were also rumors that Ghani had hired a PR firm in New York and was preparing for a series of interviews in January to rehabilitate his image.

Many Westerners like to write about the timelessness of Afghanistan, how it is the graveyard of empires and seems to them to be frozen in a previous century, but the reality is that history moves incredibly quickly. By that point, just four months after he had walked away from the presidency, fewer and fewer people seemed to care. That part of Afghan politics was now over. The Biden administration seemed mostly to hope that everyone would forget what a debacle the evacuation had been. Those who were still in Afghanistan were too busy worrying about feeding themselves that winter and hoping that the collapse of the Afghani didn't wipe out all their savings. Those who had made it to the United States or other Western countries were trying to figure out how to get new IDs and jobs to support their families.

Now, six months after the collapse, as we continue to text and call each other and our friends, it does not feel like an end as much as a continuation of the disorder of the evacuation. The UN, the World Bank, and other key international organizations remain torn. Do they refuse to acknowledge the Taliban based on their opposition to their oppressive policies towards women and minorities? Or do they attempt to work with the group to assist the tens of millions of Afghans who are in danger of starvation?[6]

A few diplomatic missions have returned to Kabul, and they occasionally complain that the Taliban still have not opened secondary schools for girls, but most of these statements are rather bland and seem aimed at not offending the new government. Some international organizations have started (or restarted) projects, particularly with humanitarian aims, many trying to prevent Afghans from starving. These projects mostly try to avoid interacting with the government—for instance, there is none of the support directly to ministries that was so extensive during the Karzai and Ghani periods. Still, any project providing aid in Afghanistan is indirectly helping Taliban rule. Even if it's just by keeping the population from starving, it all supports their narrative that they can provide a stable Afghanistan that the United States and their billions of dollars could not.

We recently were on the phone with a young American who worked for a small NGO focused on generating small-scale hydropower, and he was bragging about how quickly he had been able to get his team working again in the country. "The Taliban can be reasonable," he said. "You just need to know who to talk to and how to talk to them."

Of course, what he really meant was that they had paid some bribes to get their projects moving again. Sure, he was helping some people in some of these rural areas who really do need help, but he seemed to completely ignore the fact that by working with the Taliban, and particularly by paying them bribes, he was only strengthening their position, making it likely that their oppressive rule would continue. At times we both think perhaps this is the right approach, but it's so much more complicated than he seemed to realize. Perhaps that's always been the problem with internationals in Afghanistan—it's always more complicated than they realize.

Even those international groups that have remained the most committed to opposing Taliban rule—the human rights groups and the women's groups in particular—there is so little media attention on Afghanistan that their messages often get reduced to one or two points. Many remain focused on the fact that girls' high schools are not open, but fewer are discussing the fact that non-Pashtuns are being targeted by the current regime. Retributive killings continue and minorities in particular areas have been forced from their homes.

These groups are opposed to any sort of diplomatic engagement with the Taliban, but many others in the international community seem more open to it. The Taliban remain fractured, and the more moderate members of the government have been reaching out to international groups. For the United States in particular, there is a sense among officials that so-called "normalized" relationships with the Taliban would make the Biden administration look better, since it would suggest that the decision to pull out quickly and completely was not as disastrous as it seemed at the time. Of course, in early 2022, these same moderate Taliban officials said that girls would be allowed to return to school in March. But when they arrived, the doors remained shut. The hard-liners, who remain the most powerful faction, decided at the last minute to keep them closed. So, many in the international community remain divided on how to approach the Taliban.

For Afghans, like Arsalan, who are still in the country, and for many who are out but still have family there, the debate doesn't really seem to make sense: You must do what you need to survive. If that means being respectful to a young Talib fighter at a checkpoint or trying to get a passport through the Taliban-controlled passport office, then that is what you must do. A new order has arrived, whether they like it or not.

PART VII

KABUL

ARSALAN—MARCH 13, 2022:

Spending the last seven months having long conversations and interviews with people about leaving their homes, it's hard not to despair. This time of year, as Kabul slowly warms and the snows begin to melt, is usually the most hopeful. And while there is relief that we've made it through the first winter with the Taliban, it still feels very different from last year.

I realized that in the months that followed the Taliban's takeover, we were all somewhat shell-shocked. The only way to survive was to hope that things would improve and that the Taliban would become more moderate, but they haven't. In fact, my friend who works at the Ministry of Education was outside the ministry building with one of the Taliban deputy ministers. There was a long line of teachers who had not been paid in months, hoping to get some of the salaries that they were owed. It was a hot day, and they looked miserable standing out there, holding out hope that they might get their back pay or even just a small handout.

The Taliban minister saw them and laughed. "I enjoy seeing these people suffer like this," he said, "they are the puppets of the West and deserve to sweat in the sun." For him, anyone who did anything for the previous government, even working as a teacher, was just a pawn of the Americans and deserved only misery. This is how it will be, we are starting to realize.

Last month, my wife gave birth to our first child—a girl. And things changed again for me.

While, famously, most Afghans say that they prefer sons to daughters, when we learned from the ultrasound that it was a girl, I was excited. I don't have much experience with babies, but boys seem loud and messy. Girls seem so much sweeter to me. So even though my wife expected me to be somewhat disappointed, I was thrilled when she arrived. Then I started to wonder: What would it be like to grow up here under Taliban rule?

All secondary schools remain closed to girls, and there is no way for her to get the education that her mother or I received. Even if they open the schools eventually, there are few jobs that women are permitted to have. As I thought about it and looked down at her, I realized it is impossible to even imagine a future for her here. This, more than anything else, pushed us back into action.

Almost immediately, I started to try to get a passport for her, even though everyone has been discussing how difficult it is to get a passport these days. Luckily, I had a friend who had a contact in the passport office who had gotten him passports in the past. When I contacted him, he said that for two thousand dollars, he could get me a passport. This seemed reasonable compared to what I had heard in the past. Then he sent me a message to tell me that the deal was off—the machine that printed out the passports was no longer working, and they are not sure when they can get someone with the international experience to come to fix it.

Now people are stuck with no way to get out of the country, even if they can get a visa from some country in the West.

Then I heard that a very few Afghan embassies abroad were still handing out passports. In many cases, these embassies were not loyal to the Taliban and were filled with Ghani officials who were acting almost as if the Taliban had never come. They were handing out passports with the Afghan seal on them, and, it was said, these passports were being accepted by Western countries. I wondered if there was a way to get one from one of these embassies.

Around this time, my family finally agreed that perhaps we should consider splitting up, so that some of us could get out. My younger sister applied to several universities in Turkey, but the Turkish embassy in Kabul would not issue her a visa. So instead, we got her and my mother a medical visa to Pakistan. If you tell them you need to go to some hospital in Pakistan, that is the easiest way to get there. Even then, however, the Taliban sometimes do not let women travel without a mahram, or male relative as a chaperone. The Taliban recently stopped an entire group of women from AUAF who were trying to leave the country, even though they had legitimate visas for Qatar. I had to convince a cousin of mine who has family in Pakistan to accompany them.

They are staying with his family, hoping to get my sister a student visa from the Turkish embassy there. The first time they applied at the embassy, they were rejected, because they said we did not have enough money, but we reapplied with some documents from my brother and the deed to our home. We are waiting to hear and hoping it will come through soon.

If they get there, I'm still pretty sure that I could buy a Turkish visa on the black market for $4,000 or even $6,000. It's gotten expensive, particularly for Afghans, since hundreds of commanders and politically powerful Afghans and their families have all moved to Turkey and bought these expensive houses and live these lavish lifestyles. Now the government assumes, if you are an Afghan, you have the money to pay their fees. It used to be if you bought a home for $250,000 they would give you citizenship, but now they have raised it to $400,000. Once there I could also apply to some graduate program and stay as a part-time student. My wife and I discussed going there and trying to continue my work while waiting for my SIV application to be processed, but it would be expensive.

If I buy a property in Istanbul, I can get visas for my mother and father too, but we would have no money to spend on other things. All of this will take time, and I worry about leaving my parents alone here. Plus, what will happen to our house or our farmland once we leave? We didn't want to split the family up, but perhaps if we do that in the short term, we can be together again eventually.

We had a fairly good life in Afghanistan, and I hear from friends who are struggling to adapt abroad. One of my friends in Sweden is required by the resettlement program to spend long hours studying Swedish, and he doesn't even want to stay in Sweden. It's not just an economic and cultural challenge. Most of these countries don't want to see more Afghan immigrants; we know this. One of my friends was beaten up by a police officer in Turkey recently, and the whole time he was swearing at him, telling him to go back to Afghanistan.

If we did get out, it's possible my wife would not be able to see her parents again. It would be difficult for my daughter to grow up not seeing her grandparents or cousins. If we leave anytime soon, she will have no memory of

Afghanistan. She will not know what it means to be Afghan. We can tell her about it and share photos, and certainly we will speak Dari, but she will not sit in the orchards I played in when I was growing up, nor know what the water tastes like coming down the stream from the mountain, still icy from the snow.

At the same time, somehow it seems like things are still getting worse. The Taliban came to the orphanage where I volunteer and told them they were no longer allowed to house girls there. It is "improper" for girls to be on their own, the officials told them; they should be with their families if they are under fourteen, but if they are over that they should be married. But where do they want them to go? These girls have no family or, if they did, it was family that abused them. The Taliban intend to marry the older ones off to their leaders. We've been looking for families to take the girls in. It's a slow process, since it's a lot to ask of someone these days when people can barely feed themselves.

Some mornings in Kabul, I wake up now and think, perhaps things can continue like this. But more and more, I wake up and see my sister no longer able to work, my wife and sister not free to travel alone or able to study at the university, and I think, I can't raise a child like this.

But is there really a way out that would keep us a family? Munir is now thousands of miles away from his children; Ismaeil's brothers are scattered around the world. What languages will Amena's children speak when they grow up? Will they know Dari? Will they know Afghanistan?

I think of all the things the war did, the civilians it killed, the homes it destroyed, but also the opportunities it provided, and in the end, it picked up these lives and scattered them across the globe.

It's like waking up from a deep sleep in an unfamiliar room.

And now, we are all left, trying to make some sense of it all.

AFTERWORD

The year and a half since the collapse of the Afghan Republic has brought a new type of suffering to the people of Afghanistan. This makes us all the more grateful to everyone who helped us write this book before, during, and after the collapse of the Afghan Republic.

Of course, our deepest gratitude is to those Afghans who continue to endure the repercussions of the return of the Taliban and who spent hours on the phone, over WhatsApp, and in person discussing their stories. Beginning in 2016, we interviewed over 150 SIV applicants or eligible Afghans considering applying for an SIV. In early 2021 we began to design a project that would interview and formally track around thirty Afghans who were currently going through the application process but were also considering other ways of fleeing the country. As events in Afghanistan accelerated, this project soon evolved into a series of ongoing conversations, more than two hundred additional interviews, and countless text, email, and WhatsApp exchanges with the original thirty applicants we were looking at, but also friends, colleagues, and acquaintances. We then realized we needed to tell Arsalan's story as well as the story of the others we had been in conversation with.

As such, we are profoundly grateful to everyone who spoke to us, particularly during those moments when their lives were turning upside down. There are too many to name here and doing so would be dangerous for those who remain behind, and even for those who have made it out but still have loved ones in the country. We remain hopeful that the Taliban's repressive authoritarian tactics will ultimately bring their own downfall, but until that day, most of those who contributed to this book will remain anonymous.

We are also grateful for our enthusiastic publishing team at Rowman & Littlefield, and the friends and colleagues who supported us as we worked on this book.

Our wonderful families and children, in particular, were patient and brought us joy along the way.

In the meantime, we have watched in dismay as much of the international aid to Afghanistan remains frozen and the Taliban's increasingly oppressive rule seems to have been largely accepted by the international community: After banning girls initially from secondary schools, women are now locked out of universities and cannot work for NGOs. At the same time, while many Afghans who fled are thankful for the hospitality they have received in their new homes, they continue to experience isolation and racism, many are deeply in debt and underemployed considering their educations and experiences, and they continue to try to support family members who remain behind. The international community, and Americans in particular, should not turn away.

Since finalizing the manuscript of this book, Munir moved to Los Angeles to find better work. He has not yet been able to see his wife or children, including his daughter who was born after he left the country.

After spending eight months in the processing center in Dubai, Najeeb's wife and brother both were finally able to reunite with Najeeb in Texas. Najeeb is on track to graduate from law school this year.

Amena and her family are still in Germany, where she hopes to again be allowed to practice medicine one day.

Ismaeil was able to visit his granddaughters last summer, but he has little hope of reuniting with the rest of his family.

Jalil and Sahar have not been able to find a way out of Afghanistan, and the stress of the situation has led them to separate.

Zeinab was reunited with her husband, Ali, after almost a year of separation, and in October she finished the half Ironman world championships in Utah.

Arsalan, Farah, and their baby daughter remain in Kabul.

—*Kabul and Brattleboro, February 2023*

Notes

Chapter 1

1. Monsutti, *War and Migration*.
2. Some of the best accounts of this era include, Suhrke, *When More Is Less*; Rashid, *Descent into Chaos*; Gopal, *No Good Men among the Living*; Chandrasekaran, *Little America*; Strick van Linschoten and Kuehn, *An Enemy We Created*.
3. Strick van Linschoten and Kuehn, *An Enemy We Created*.
4. Coburn, *Losing Afghanistan*.
5. UN High Commissioner for Refugees, "UNHCR Afghan Refugee Statistics."
6. Abu-Lughod, *Do Muslim Women Need Saving?*
7. Wimpelmann, *The Pitfalls of Protection*.
8. For a thorough discussion of Afghan feminisms and their fraught relationship with Western versions of feminism, see Ahsan-Tirmizi, *Pious Peripheries*.
9. World Health Organization, "Health System Programmes—Afghanistan."
10. Hoodfar and Oates, "Protecting Education Should Be at the Centre of Peace Negotiations in Afghanistan."
11. Ruttig, "Schools on the Frontline."
12. USAID, "Education—Afghanistan."
13. World Bank, "Women's Role in Afghanistan's Future: Taking Stock of Achievements and Continued Challenges."
14. Woodward, *Obama's Wars*; Malkasian, *The American War in Afghanistan*.

Chapter 2

1. Stack, "The Soldiers Came Home Sick. The Government Denied It Was Responsible."
2. Coburn, *Under Contract*.
3. Filkins, "'The Poo Pond.'"
4. Chatterjee, "Mission Essential, Translators Expendable."
5. Shachtman, "Unlimited Talk, Only $679 Million."
6. Coburn, *Under Contract*.
7. Chatterjee, "Mission Essential, Translators Expendable."
8. See chapters 6 and 13 in particular in Malkasian, *The American War in Afghanistan*.

9. Malkasian, *The American War in Afghanistan*, 295.

10. Shachtman, "Unlimited Talk, Only $679 Million."

11. Watkins, "Lessons from the Collapse of Afghanistan's Security Forces."

Chapter 3

1. Rashid, *Taliban*.

2. USAID, "Promote."

3. Ariana News, "Taliban Abduct 30 Passengers in Zabul."

4. European Asylum Support Office, *Afghanistan Key Socio-Economic Indicators, Focus on Kabul City, Mazar-e Sharif and Herat City*.

5. World Inequality Database, "Afghanistan."

6. European Asylum Support Office, *Afghanistan Key Socio-Economic Indicators, Focus on Kabul City, Mazar-e Sharif and Herat City*.

7. Asey, "The Price of Inequality."

8. Purkiss, "The Afghan Officials' Families with Luxury Pads in Dubai."

9. US Embassy in Kabul, "US Embassy Cables."

10. Rasmussen, "Afghanistan's Female Marathon Runner Defies Danger to Go the Distance."

Chapter 4

1. Najafizada, "Afghan Youth, the Face of a Transformed Nation."

2. Reid, "Afghanistan 1400."

3. Falke, "Where There's a Will, There's a Way to Go Online."

4. For more on patterns of local governance in Afghanistan, see Barfield, *Afghanistan*; Murtazashvili, *Informal Order and the State in Afghanistan*.

5. Coburn and Larson, *Derailing Democracy in Afghanistan*.

6. Mohib, "A Grassroots Democracy for Afghanistan."

Chapter 5

1. Oppel, Wafa, and Rahimi, "20 Dead as Taliban Attackers Storm Kabul Offices."

2. Janofsky, "Bush Proposes Broader Language Training."

3. US Government Accountability Office, "Afghan and Iraqi Special Immigrants: More Information on Their Resettlement Outcomes Would Be Beneficial."

4. Congressional Research Service, "Iraqi and Afghan Special Immigrant Visa Programs."

5. US Department of State, "Special Immigrant Visas for Afghans—Who Were Employed by/on Behalf of the U.S. Government."

6. Coburn and Gill, "Uncompensated Allies."

Chapter 6

1. Coburn, *Losing Afghanistan*.

2. Brown, "Aiding Afghan Local Governance: What Went Wrong?"

3. Brown.
4. Jackson, *Negotiating Survival.*
5. Fishstein and Wilder, "Winning Hearts and Minds?"
6. Jackson.
7. World Bank, "Development Projects."
8. Ghani, "Innovations for Successful Societies—interview."
9. Ghani, "Innovations for Successful Societies—interview."
10. Jeong, "The Man Who Thought He Could Fix Afghanistan."
11. Bjelica, "Is the Citizens' Charter the Right Vehicle for Reconciliation?"
12. Beath, Christia, and Enikolopov, "The National Solidarity Program."
13. Afghan government website, "Citizens' Charter Program."
14. "Afghanistan's Citizens' Charter Program."
15. Bjelica, "Is the Citizens' Charter the Right Vehicle for Reconciliation?"
16. Graf, "What Afghanistan Teaches Us about Evidence-Based Policy."

CHAPTER 7

1. BBC News, "Trump Visits US Troops in Afghanistan on Thanksgiving."
2. Clark, "The Eid Ceasefire."
3. Yaad, "Peace Movement Blames Foreign Countries for Afghan War."
4. Sabawoon, "Going Nationwide."
5. Clark, "The Eid Ceasefire."
6. Crowley, "A Veteran Diplomat, a 'Tragic Figure,' Battles Critics in the U.S. and Afghanistan."
7. Radio Free Europe/Radio Liberty, "U.S. 'to End Contacts' with Afghan Security Adviser Mohib Following Verbal Attack."
8. Coll and Entous, "The Secret History of the U.S. Diplomatic Failure in Afghanistan."
9. In April 2019, talks between the Taliban and the government again collapsed due to arguments over the size of the delegation coming from Kabul. The halt due to this seemingly minor issue led some to question whether either side was really committed to peace in that moment—the Taliban because they had military momentum and were taken new territory daily and Ghani because he was up for reelection that year and by being reelected would have a stronger mandate at the negotiating table. Walsh, "Amid a Spike in Violence, Have Afghan Peace Talks Lost Momentum?"
10. Miller and Smith, "Behind Trump's Taliban Debacle."
11. Coll and Entous, "The Secret History of the U.S. Diplomatic Failure in Afghanistan."
12. US Department of State, "Agreement for Bringing Peace to Afghanistan between the Islamic Emirate of Afghanistan Which Is Not Recognized by the United States as a State and Is Known as the Taliban and the United States of America."
13. UNAMA and UNHCR, "Afghanistan: Protection of Civilians in Armed Conflict."
14. BBC News, "Taliban Prisoner Release."
15. Gibbons-Neff, Barnes, and Goldman, "She Killed an American in 2012. Why Was She Freed in the Taliban Deal?"; Brooking, "Why Was a Negotiated Peace Always Out

of Reach in Afghanistan?: Opportunities and Obstacles, 2001–21"; Lee and Tucker, "Was Biden Handcuffed by Trump's Taliban Deal in Doha?"

16. Mashal and Faizi, "Afghanistan to Release Last Taliban Prisoners, Removing Final Hurdle to Talks."

17. Radio Azadi, "Afghan Government Unveils Negotiating Team for Taliban Talks."

18. Coll and Entous, "The Secret History of the U.S. Diplomatic Failure in Afghanistan."

19. Coll and Entous, "The Secret History of the U.S. Diplomatic Failure in Afghanistan."

20. Bezhan, "Ashraf Ghani."

21. Murtazashvili, "The Collapse of Afghanistan."

22. Shear, Jakes, and Sullivan, "Inside the Afghan Evacuation."

CHAPTER 8

1. In the years that have followed, several resettlement agencies have focused on helping Afghans get their transcripts and credentials translated into English to help them secure positions more in line with their experiences. Despite these efforts, however, many Afghan immigrants found that Najeeb's path was the most effective: Study at a local community college, gain some initial credits, and use that to begin building your resume all over again. It was disheartening, but for many, it seemed like the only way.

2. Forty-eight percent had worked for the US military, the rest had worked for the State Department, USAID, or in support of US efforts in some other way. No One Left Behind, "No One Left Behind 2020 Annual SIV Research Survey."

3. US Government Accountability Office, "Afghan and Iraqi Special Immigrants: More Information on Their Resettlement Outcomes Would Be Beneficial."

4. No One Left Behind, "No One Left Behind 2020 Annual SIV Research Survey."

CHAPTER 9

1. UNHCR, "Frequently Asked Questions: Asylum and Refugee Status."

2. While there was no formal process that gave those who had served in combat zones any special status, it did become clear to many applicants that if you had a US service member, in particular, pushing your case, there were informal ways to get the process sped up. Speaking with the director of No One Left Behind in 2016, he told Noah that each veteran, if they lobbied their congresspeople, could potentially put enough pressure on the system to get an application processed faster, but that this was really only true on a case-by-case basis—each veteran could effectively get one translator or contractor out, if they put their minds to it. And many military service people were doing this, sending letters and making phone calls, and there were certainly cases where this approach was successful.

3. US Department of State, "Special Immigrant Visas for Afghans—Who Were Employed by/on Behalf of the U.S. Government."

4. Islamic Emirate of Afghanistan, "Urgent Warning: Taliban Night Letter—Paktika."

5. International Refugee Assistance Project, "IRAP Lawsuit Reveals Government Flouts Congress, Reports Inaccurate Processing Times in SIV Program."

6. International Refugee Assistance Project, "Afghan and Iraqi Allies v. Pompeo."

7. Babur and O'Donnell, "Afghans Seeking Asylum Buy Fake Taliban Threat Letters."

8. Matthieu Aikins provides an in depth look at several of these pathways in *The Naked Don't Fear the Water*.

9. Childs, "European Countries Deported 70,000 People to Afghanistan Because It Was 'Safe'"; Duetsche Welle, "Second Collective Deportation of Rejected Asylum Seekers from Germany Arrives in Afghanistan."

10. Siebold and Chalmers, "Six EU Countries Warn against Open Door for Afghan Asylum Seekers."

CHAPTER 10

1. Lawrence, "Understaffed, Uncoordinated."

2. Bier, "Trump Cut Muslim Refugees 91%, Immigrants 30%, Visitors by 18%."

3. US Department of State, "Review of the Afghan Special Immigrant Visa Program."

4. US Department of State and Department of Homeland Security, "Joint Department of State/Department of Homeland Security Report: Status of the Afghan Special Immigrant Visa Program."

5. US Department of State, "Review of the Afghan Special Immigrant Visa Program."

CHAPTER 11

1. Watkins, "Lessons from the Collapse of Afghanistan's Security Forces."

2. Nordland, "Taliban End Takeover of Kunduz after 15 Days."

3. Amnesty International, "No Escape: War Crimes and Civilian Harm during the Fall of Afghanistan to the Taliban."

4. White House, "Executive Order on Rebuilding and Enhancing Programs to Resettle and Refugees and Planning for the Impact of Climate Change on Migration."

5. White House.

6. Shear et al., "Miscue after Miscue, U.S. Exit Plan Unravels."

7. Vittori, "Corruption and Self-Dealing in Afghanistan and Other U.S.-Backed Security Sectors."

8. Gannon, "US Left Afghan Airfield at Night, Didn't Tell New Commander."

9. Shear et al., "Miscue after Miscue, U.S. Exit Plan Unravels."

10. Shear et al.

11. US Department of State, "Operation Allies Refuge."

12. Schmitt and Steinhauer, "Afghan Visa Applicants Arrive in U.S. after Years of Waiting."

13. US Department of State, "U.S. Refugee Admissions Program Priority 2 Designation for Afghan Nationals."

14. US Department of State, "Briefing with Senior State Department Officials on the U.S. Refugee Admissions Program Priority 2 (P-2) Designation for Afghan Nationals."

15. Hartung, "Profits of War: Corporate Beneficiaries of the Post-9/11 Pentagon Spending Surge."

16. Coburn, *Under Contract*.

CHAPTER 12

1. While many remained silent, a few members of Ghani's inner circle later did come forward with their own accounts of Ghani's actions on those final days. The most notable and widely discussed in the early days after the collapse was a series of long interviews by Ghani's finance minister, Khalid Payenda. These accounts largely confirmed what many others in the country already suspected about the disarray of the government in its final days.

2. Madi, Khalid, and Nizami, "Chaos and Confusion."

3. Cullison and Shah, "Taliban Commander Who Led Attack on Afghan City Was Released from Prison Last Year, Officials Say."

4. Watkins, "Lessons from the Collapse of Afghanistan's Security Forces."

5. *PBS NewsHour*, "Afghanistan 'Ready' for Taliban Violence after US Withdrawal, Afghan President Says."

6. Shear, Jakes, and Sullivan, "Inside the Afghan Evacuation."

7. Sohail, "Exclusive: The Untold Story of How Afghan President Ashraf Ghani Fled the Country."

8. Shashikumar, "The Great Afghan Betrayal"; Shear, Jakes, and Sullivan, "Inside the Afghan Evacuation."

9. Rasooli, "Doha Deal Led to Collapse of Former Govt: Mohib."

10. Madi, Khalid, and Nizami, "Chaos and Confusion."

11. Ray and Dangor, "Afghanistan Embassy in Tajikistan Demands Arrest of Ashraf Ghani over 'Treasury Theft.'"

12. Al Jazeera, "Ghani Unlikely to Have Fled Kabul with Millions in Cash."

13. Salem, John, Lister, and Ritchie, "Former Afghan President Ashraf Ghani Emerges in the UAE."

CHAPTER 13

1. Coleman, "Video Shows a Crowd Scaling a Jet Bridge to Try to Force Its Way onto a Flight out of Kabul as Afghanistan Falls to the Taliban."

2. According to the Turkish press, there were forty Afghan government officials on the flight. Atilla, "Turkey Helps Senior Afghan Officials Leave Country."

CHAPTER 14

1. White House, "Remarks by President Biden on Afghanistan."

2. Ali and Pamuk, "Hundreds of Afghan Security Forces Help at Kabul Airport, U.S. Says."

3. Shear et al., "Miscue after Miscue, U.S. Exit Plan Unravels."

4. Mahshie, "Evacuating to Freedom."

5. Mahshie.

6. Seligman, Desiderio, and Banco, "Hundreds of U.S. Citizens, Afghan Commandos Successfully Evacuated through Secret CIA Base."

7. Shear, Jakes, and Sullivan, "Inside the Afghan Evacuation."

8. Shear et al., "Miscue after Miscue, U.S. Exit Plan Unravels."

9. Akerman, *The Fifth Act.*

10. Mann, *Operation Pineapple Express.*

11. Nissenbaum, "In Kabul, Private Rescue Efforts Grow Desperate as Time to Evacuate Afghans Runs Out; Defense Contractor Erik Prince Charges $6,500 a Person, Other Groups' Planes Leave Kabul Empty."

12. Cooper and Schmitt, "Witnesses to the End."

CHAPTER 15

1. Joscelyn and Roggio, "Taliban's Special Forces Outfit Providing 'Security' at Kabul Airport."

2. Shear, Jakes, and Sullivan, "Inside the Afghan Evacuation"; Hashemi et al., "American Forces Keep up Airlift under High Threat Warnings."

3. Shear, "'We Will Not Forgive,' Biden Says, Vowing Retaliation for Kabul Attack."

4. Schmitt and Cooper, "Pentagon Acknowledges Aug. 29 Drone Strike in Afghanistan Was a Tragic Mistake That Killed 10 Civilians."

5. GIZ. "Afghanistan: Efforts to Find Alternative Evacuation Routes Continue."

6. Pikulicka-Wilczewska, "International Employers Accused of Abandoning Afghan Staff."

7. Kirka and Lawless, "Whistleblower: As Afghanistan Fell, UK Abandoned Supporters."

8. Nissenbaum, "In Kabul, Private Rescue Efforts Grow Desperate as Time to Evacuate Afghans Runs Out; Defense Contractor Erik Prince Charges $6,500 a Person, Other Groups' Planes Leave Kabul Empty."

9. Swaine, "How an Instagram Star's $7 Million Mission to Rescue Afghan Civilians Struggled to Get off the Ground."

10. Tarabay and Wadhams, "Facebook and a LinkedIn Co-Founder Funded a Suddenly Packed Afghan Airlift."

CHAPTER 16

1. Glinski, "12 Million Angry Men."

2. Shaheed, "Sources Allege 100 Civilians Killed after Fall of Spin Boldak."

3. Cheng and Khan, "Hundreds of Afghans Gather Outside Passport Office as Taliban Resumes Issuing Travel Documents."

4. Watkins, "An Assessment of Taliban Rule at Three Months."

CHAPTER 17

1. Johnson, Nichols, and Swan, "'A Living Hell.'"

2. Machi, "'Tonight, We'll Be Maxed Out.' Inside Ramstein Air Base's Push to Host Thousands of Evacuees from Afghanistan."

3. Feroz, "A Notorious CIA-Armed Militia Finds a Home in the U.S."

4. Eddy, "'Finally, I Am Safe.'"

5. Lawson, "'An Unprecedented Mobilization.'"

6. Seligman et al., "FBI Agents Question Afghan Rescue Groups."

7. Joint Base McGuire-Dix, "Final Environmental Assessment for Temporary Shelter of Afghan Special Immigrants."

CHAPTER 18

1. Saif, "Taliban Asks Women Healthcare Workers to Resume Duties."

2. Pal, "Afghan Women Should Not Work alongside Men, Senior Taliban Figure Says."

3. Franklin, "Female Government Workers in Kabul Told to Stay Home in Latest Taliban Rule."

4. Blue and Zucchino, "A Harsh New Reality for Afghan Women and Girls in Taliban-Run Schools."

5. Amnesty International, "No Escape: War Crimes and Civilian Harm during the Fall of Afghanistan to the Taliban."

CHAPTER 19

1. Solis, "Cornyn Meets with Afghans, Who Tell Him of the Many Left Behind in Their Homeland."

2. US Department of State, "Launch of the Sponsor Circle Program for Afghans."

3. International Refugee Assistance Project, "Private Sponsorship."

4. Associated Press, "Thousands of Afghans Seek Temporary US Entry, Only 100 Approved."

5. Cai and Kight, "U.S. Begins Denying Afghan Immigrants Seeking Humanitarian Parole."

6. Kight, "U.S. Will Now Allow Private Citizens to Sponsor Afghan Refugees."

7. International Refugee Assistance Project, "IRAP Files Lawsuit Demanding U.S. Government Protect Afghan Ally's Children from Taliban."

8. AfghanEvac, "Open Letter."

9. Mohibi, "Thousands Afghan Evacuees at Emirates Humanitarian City Seek Answers to Their U.S. Entry Status."

CHAPTER 20

1. In the months that followed, the Taliban began enforcing this requirement more forcefully in many areas.

2. Brennan and Schick, "Zalmay Khalilzad Sticks by His Taliban Deal, Says the U.S. Should Have Pressed President Ghani Harder."

3. Crowley, "A Veteran Diplomat, a 'Tragic Figure,' Battles Critics in the U.S. and Afghanistan."

4. Rasooli, "Doha Deal Led to Collapse of Former Govt: Mohib."

5. Watson,"Former Ghani Adviser Says Afghan Leaders Didn't See 'Writing on the Wall' of U.S. Withdrawal."

6. Coll, "A Year after the Fall of Kabul."

BIBLIOGRAPHY

Abu-Lughod, Lila. *Do Muslim Women Need Saving?* Cambridge: Harvard University Press, 2015.

AfghanEvac. "Open Letter." December 1, 2021. https://afghanevac.org/openletter/.

Ahsan-Tirmizi, Sonia. *Pious Peripheries: Runaway Women in Post-Taliban Afghanistan.* Stanford: Stanford University Press, 2021.

Aikins, Matthieu. *The Naked Don't Fear the Water: An Underground Journey with Afghan Refugees.* New York: Harper, 2022.

Akerman, Elliot. *The Fifth Act: America's End in Afghanistan:* New York: Penguin, 2022.

Ali, Idrees, and Humeyra Pamuk. "Hundreds of Afghan Security Forces Help at Kabul Airport, U.S. Says." Reuters, August 18, 2021. https://www.reuters.com/world/asia -pacific/hundreds-afghan-security-forces-help-kabul-airport-pentagon-says-2021 -08-17/.

Amnesty International. "No Escape: War Crimes and Civilian Harm during the Fall of Afghanistan to the Taliban." Amnesty International, 2021. https://www.amnesty .org/en/wp-content/uploads/2021/12/ASA1150252021ENGLISH.pdf.

Ariana News. "Taliban Abduct 30 Passengers in Zabul." February 24, 2015. https://www .ariananews.af/taliban-abduct-30-passengers-in-zabul/.

Asey, Tamim. "The Price of Inequality: The Dangerous Rural-Urban Divide in Afghanistan." *Global Security Review,* March 5, 2019. https://www.globalsecurityreview .com/inequality-dangerous-rural-urban-divide-afghanistan/.

Associated Press. "Thousands of Afghans Seek Temporary US Entry, Only 100 Approved." November 19, 2021. https://www.aljazeera.com/news/2021/11/19/ thousands-of-afghans-seek-temporary-us-entry-few-approved.

Atilla, Toygun. "Turkey Helps Senior Afghan Officials Leave Country." *Hürriyet Daily News,* August 20, 2021. https://www.hurriyetdailynews.com/turkey-helps-senior -afghan-officials-leave-country-167204.

Babur, Humayoon, and Lynne O'Donnell. "Afghans Seeking Asylum Buy Fake Taliban Threat Letters." AP News, November 22, 2015. https://apnews.com/article/6c4fd4 eae7284ac9b9453ce0040457dc.

Barfield, Thomas. *Afghanistan: A Cultural and Political History.* Princeton: Princeton University Press, 2012.

BBC News. "Taliban Prisoner Release: Afghan Government Begins Setting Free Last 400." August 14, 2020. https://www.bbc.com/news/world-asia-53775035.

BBC News. "Trump Visits US Troops in Afghanistan on Thanksgiving." November 29, 2019. https://www.bbc.com/news/world-asia-50594943.

Beath, Andrew, Fotini Christia, and Ruben Enikolopov. "The National Solidarity Program: Assessing the Effects of Community-Driven Development in Afghanistan." The World Bank, Office of the Chief Economist, September 18, 2015. https://doi.org/10.1596/1813-9450-7415.

Bezhan, Frud. "Ashraf Ghani: The Deeply Polarizing President Who Oversaw the Fall of Afghanistan." Radio Free Europe/Radio Liberty. Accessed December 7, 2021. https://gandhara.rferl.org/a/ashraf-ghani-afghan-president/31413459.html.

Bier, David J. "Trump Cut Muslim Refugees 91%, Immigrants 30%, Visitors by 18%." Cato Institute, December 7, 2018. https://www.cato.org/blog/trump-cut-muslim-refugees-91-immigrants-30-visitors-18.

Bjelica, Jelena. "Is the Citizens' Charter the Right Vehicle for Reconciliation? The Risks of Monetising Peace." Afghanistan Analysts Network, May 31, 2020. https://www.afghanistan-analysts.org/en/reports/rights-freedom/is-the-citizens-charter-the-right-vehicle-for-reconciliation-the-risks-of-monetising-peace/.

Blue, Victor J., and David Zucchino. "A Harsh New Reality for Afghan Women and Girls in Taliban-Run Schools." New York Times, September 20, 2021. https://www.nytimes.com/2021/09/20/world/asia/afghan-girls-schools-taliban.html.

Brennan, Margaret, and Camilla Schick. "Zalmay Khalilzad Sticks by His Taliban Deal, Says the U.S. Should Have Pressed President Ghani Harder." October 23, 2021. https://www.cbsnews.com/news/zalmay-khalilzad-sticks-by-taliban-deal-says-the-u-s-should-have-pressed-president-ghani-harder/.

Brooking, Steve. "Why Was a Negotiated Peace Always Out of Reach in Afghanistan?: Opportunities and Obstacles, 2001–21." Peaceworks. Washington, DC: US Institute of Peace, August 30, 2022.

Brown, Frances Z. "Aiding Afghan Local Governance: What Went Wrong?" Carnegie Endowment for International Peace, November 2021.

Cai, Sophia, and Stef W. Kight. "U.S. Begins Denying Afghan Immigrants Seeking Humanitarian Parole." Axios, December 9, 2021. https://www.axios.com/us-turns-away-afghans-66bf3aac-4c93-46b1-828b-e08d503c007c.html.

Chandrasekaran, Rajiv. Little America: The War within the War for Afghanistan. New York: Vintage, 2013.

Chatterjee, Pratap. "Mission Essential, Translators Expendable." Corpwatch, August 11, 2009. https://www.corpwatch.org/article/mission-essential-translators-expendable-0.

Cheng, Amy, and Haq Nawaz Khan. "Hundreds of Afghans Gather Outside Passport Office as Taliban Resumes Issuing Travel Documents." Washington Post. Accessed November 22, 2021. https://www.washingtonpost.com/world/2021/10/06/afghanistan-taliban-passport-refugee/.

Childs, Simon. "European Countries Deported 70,000 People to Afghanistan Because It Was 'Safe.'" Vice, August 19, 2021. https://www.vice.com/en/article/n7bmq7/europe-deported-70000-to-afghanistan-deeming-it-safe.

Chomsky, Noam, and Vijay Prashad. *The Withdrawal: Iraq, Libya, Afghanistan, and the Fragility of U.S. Power.* New York: The New Press, 2022.

Clark, Kate. "The Eid Ceasefire: Allowing Afghans to Imagine Their Country at Peace." Afghanistan Analysts Network, June 19, 2018. https://www.afghanistan-analysts.org/en/reports/war-and-peace/the-eid-ceasefire-allowing-afghans-to-imagine-their-country-at-peace/.

Coburn, Noah. *Losing Afghanistan: An Obituary for the Intervention.* Stanford: Stanford University Press, 2016.

———. "The Costs of Working with the Americans in Afghanistan: The United States' Broken Special Immigrant Visa Process." Brown University: Costs of War Project, 2021. https://watson.brown.edu/costsofwar/files/cow/imce/papers/2021/Costs%20of%20Working%20with%20Americans_Coburn_Costs%20of%20War.pdf.

———. *Under Contract: The Invisible Workers of America's Global War.* Stanford: Stanford University Press, 2018.

Coburn, Noah, and Peter Gill. "Uncompensated Allies: How Contracting Companies and U.S. Government Agencies Failed Third-Country Nationals in Afghanistan." Brown University: Costs of War Project, 2022.

Coburn, Noah, and Anna Larson. *Derailing Democracy in Afghanistan: Elections in an Unstable Political Landscape.* New York: Columbia University Press, 2014.

Coburn, Noah, and Timor Sharan. "Out of Harm's Way? Perspectives of the Special Immigrant Visa Program for Afghanistan." The Hollings Center for International Dialogue, July 2016.

Coleman, Ashley. "Video Shows a Crowd Scaling a Jet Bridge to Try to Force Its Way onto a Flight Out of Kabul as Afghanistan Falls to the Taliban." *Insider,* August 16, 2021. https://www.businessinsider.com/kabul-airport-crowd-scales-jet-bridge-try-escape-afghanistan-video-2021-8.

Coll, Steve. "A Year after the Fall of Kabul." *The New Yorker,* August 27, 2022. https://www.newyorker.com/news/daily-comment/a-year-after-the-fall-of-kabul.

Coll, Steve, and Adam Entous. "The Secret History of the U.S. Diplomatic Failure in Afghanistan." *The New Yorker,* December 10, 2021. https://www.newyorker.com/magazine/2021/12/20/the-secret-history-of-the-us-diplomatic-failure-in-afghanistan.

Congressional Research Service. "Iraqi and Afghan Special Immigrant Visa Programs." April 2, 2020.

Cooper, Helene, and Eric Schmitt. "Witnesses to the End." *New York Times,* November 7, 2021. https://www.nytimes.com/2021/11/07/us/politics/afghanistan-war-marines.html.

Crowley, Michael. "A Veteran Diplomat, a 'Tragic Figure,' Battles Critics in the U.S. and Afghanistan." *New York Times,* November 16, 2021. https://www.nytimes.com/2021/11/16/us/politics/zalmay-khalilzad-afghanistan-war.html.

Cullison, Alan, and Saeed Shah. "Taliban Commander Who Led Attack on Afghan City Was Released from Prison Last Year, Officials Say." *Wall Street Journal,* August 3, 2021. https://www.wsj.com/articles/taliban-commander-who-led-attack-on-afghan-city-was-released-from-prison-last-year-officials-say-11628010527.

Deutsche Welle. "Second Collective Deportation of Rejected Asylum Seekers from Germany Arrives in Afghanistan." January 24, 2017. https://www.dw.com/en /second-collective-deportation-of-rejected-asylum-seekers-from-germany-arrives -in-afghanistan/a-37248018.

Eddy, Melissa. "'Finally, I Am Safe': U.S. Air Base Becomes Temporary Refuge for Afghans." *New York Times*, September 1, 2021. https://www.nytimes.com/2021/09 /01/world/europe/us-airbase-germany-afghanistan.html.

European Asylum Support Office. *Afghanistan Key Socio-Economic Indicators, Focus on Kabul City, Mazar-e Sharif and Herat City: Country of Origin Information Report.* LU: Publications Office, 2020. https://data.europa.eu/doi/10.2847/497573.

Falke, Theresa. "Where There's a Will, There's a Way to Go Online: Afghanistan's Youth and New Media." Afghanistan Analysts Network, November 13, 2014. https: //www.afghanistan-analysts.org/en/reports/context-culture/where-theres-a-will -theres-a-way-to-go-online-afghanistans-youth-and-new-media/.

Feroz, Emran. "A Notorious CIA-Armed Militia Finds a Home in the U.S." *The American Prospect*, November 3, 2021. https://prospect.org/api/content/1b0a3746-3c2e-11ec -94cb-12f1225286c6/.

Filkins, Dexter. "'The Poo Pond.'" *New York Times*, At War Blog, May 26, 2010. https:// atwar.blogs.nytimes.com/2010/05/26/the-poo-pond/.

Fishstein, Paul, and Andrew Wilder. "Winning Hearts and Minds? Examining the Relationship between Aid and Security in Afghanistan." Medford, MA: Feinstein International Center, January 2012.

Franklin, Jonathan. "Female Government Workers in Kabul Told to Stay Home in Latest Taliban Rule." NPR, September 19, 2021. https://www.npr.org/2021/09/19 /1038685721/female-workers-kabul-stay-home-taliban-rule.

Gannon, Kathy. "US Left Afghan Airfield at Night, Didn't Tell New Commander." AP News, July 5, 2021. https://apnews.com/article/bagram-afghanistan-airfield-us -troops-f3614828364f567593251aaaa167e623.

Ghani, Ashraf. "Innovations for Successful Societies—Interview," Rushda Majeed. Princeton University, November 3, 2013. https://successfulsocieties.princeton.edu/ interviews/ashraf-ghani.

Gibbons-Neff, Thomas, Julian E. Barnes, and Adam Goldman. "She Killed an American in 2012. Why Was She Freed in the Taliban Deal?" *New York Times*, January 15, 2021. https://www.nytimes.com/2021/01/15/world/asia/afghanistan-prisoner -exchange-taliban.html.

GIZ (Deutsche Gesellschaft für Internationale Zusammenarbeit). "Afghanistan: Efforts to Find Alternative Evacuation Routes Continue." August 27, 2021. https://www .giz.de/en/mediacenter/100485.html.

Glinski, Stefanie. "12 Million Angry Men." *Foreign Policy*, October 28, 2021. https:// foreignpolicy.com/2021/10/28/afghanistan-taliban-justice-sharia/.

Gopal, Anand. *No Good Men among the Living: America, the Taliban, and the War through Afghan Eyes.* New York: Picador, 2015.

Government of the Islamic Republic of Afghanistan. "Citizens' Charter Program." Accessed August 25, 2022. https://www.ccnpp.org/.

Graf, Corinne. "What Afghanistan Teaches Us about Evidence-Based Policy." US Institute of Peace, December 2, 2021. https://www.usip.org/publications/2021/12/what-afghanistan-teaches-us-about-evidence-based-policy.

Hartung, William. "Profits of War: Corporate Beneficiaries of the Post-9/11 Pentagon Spending Surge." Watson Institute, September 13, 2021. https://watson.brown.edu/costsofwar/files/cow/imce/papers/2021/Profits%20of%20War_Hartung_Costs%20of%20War_Sept%2013%2C%202021.pdf.

Hashemi, Sayed Ziarmel, Lolita Baldor, Kathy Gannon, and Ellen Knickmeyer. "American Forces Keep up Airlift under High Threat Warnings." AP News, August 27, 2021. https://apnews.com/article/bombings-evacuations-kabul-bb32ec2b65b54ec24323e021c9b4a553.

Hoodfar, Homa, and Lauryn Oates. "Protecting Education Should Be at the Centre of Peace Negotiations in Afghanistan." The Conversation. Accessed June 16, 2021. http://theconversation.com/protecting-education-should-be-at-the-centre-of-peace-negotiations-in-afghanistan-161769.

International Refugee Assistance Project (IRAP). "Afghan and Iraqi Allies v. Pompeo: Challenging Systemic Delays in Deciding Special Immigrant Visa Applications." No date. Accessed December 4, 2021. https://refugeerights.org/news-resources/afghan-and-iraqi-allies-v-pompeo-challenging-the-systematic-delay-in-processing-of-special-immigrant-via-applications.

———. "IRAP Files Lawsuit Demanding U.S. Government Protect Afghan Ally's Children from Taliban." October 7, 2021. https://refugeerights.org/news-resources/irap-files-lawsuit-demanding-u-s-government-protect-afghan-allys-children-from-taliban.

———. "IRAP Lawsuit Reveals Government Flouts Congress, Reports Inaccurate Processing Times in SIV Program." June 12, 2019. https://refugeerights.org/news-resources/irap-lawsuit-reveals-government-flouts-congress-reports-inaccurate-processing-times-in-siv-program.

———. "Private Sponsorship." No date. Accessed December 9, 2021. https://refugeerights.org/issue-areas/private-sponsorship.

Islamic Emirate of Afghanistan. "Urgent Warning: Taliban Night Letter—Paktika." The Combating Terrorism Center, West Point. Accessed December 3, 2021. https://ctc.usma.edu/harmony-program/taliban-night-letter_paktika_one-original-language-2/.

Jackson, Ashley. *Negotiating Survival: Civilian-Insurgent Relations in Afghanistan.* London: Hurst, 2021.

Janofsky, Michael. "Bush Proposes Broader Language Training." *New York Times,* January 6, 2006. https://www.nytimes.com/2006/01/06/politics/bush-proposes-broader-language-training.html.

Al Jazeera. "Ghani Unlikely to Have Fled Kabul with Millions in Cash: Report." June 7, 2022. https://www.aljazeera.com/news/2022/6/7/ghani-unlikely-to-have-fled-kabul-with-millions-in-cashus-report.

Jeong, May. "The Man Who Thought He Could Fix Afghanistan." *POLITICO Magazine,* November/December 2017. http://politi.co/2iDOIV6.

Johnson, Glen, Hans Nichols, and Jonathan Swan. "'A Living Hell': Leaked Email Describes Squalid Afghan Refugee Conditions." *Axios*, August 24, 2021. https://www.axios.com/afghan-refugees-conditions-qatar-89cf31b7-3ff4-46f3-82e9-a6fc06494a2e.html.

Joint Base McGuire-Dix. "Final Environmental Assessment for Temporary Shelter of Afghan Special Immigrants." Lakehurst, NJ: Department of the Air Force. Accessed November 24, 2021. https://www.jbmdl.jb.mil/Portals/47/Final%20EA_Afghan%20Special%20Immigrants%20at%20JBMDL_With%20Appendices_30Aug2021.pdf.

Joscelyn, Thomas, and Bill Roggio. "Taliban's Special Forces Outfit Providing 'Security' at Kabul Airport." FDD's Long War Journal, August 22, 2021. https://www.longwarjournal.org/archives/2021/08/talibans-special-forces-outfit-providing-security-at-kabul-airport.php.

Kight, Stef W. "U.S. Will Now Allow Private Citizens to Sponsor Afghan Refugees." *Axios*, October 25, 2021. https://www.axios.com/afghan-refugee-private-sponsorship-biden-ed9a2793-4482-42c0-8b73-aedf4cd9ce45.html.

Kirka, Danica, and Jill Lawless. "Whistleblower: As Afghanistan Fell, UK Abandoned Supporters." AP News, December 7, 2021. https://apnews.com/article/afghanistan-europe-evacuations-kabul-taliban-9dc6d24e464f8f3a08222c175aedd759.

Lawrence, J. P. "Understaffed, Uncoordinated: IG Outlines Flaws in Visa Program for War Zone Interpreters." *Stars and Stripes*, June 19, 2020. https://www.stripes.com/news/understaffed-uncoordinated-ig-outlines-flaws-in-visa-program-for-war-zone-interpreters-1.634409.

Lawson, Charlotte. "'An Unprecedented Mobilization.'" *The Dispatch*, October 25, 2021. https://thedispatch.com/p/americans-stranded-afghanistan.

Lee, Matthew, and Eric Tucker. "Was Biden Handcuffed by Trump's Taliban Deal in Doha?" AP News, August 19, 2021. https://apnews.com/article/joe-biden-middle-east-taliban-doha-e6f48507848aef2ee849154604aa11be.

Machi, Vivienne. "'Tonight, We'll Be Maxed Out.' Inside Ramstein Air Base's Push to Host Thousands of Evacuees from Afghanistan." *Air Force Times*, August 27, 2021. https://www.airforcetimes.com/news/your-air-force/2021/08/27/tonight-well-be-maxed-out-inside-ramstein-air-bases-push-to-host-thousands-of-evacuees-from-afghanistan/.

Madi, Mohamed, Ahmad Khalid, and Sayed Abdullah Nizami. "Chaos and Confusion: The Frenzied Final Hours of the Afghan Government." BBC News, September 8, 2021. https://www.bbc.com/news/world-asia-58477131.

Mahshie, Abraham. "Evacuating to Freedom." *Air Force Magazine*, November 4, 2021. https://www.airforcemag.com/article/evacuating-to-freedom/.

Malkasian, Carter. *The American War in Afghanistan*. New York: Oxford University Press, 2021.

Mann, Scott. *Operation Pineapple Express: The Incredible Story of a Group of Americans Who Undertook One Last Mission and Honored a Promise in Afghanistan*. New York: Simon & Schuster, 2022.

Mashal, Mujib, and Fatima Faizi. "Afghanistan to Release Last Taliban Prisoners, Removing Final Hurdle to Talks." *New York Times*, August 9, 2020. https://www.nytimes.com/2020/08/09/world/asia/afghanistan-taliban-prisoners-peace-talks.html.

Miller, Laurel, and Graeme Smith. "Behind Trump's Taliban Debacle." International Crisis Group, September 10, 2019. https://www.crisisgroup.org/asia/south-asia/afghanistan/behind-trumps-taliban-debacle.

Mohib, Hamdullah. "A Grassroots Democracy for Afghanistan." *Foreign Policy*, June 27, 2011.

Mohibi, Ahmad. "Thousands Afghan Evacuees at Emirates Humanitarian City Seek Answers to Their U.S. Entry Status." Rise to Peace, November 14, 2021. https://www.risetopeace.org/2021/11/14/afghans-stuck-in-emirates-humanitarian-city-seek-answers/shah1505/.

Monsutti, Alessandro. *War and Migration: Social Networks and Economic Strategies of the Hazaras of Afghanistan*. 1st ed. Middle East Studies: History, Politics, and Law. New York: Routledge, 2005.

Murtazashvili, Jennifer Brick. "The Collapse of Afghanistan." *The Journal of Democracy* 33:1. January 2022.

———. *Informal Order and the State in Afghanistan*. Cambridge: Cambridge University Press, 2018.

Najafizada, Lotfullah. "Afghan Youth, the Face of a Transformed Nation." *TEDxKabul*, 2014. https://www.youtube.com/watch?v=3xcqvvA6cPM.

Nissenbaum, Dion. "In Kabul, Private Rescue Efforts Grow Desperate as Time to Evacuate Afghans Runs Out; Defense Contractor Erik Prince Charges $6,500 a Person, Other Groups' Planes Leave Kabul Empty." *Wall Street Journal*, August 25, 2021. https://www.wsj.com/articles/in-kabul-private-rescue-efforts-grow-desperate-as-time-to-evacuate-afghans-runs-out-11629875097.

No One Left Behind. "No One Left Behind 2020 Annual SIV Research Survey" January 29, 2021.

Nordland, Rod. "Taliban End Takeover of Kunduz after 15 Days." *New York Times*, October 13, 2015. https://www.nytimes.com/2015/10/14/world/asia/taliban-afghanistan-kunduz.html.

Oppel, Richard, Abdul Waheed Wafa, and Sangar Rahimi. "20 Dead as Taliban Attackers Storm Kabul Offices." *New York Times*, February 11, 2009. https://www.nytimes.com/2009/02/12/world/asia/12afghan.html.

Pal, Alasdair. "Afghan Women Should Not Work alongside Men, Senior Taliban Figure Says." Reuters, September 13, 2021. https://www.reuters.com/world/asia-pacific/exclusive-afghan-women-should-not-work-alongside-men-senior-taliban-figure-says-2021-09-13/.

PBS NewsHour. "Afghanistan 'Ready' for Taliban Violence after US Withdrawal, Afghan President Says." May 17, 2021. https://www.pbs.org/newshour/show/afghanistan-ready-for-taliban-violence-after-us-withdrawal-afghan-president-says.

Pikulicka-Wilczewska, Agnieszka. "International Employers Accused of Abandoning Afghan Staff." Al Jazeera, August 27, 2021. https://www.aljazeera.com/news/2021/8/27/afghan-local-staff-left-behind-as-evacuation-deadline-looms.

Purkiss, Jessica. "The Afghan Officials' Families with Luxury Pads in Dubai." Bureau of Investigative Journalism, November 4, 2019. https://www.thebureauinvestigates.com/stories/2019-11-04/the-afghan-officials-families-with-luxury-pads-in-dubai.

Radio Azadi. "Afghan Government Unveils Negotiating Team for Taliban Talks." Radio Free Europe/Radio Liberty, March 27, 2020. https://www.rferl.org/a/afghan-government-unveils-negotiating-team-for-taliban-talks/30513633.html.

Radio Free Europe/Radio Liberty. "U.S. 'to End Contacts' with Afghan Security Adviser Mohib Following Verbal Attack." March 19, 2019. https://www.rferl.org/a/us-ends-contacts-afghan-security-adviser-mohib/29829238.html.

Rashid, Ahmed. *Descent into Chaos: The U.S. and the Disaster in Pakistan, Afghanistan, and Central Asia.* New York: Penguin Books, 2009.

———. *Taliban: Militant Islam, Oil and Fundamentalism in Central Asia.* 2nd ed. New Haven, CT: Yale University Press, 2010.

Rasooli, Shirshah. "Doha Deal Led to Collapse of Former Govt: Mohib." TOLOnews, December 17, 2021. https://tolonews.com/afghanistan-175929.

Rasmussen, Sune Engel. "Afghanistan's Female Marathon Runner Defies Danger to Go the Distance." *The Guardian,* October 28, 2015. https://www.theguardian.com/global-development/the-running-blog/2015/oct/28/afghanistans-female-marathon-runner-defies-danger-to-go-the-distance.

Ray, Siladitya, and Graison Dangor. "Afghanistan Embassy in Tajikistan Demands Arrest of Ashraf Ghani over 'Treasury Theft.'" *Forbes,* August 18, 2021. Accessed December 5, 2021. https://www.forbes.com/sites/siladityaray/2021/08/18/afghan-embassy-in-tajikistan-demands-interpol-arrest-escaped-former-president-ashraf-ghani/.

Reid, Rachel. "Afghanistan 1400: The Dawn and Decline of a Political Movement." Afghanistan Analysts Network, March 24, 2021. https://www.afghanistan-analysts.org/en/reports/rights-freedom/afghanistan-1400-the-dawn-and-decline-of-a-political-movement/.

Roggio, Bill. "Mapping Taliban Contested and Controlled Districts in Afghanistan." FDD's Long War Journal, August 29, 2017. https://www.longwarjournal.org/mapping-taliban-control-in-afghanistan.

Ruttig, Thomas. "Schools on the Frontline: The Struggle over Education in the Afghan Wars." In *Education and Development in Afghanistan,* edited by Uwe H. Bittlingmayer, Anne-Marie Grundmeier, Reinhart Kößler, Diana Sahrai, and Fereschta Sahrai, 101–40. Transcript Verlag, 2019. https://doi.org/10.14361/9783839436370-007.

Sabawoon, Ali Mohammad. "Going Nationwide: The Helmand Peace March Initiative." Afghan Analysts Network, April 23, 2018. https://www.afghanistan-analysts.org/en/reports/war-and-peace/going-nationwide-the-helmand-peace-march-initiative/.

Saif, Shadi Khan. "Taliban Asks Women Healthcare Workers to Resume Duties." Anadolu Agency, August 28, 2021. https://www.aa.com.tr/en/asia-pacific/taliban-asks-women-healthcare-workers-to-resume-duties/2349122.

Salem, Mostafa, Tara John, Tim Lister, and Hannah Ritchie. "Former Afghan President Ashraf Ghani Emerges in the UAE." CNN, August 18, 2021. https://www.cnn .com/2021/08/18/asia/afghanistan-taliban-ashraf-ghani-intl/index.html.

Schmitt, Eric, and Helene Cooper. "Pentagon Acknowledges Aug. 29 Drone Strike in Afghanistan Was a Tragic Mistake That Killed 10 Civilians." New York Times, September 17, 2021. https://www.nytimes.com/2021/09/17/us/politics/pentagon -drone-strike-afghanistan.html.

Schmitt, Eric, and Jennifer Steinhauer. "Afghan Visa Applicants Arrive in U.S. after Years of Waiting." New York Times, July 30, 2021. https://www.nytimes.com/2021/07/30/ us/politics/afghan-interpreters-evacuated.html.

Seligman, Lara, Andrew Desiderio, and Erin Banco. "Hundreds of U.S. Citizens, Afghan Commandos Successfully Evacuated through Secret CIA Base." POLITICO, September 1, 2021.

Seligman, Lara, Betsy Woodruff Swan, Erin Banco, and Alexander Ward. "FBI Agents Question Afghan Rescue Groups." POLITICO, September 24, 2021. https:// www.politico.com/news/2021/09/24/fbi-agents-question-afghan-rescue-groups -514151.

Shachtman, Noah. "Unlimited Talk, Only $679 Million: Inside the No-Bid Deal for Afghan Interpreters." Wired, n.d. Accessed October 20, 2021.

Shaheed, Anisa. "Sources Allege 100 Civilians Killed after Fall of Spin Boldak." TOLOnews, July 22, 2021. https://tolonews.com/afghanistan-173674.

Shashikumar, VK. "The Great Afghan Betrayal: A Palace Coup?" Indian Defence Review, September 24, 2021. http://www.indiandefencereview.com/spotlights/the-great -afghan-betrayal-a-palace-coup/.

Shear, Michael D. "'We Will Not Forgive,' Biden Says, Vowing Retaliation for Kabul Attack." New York Times, August 26, 2021. https://www.nytimes.com/live/2021/08 /26/world/afghanistan-taliban-biden-news.

Shear, Michael D., Lara Jakes, and Eileen Sullivan. "Inside the Afghan Evacuation: Rogue Flights, Crowded Tents, Hope and Chaos." New York Times, September 3, 2021. https://www.nytimes.com/2021/09/03/us/politics/afghanistan-evacuation .html.

Shear, Michael D., David E. Sanger, Helene Cooper, Eric Schmitt, Julian E. Barnes, and Lara Jakes. "Miscue after Miscue, U.S. Exit Plan Unravels." New York Times, August 21, 2021. https://www.nytimes.com/2021/08/21/us/politics/biden-taliban -afghanistan-kabul.html.

Siebold, Sabine, and John Chalmers. "Six EU Countries Warn against Open Door for Afghan Asylum Seekers." Reuters, August 10, 2021. https://www.reuters.com /world/six-countries-urge-eu-not-stop-deportations-afghanistan-belgium-says -2021-08-10/.

Sohail, Sanjar. "Exclusive: The Untold Story of How Afghan President Ashraf Ghani Fled the Country." Hasht-E Subh Daily, October 2, 2021. https://8am.af/eng/exclusive -the-untold-story-of-how-afghan-president-ashraf-ghani-fled-the-country/.

Solis, Dianne. "Cornyn Meets with Afghans, Who Tell Him of the Many Left Behind in Their Homeland." Dallas News, October 15, 2021. https://www.dallasnews.com

/news/immigration/2021/10/15/texas-sen-cornyn-meets-with-afghans-who-tell
-him-of-the-many-left-behind-in-their-homeland/.

Stack, Megan K. "The Soldiers Came Home Sick. The Government Denied It Was Responsible." *New York Times*, January 11, 2022. https://www.nytimes.com/2022 /01/11/magazine/military-burn-pits.html.

Strick van Linschoten, Alex, and Felix Kuehn. *An Enemy We Created: The Myth of the Taliban-al Qaeda Merger in Afghanistan.* Oxford; New York: Oxford University Press, 2012.

Suhrke, Astri. *When More Is Less: The International Project in Afghanistan.* New York: Columbia University Press, 2011.

Swaine, Jon. "How an Instagram Star's $7 Million Mission to Rescue Afghan Civilians Struggled to Get Off the Ground." *Washington Post*, September 29, 2021. https: //www.washingtonpost.com/investigations/flyaway-afghanistan-rescue-quentin -quarantino/2021/09/29/2e94666a-1b22-11ec-bcb8-0cb135811007_story.html.

Tarabay, Jamie, and Nick Wadhams. "Facebook and a LinkedIn Co-Founder Funded a Suddenly Packed Afghan Airlift." Bloomberg News, September 24, 2021. https:// www.bloomberg.com/news/articles/2021-09-24/why-155-extra-afghans-boarded -facebook-funded-flight-thanks-to-the-airline.

UNAMA, and UNHCR. "Afghanistan: Protection of Civilians in Armed Conflict." Annual Report. Kabul, Afghanistan, 2020. https://unama.unmissions.org/sites /default/files/executive_summary_afghanistan_protection_of_civilians_annual _report_2020_eng_0.pdf.

UNHCR. "Frequently Asked Questions: Asylum and Refugee Status." Accessed August 29, 2022. https://help.unhcr.org/faq/how-can-we-help-you/asylum-and-refugee -status/.

———. "UNHCR Afghan Refugee Statistics." Situation Report, September 10, 2001. https://www.unhcr.org/en-us/afghanistan.html.

USAID. "Education—Afghanistan." September 10, 2019. https://www.usaid.gov/ afghanistan/education.

———. "Promote." August 13, 2021. https://www.usaid.gov/afghanistan/promote.

US Department of State. "Agreement for Bringing Peace to Afghanistan between the Islamic Emirate of Afghanistan Which Is Not Recognized by the United States as a State and Is Known as the Taliban and the United States of America." February 29, 2020. https://www.state.gov/wp-content/uploads/2020/02/Agreement-For -Bringing-Peace-to-Afghanistan-02.29.20.pdf.

———. "Briefing with Senior State Department Officials on the U.S. Refugee Admissions Program Priority 2 (P-2) Designation for Afghan Nationals." Accessed November 1, 2021. https://www.state.gov/briefing-with-senior-state-department -officials-on-the-u-s-refugee-admissions-program-priority-2-p-2-designation-for -afghan-nationals/.

———. "Launch of the Sponsor Circle Program for Afghans." October 25, 2021. https: //www.state.gov/launch-of-the-sponsor-circle-program-for-afghans/.

———. "Operation Allies Refuge." U.S. Embassy in Afghanistan, July 17, 2021. https:// af.usembassy.gov/operation-allies-refuge/.

———. "Review of the Afghan Special Immigrant Visa Program." Office of Inspector General, June 2020. https://www.oversight.gov/sites/default/files/oig-reports/AUD-MERO-20-35.pdf.

———. "Special Immigrant Visas for Afghans—Who Were Employed by/on Behalf of the U.S. Government." Accessed March 2, 2021. https://travel.state.gov/content/travel/en/us-visas/immigrate/special-immg-visa-afghans-employed-us-gov.html.

———. "U.S. Refugee Admissions Program Priority 2 Designation for Afghan Nationals." Accessed October 31, 2021. https://www.state.gov/u-s-refugee-admissions-program-priority-2-designation-for-afghan-nationals/.

US Department of State and Department of Homeland Security. "Joint Department of State/Department of Homeland Security Report: Status of the Afghan Special Immigrant Visa Program," October 2020. https://travel.state.gov/content/dam/visas/SIVs/Afghan-Public-Quarterly-Report-Q4-October-2021.pdf.

US Embassy in Kabul. "US Embassy Cables: Money Smuggling Out of Afghanistan." Accessed through *The Guardian*, December 2, 2010. https://www.theguardian.com/world/us-embassy-cables-documents/230265.

US Government Accountability Office. "Afghan and Iraqi Special Immigrants: More Information on Their Resettlement Outcomes Would Be Beneficial." GAO-18-107, February 2018. https://www.gao.gov/products/gao-18-107.

Vittori, Jodi. "Corruption and Self-Dealing in Afghanistan and Other U.S.-Backed Security Sectors." Carnegie Endowment for International Peace, September 9, 2021. https://carnegieendowment.org/2021/09/09/corruption-and-self-dealing-in-afghanistan-and-other-u.s.-backed-security-sectors.

Walsh, Johnny. "Amid a Spike in Violence, Have Afghan Peace Talks Lost Momentum?" US Institute of Peace, June 19, 2019. Accessed November 30, 2021. https://www.usip.org/publications/2019/06/amid-spike-violence-have-afghan-peace-talks-lost-momentum.

Watkins, Andrew. "An Assessment of Taliban Rule at Three Months." Combating Terrorism Center at West Point, November 11, 2021. https://ctc.usma.edu/an-assessment-of-taliban-rule-at-three-months/.

———. "Lessons from the Collapse of Afghanistan's Security Forces." Combating Terrorism Center at West Point, October 21, 2021. https://ctc.usma.edu/lessons-from-the-collapse-of-afghanistans-security-forces/.

Watson, Kathryn. "Former Ghani Adviser Says Afghan Leaders Didn't See 'Writing on the Wall' of U.S. Withdrawal." CBS News, December 16, 2021. https://www.cbsnews.com/news/afghanistan-leadership-mistakes-u-s-withdrawal/.

White House. "Executive Order on Rebuilding and Enhancing Programs to Resettle and Refugees and Planning for the Impact of Climate Change on Migration." The Briefing Room: Presidential Actions, February 4, 2021. https://www.whitehouse.gov/briefing-room/presidential-actions/2021/02/04/executive-order-on-rebuilding-and-enhancing-programs-to-resettle-refugees-and-planning-for-the-impact-of-climate-change-on-migration/.

———. "Remarks by President Biden on Afghanistan." The Briefing Room: Speeches and Remarks, August 16, 2021. https://www.whitehouse.gov/briefing-room/speeches-remarks/2021/08/16/remarks-by-president-biden-on-afghanistan/.

Wimpelmann, Torunn. *The Pitfalls of Protection: Gender, Violence, and Power in Afghanistan.* Oakland: University of California Press, 2017.

Wissing, Douglas A. *Funding the Enemy: How US Taxpayers Bankroll the Taliban.* Amherst, NY: Prometheus Books, 2012.

Woodward, Bob. *Obama's Wars.* New York: Simon & Schuster, 2011.

World Bank. "Development Projects: Citizens' Charter Afghanistan Project—P160567." Text/HTML. World Bank. Accessed October 8, 2021. https://projects.worldbank.org/en/projects-operations/project-detail/P160567.

———. "Women's Role in Afghanistan's Future: Taking Stock of Achievements and Continued Challenges." February 14, 2014.

World Health Organization. "Health System Programmes—Afghanistan." Accessed July 7, 2021. http://www.emro.who.int/afg/programmes/health-system-strengthening.html.

World Inequality Database. "Afghanistan." Accessed November 12, 2021. https://wid.world/country/afganistan/.

Yaad, Ziar Khan. "Peace Movement Blames Foreign Countries for Afghan War." TOLOnews, March 24, 2019. https://tolonews.com/afghanistan/peace-movement-blames-foreign-countries-afghan-war.

INDEX

Abbey Gate, 193, 195, 197, 200, 209, 259
Abdullah, Abdullah, 67
Abu Dhabi: Humanitarian City camp, 255, 259, 260–61, 262; legal limbo of, 213, 256; Zeinab and, 137, 240
Afghan Allies Protection Act, 73, 154–55, 258
Afghan Children Read Project (ACR), 54
Afghan Civil War, 12, 15, 16, 60, 64, 96, 115
#AfghanEvac, 258
Afghan Football Federation, 166
Afghanistan 1400, 61–62
Afghanistan Human Rights Independent Commission, 215
Afghanistan Research and Evaluation Unit (AREU), 66, 80, 104
Afghan National Army (ANA), 110, 163, 165, 203; contractors and, 40–41; evacuation of ANA members, 192, 210; ghost soldiers of, 9–10; US troops, working with, 141, 154

Afghan National Police (ANP), 41, 110
Afghan Special Forces, 105–6
Afghan Transitional Administration, 17
Akhunzada, Haibatullah, 9
Ali, 170, 192, 193; COVID test, obtaining, 168–69; evacuation attempts, 239–40; Kabul airport, journey to, 179–82, 183; spousal visa, applying for, 261–62; Zeinab, marriage to, 167, 280
Al Jazeera news agency, 257
Al Qaeda, 22–23, 207
Al Udeid Air Base, 235
Amena. *See* Hakimi, Ameena
American University of Afghanistan (AUAF), 68, 108, 164, 193; attack on campus, 104–7; female students of, 169, 276; kidnapping of professors from, 103; Najeeb as attending, 76, 119; opportunities, providing, 44–45; Zeinab and, 46, 113, 137, 151, 263
Arsalan. *See* Noori, Arsalan

255, 265, 280; Ghazni as home village, 72, 87; Iran, as a refugee from, 21–24, 27–28, 43, 70; Ismaeil as father-in-law, 74, 125, 126, 130, 250, 265; Ministry of Justice attack, surviving, 70–72, 104, 151; MSH, working for, 28–31, 128, 129, 130; Murtaza, marriage to, 69–70; national collapse, as a witness to, 163–64; Organization for Migration, contacted by, 249–50; Pakistan, viewing as a place of refuge, 219–22, 224; Qatar, flight to, 252–53; SIV, applying for, 130–31, 133; as targeted, 128–29, 133, 215; in Turkey, 130, 136; value diminished under Taliban, 217–18

Hakimi, Ismaeil, 70, 108, 119, 130, 248; Amena as daughter-in-law, 74, 125, 126, 130, 250, 265; grandchildren of, 126, 280; San Diego, resettling in, 76, 120–23; Utah, relocating to, 125–26

Hakimi, Murtaza, 70, 125; Afghanistan, departure from, 215–16, 250; family separation, 69–70, 75–76, 278; first child, birth of, 126; Qatar, flight to, 252, 265

Hamid Karzai International Airport (HKIA), 36, 173, 192,

214, 235; children, processing through, 203–4, 207–8; German assistance at, 210–12; Mazar airport, comparing to, 154, 241–42; military officials, early entrance offered to, 190–91; suicide bombing, 12, 209–10; Sahar, ordeal at, 196–201; Zeinab, journey through, 180–86

Haqqani network, 9, 71, 103, 207, 268

Haseeb (brother of Najeeb), 255, 259–61

Hazara ethnic group, 23, 28, 59; in Bamiyan, 43, 48; Ismaeil as Hazara, 122–23; Kabul, Hazara neighborhood of, 24, 164; as targeted, 21, 45, 72, 222, 248–49, 263

Helmand Province, 39, 109, 165

Herat, city of, 142, 218, 229; peace protesters in, 109; Taliban, falling to, 141, 165, 179; Zeinab, as hometown of, 44, 103, 107, 137, 262

heroin, 46

Hizbe Islami party, 65

Hoffman, Reid, 213

Holbrooke, Richard, 111

Humanitarian City processing camp, 255, 259–60, 261

Humanitarian Parole, 160, 231, 244–45, 255, 257, 265

International Narcotics and Law
Enforcement Affairs (INL),
80–81, 82
International Organization for
Migration (IOM), 120, 249
International Refugee Assistance
Project (IRAP), 133, 147, 153,
257–58
International Security Assistance
Forces (ISAF), 51, 109
Iran, 46, 96, 135, 266; Amena as
a refugee from, 21–24, 27–28,
43, 70; fleeing to, 194, 218, 262;
Ismaeil living in, 121, 122, 125;
Taliban on the border of, 165,
219; Zeinab as a refugee from,
43, 44
Iraq, 73, 133, 152; Abu Ghraib
torture in, 81; Iraqi SIVs,
72–73, 75; Khalilzad as
ambassador to, 111
Islamic Republic of Afghanistan,
11, 18
Islamic State-Khorasan (IS-K),
209, 225, 263
Ismaeil. *See* Hakimi, Ismaeil

J-1 exchange visa, 167
Jackson, Ashley, 87, 88
Jalil, 193–201, 203, 209
Jawzjan province, 165
Johnson, Boris, 212

Kabir, 100–101, 226, 229, 233

Kabul, city of, 42, 46, 54, 69, 75,
117, 126, 223; as dangerous,
9, 74–75, 76, 77, 112, 147,
267; diplomatic missions in,
25, 273; families left behind,
243, 255, 266, 267, 269, 278,
280; Hazara community of, 24,
164; Ministry of Justice attack,
70–71, 104; Munir in, 7, 65–66,
68, 82; Najeeb in, 42, 76, 77,
134, 155, 259; poverty of, 46,
52, 103; professional workers of,
57, 60, 67, 93; protest march to,
109–10; suicide attacks in, 31,
71; swimming pools of, 136–37;
Taliban control of city, 16, 38,
247–48, 262, 267–68, 275–78;
Taliban take-over of city, 10,
30, 82, 95, 98–99, 104–7,
168–69, 171, 189–90, 191;
Turkish embassy in, 276, 277;
World Bank offices in, 90, 92;
Zeinab in, 47–48, 50–51, 107.
See also American University of
Afghanistan
Kabul Airport. *See* Hamid Karzai
International Airport
Kam airlines, 185, 213
Kandahar, 37, 165, 267; air base,
33, 34, 36, 76, 154; Amena,
travel through, 219–20, 223;
Forward Operating Base in,
38–39; road to, 35, 229
Kankor entrance exams, 26–27,
38, 44, 218

factor in application process,
130–31, 132; "travel agent"
assistance with applying, 134,
135; Turkey, waiting for SIV
processing in, 128, 277
Spin Boldak border crossing, 39,
219, 220

Tajikistan, 4, 171
Talib, Mawlavi, 165
Taliban, 9, 53, 76, 93, 112, 209,
217, 238, 258; Al Qaeda,
conflating with, 22–23; ANA
as enemies of, 110, 165; Arsalan
and, 1–5, 222–23, 225–29,
232–33; checkpoints, manning,
53, 99, 179–80, 190, 192, 195,
206–7, 211, 219–20, 247, 248,
274; control over Kabul, 16, 38,
247–48, 262, 267–68, 275–78;
fearful existence under Taliban
rule, 186, 193, 216, 221, 230;
first Taliban era, 12–13, 15, 17,
23, 43, 60, 64, 111; foreign ties,
targeting Afghans with, 40,
59, 62, 65, 68, 73, 77, 80, 83,
87, 95, 104, 117, 136, 153, 155,
194, 205, 215, 241; Hazaras,
persecuting, 21, 45, 59, 72, 222,
248, 263; Kabul, taking of,
10, 30, 82, 95, 98–99, 104–7,
168–69, 171, 189–90, 191;
life under Taliban rule, 15–20,
116, 225–33, 247; *mahram*,
requiring for women's activities,
268, 276; negotiating with,
87, 99, 109–16, 143, 171, 190,
268; Night Letters left by, 132,
134–35; orphanages, attitude
towards, 250–52, 278; release
of prisoners, 114, 151, 165, 206,
225–26; restrictions imposed
by, 117, 170; rise of, 39, 85–86,
178, 267; second coming of, 53,
95–101; Taliban government,
17, 23, 64, 96, 98, 154, 222,
226, 230, 233, 241, 242, 252,
267; Taliban leaders, 95,
140–41, 171, 226, 230; Taliban
soldiers, 17, 110, 168, 182, 195,
206, 208, 214, 229, 233, 267;
Taliban violence, 11, 36, 39,
157, 173, 201, 240; territory,
gaining, 31, 65, 88, 89, 127,
141–44, 151, 156, 164–65, 167,
179; US-Taliban relations, 182,
242, 271; women, faring under
Taliban rule, 21, 28, 30, 53,
56–57, 164, 187, 217–18, 231,
247–49, 280
Taskforce Pineapple, 193
Titan contracting company, 37
TOLO (Afghan television
station), 205
Trump, Donald, 160, 165, 213;
Camp David, inviting Taliban
to, 112, 114, 141; Ghani,
relations with, 108–9, 114;
immigration policies, 74,
147–48; Khalilzad and, 111,